An endless adventure . . .

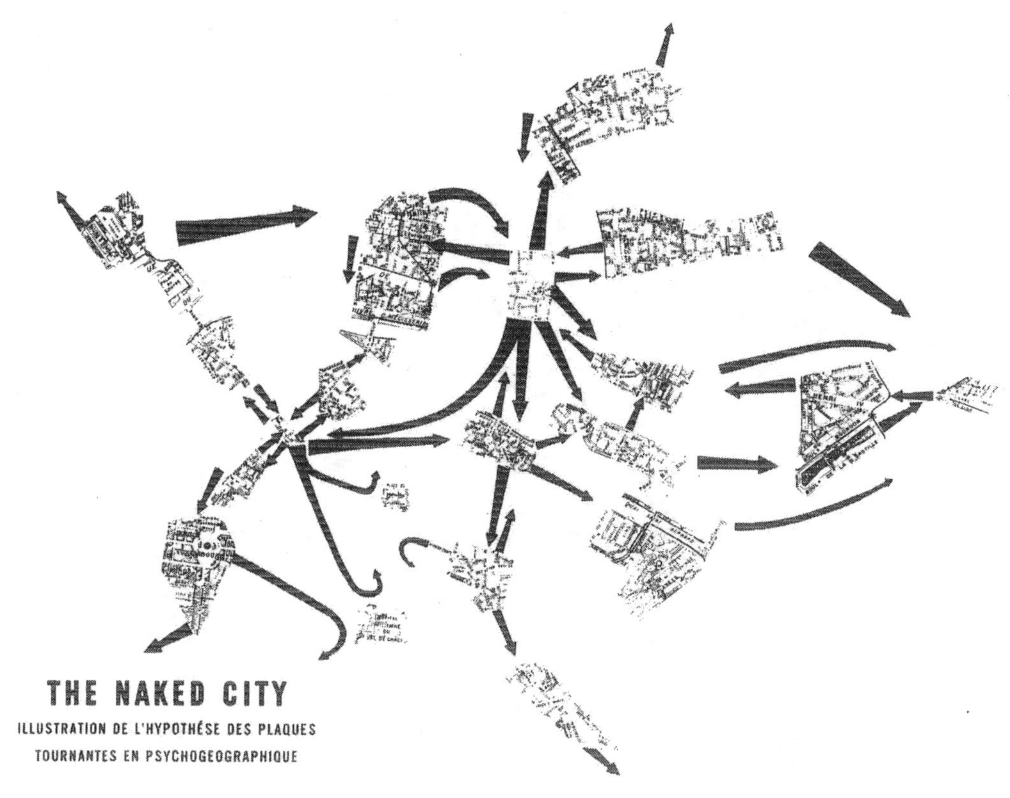

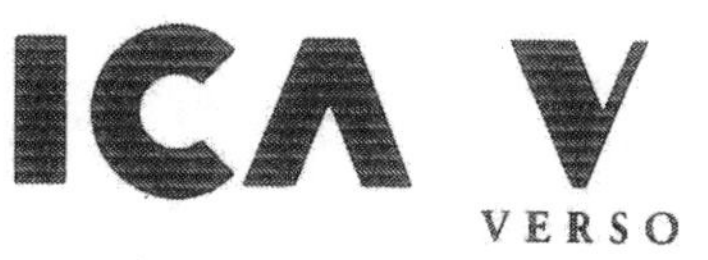
ICA
London
VERSO
London . New York

an endless passion . . .

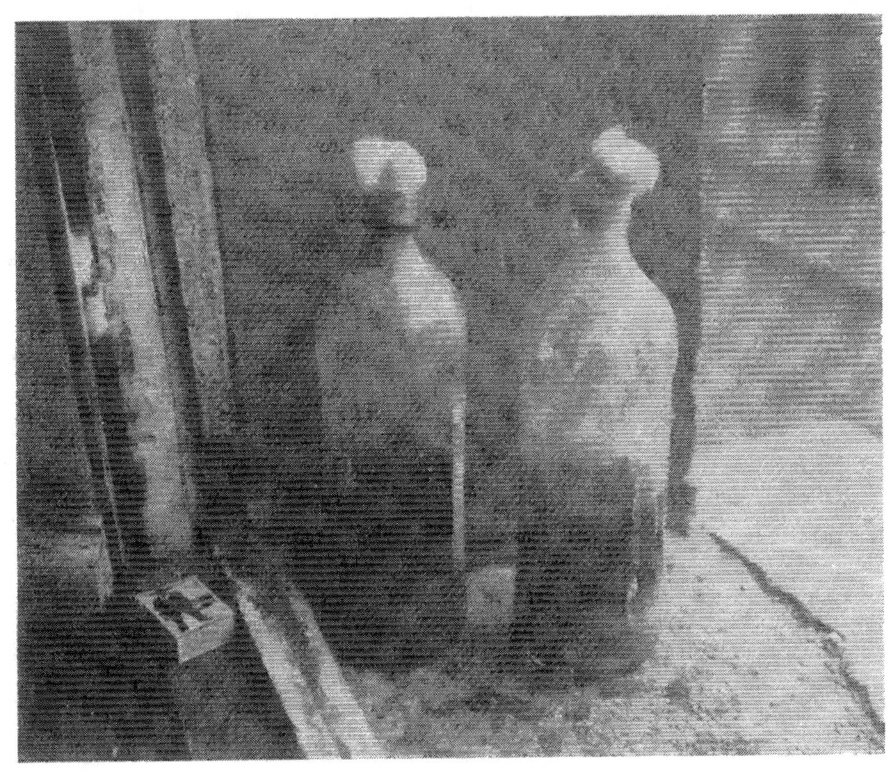

A situationist scrapbook

an endless banquet

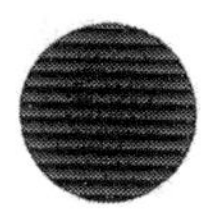

The Situationist International
Selected documents from 1957 to 1962

Documents tracing the impact on
British culture from the 1960s to the 1980s

'Plagiarism is necessary –
progress implies it.'
Lautréamont

Edited by Iwona Blazwick
in consultation with Mark Francis,
Peter Wollen and Malcolm Imrie

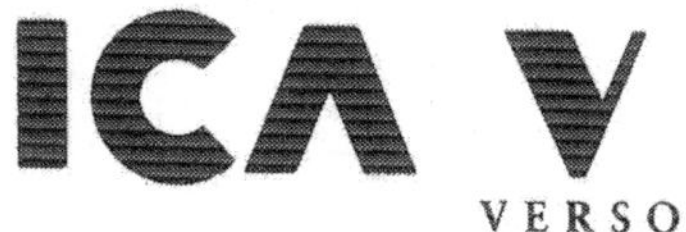

VERSO

Contents

Fall Out:
A British Inheritance 1966–1988

It's all over

The material (and anti-material) evidence

In the archives of the Silkeborg Museum in Denmark can be found a hand-written note titled *Plan général de la Bibliothèque situationniste de Silkeborg*. It lists clearly, with sections and sub-sections (Pre-Situationist/Situationist/historical/copies) the items which were printed and produced by the members of the *Internationale Situationniste* before the group's formation in 1957, and during the first four years of its existence. The note is dated 10 March 1961 and initialled GD. Almost all the items listed by Guy Debord were given by him to the museum's archive, and the basic collection has been supplemented by Asger Jorn's own collection, and by gifts from Guy Atkins, Jorn's biographer, and others.

Here the trajectory of the group can be reconstructed – the 'passage de quelques personnes' which we have plagiarised for the title of this exhibition.[1] Two aspects of the discovery of these notes seem apposite to any remarks about the intentions and purposes of an exhibition such as this. The first is the very existence of this archive, in the 'public domain', and clearly intended for reference; the second is its clear and even dialectical method or organisation (eg 'section III, division B: anti-Situationist polemics'). It lent credence to our supposition that collecting and presenting that collection of models, films, tracts, art-works, books and leaflets which were issued in the name of the IS, or which specifically used the strategies and methods they developed, such as the 'modifications' of Jorn, or the 'industrial painting' of Pinot-Gallizio could and should be attempted. Their publications, even after 1961, such as the books comprising the Bibliothèque d'Alexandrie, on Constant, Pinot-Gallizio, *Le long voyage de Jorn et Wemaere*, and Debord's *Contre le Cinéma*, can of course be found in many public domains, and indeed the facsimile collected edition of the original 12 issues of the *Internationale Situationniste* bulletin itself is still in print and readily available.[2] On the other hand, many of the works of art had disappeared from view and are almost forgotten. Such was the fate, for example, of the *Caverne du Anti-Matière* of Pinot-Gallizio, which was originally installed at the Galerie René Drouin in rue Visconti, Paris in May 1959, and hardly ever seen since. It has not been shown in public for 15 years, since the retrospective of Pinot-Gallizio in Torino in 1974.

When Peter Wollen and I started to discuss the possibilities and justification for an exhibition about the IS some years ago, we did not fully anticipate the plethora of references to the IS and their role in more or less well-known public events over the last twenty or more years, which have subsequently appeared. The all-pervasive 'society of the spectacle', as predicted by Debord in 1967, has been accompanied, as if by a spectre at the feast of consumption, by acknowledgements to the concept of *détournement* and the spectacle in all departments of the culture industry, from the art, art-historical and architectural press to the fanzines and clubs of pop-music, at least since the mid-1970s onwards.

Doubtless the exhibition will also be seen to contribute to this accumulation of 'mediatised' images. But while the IS themselves recognised, as early as the 5th conference in Göteborg in August 1961,[3] that their ideas would be claimed by others and put to uses directly contrary to those intended, it can also be argued that this is what they themselves had done with pre-existing images and texts. Copyright was a legal proscription absolutely opposed to the distributive principles of potlatch and plagiarism, which had first been elaborated by the Lettriste Internationale. The only way to proceed, then, for us, thirty years after the foundation of the IS in Cosio d'Arroscia, was not to consider their *passage* a closed chapter, nor to be deflected by the lenses of another time, another place. While it is inevitable that later attempts to reflect upon these matters are a *commentary*, we may aspire also to being one of the *études objectives* prefigured in Debord's note of 1961, insofar as we have exhibited only the original documents and projects. The key concepts of *dérive, détournement, urbanisme unitaire*, and the construction of *situations*, were all elaborated before the nominal foundation of the IS in 1957. The concept of *spectacle*, and especially the potential role of cinema working against its 'accumulation of images' was developed through the 1960s. It has become a part of the mythology surrounding the IS that the theory became a reality only in 1967-68, but we can now see how their principles were clarified and reformulated in the light of works first produced in the late 1950s – in the collaborative books *Fin de Copenhague, Mémoires* and *Stavrim Sonetter,* in the experiments of industrial painting and modifications, even perhaps in the expectations which one can imagine were held for the ambiance of *La Méthode,* the café-bar in rue Descartes which was planned by Michèle Bernstein and Guy Debord in 1958, but which lasted only a few weeks.

How can these objects, events, journeys, stunts, still signify after a historical gap of twenty or thirty years? The problem here is substantially more acute than the standard museological problem of recontextualising historical material. Like radio currents, the situationist concepts have been emitted, and remain alive but invisible until picked up by a receiver. Tuned to the right wavelength, the message can be transmitted. Our approach then, as a result of our researches in Paris, Silkeborg, Amsterdam, Alba, Torino, Munich, London, New York and Los Angeles, was to organise the material into coherent sections. These are specifically those concepts of *détournement,* (demonstrated by the paintings of Asger Jorn, the films of Debord and René Viénet, and the comic strips and photographs *détourned* in Bertrand and Joannes' 'Retour de la colonne Durruti'), *dérive* and *psychogeography,* (shown by Ralph Rumney's Venice photo-collage, Debord's *Guide Psychogéographique de Paris* and *The Naked City Map,* and JV Martin's *Golden Fleet* constructions), rolls of *Pittura Industriale* and the Cavern of Anti-Matter of Pinot-Gallizio, *Unitary Urbanism* (Constant's New Babylon models, drawings and maps), the tracts and posters produced by the Council for the Maintenance of the Occupations at the Sorbonne in May 1968 (which included some of the Situationists).

All this implied a chronological trajectory articulated in spatial terms – a simple and comprehensive organisation of objects, as the Bibliothèque in Silkeborg had indicated and indeed made imperative – not to reconstruct time past but to expose to the light things which have run the risk of acquiring the patina of nostalgia and the glamour of neglect.

The exhibition concludes with some indications – obviously not exhaustive – of the areas in which the ideas articulated by the IS have penetrated, in urbanism, among artists, radical political groups, and during the short-lived eruption of punk. While the IS material is arranged according to sense, there is also a diachronic structure, corresponding to the *Laboratory* period, centred (if at all) in Alba, the *detonator* period, which refers to Debord's statement that he provided the explosive machinery which ignited in May 1968, and the *fallout* period, after the IS disbanded in 1972. In this section are included works by Marcel Broodthaers, Mario Merz, Daniel Buren and Art and Language, who all had some direct or indirect contact with the IS, various items by Jamie Reid, including the Sex Pistols mural, and from Tony Wilson's Factory Records, including the sandpaper record cover of Vini Reilly's group, the Durutti Column. Jamie Reid had designed 'Leaving the 20th Century – the incomplete work of the Situationist International', while working at Suburban Press in Croydon. Both he and Tony Wilson have explicitly made use of situationist tactics and diversions.

Over these last thirty years what has changed? Everything, and yet nothing. *Tout reste à faire.* To visualise the problems which remain unresolved, and to see how the hopes and aspirations of those few people who were closely involved with the IS are still unfulfilled and indeed continually inverted, one might try to compare the ambiance of the Haçienda Club in Manchester, open for business since the late 1970s, with the imaginary *haçienda* dreamt of by Ivan Chtcheglov in his 'Formula for a new urbanism'.

Here in the text of 1953[4], the distance between delirious dream and spectacular reality can be practically measured. It should become clear the spectacle is always with us, and the urgency of transforming the relations of everyday life, work and art into a continuous spontaneity can never be left to others.

© Mark Francis
Paris, April 1989

Foot notes

1 'Plagiarism is necessary. Progress implies it': one of the aphorisms Guy Debord lifted from Lautréamont in the proto-Situationist period.

2 Through Editions Gérard Lebovici, 27, rue St Sulpice, 75006 Paris. They have also recently published Jean-François Martos 'Histoire de l'Internationale Situationniste'.

3 See IS n° 7, pp. 25-31.

4 'Maintenant c'est joué. L'Haçienda, tu ne la verras pas. Elle n'existe pas. Il faut construire l'Haçienda'. Gilles Ivain, 'Formulaire pour un urbanisme nouveau', IS n° 1, page 15.

ELCOME TO DENMARK

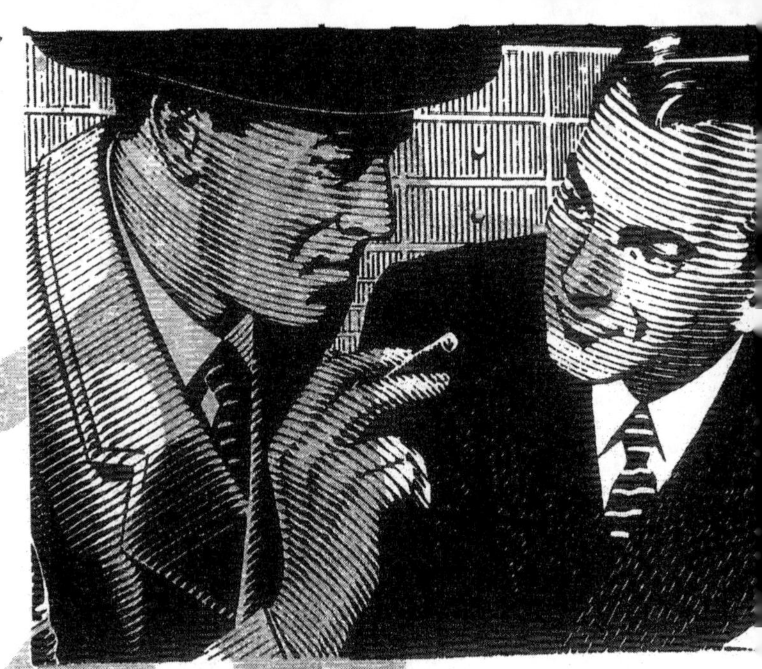

C'EST DE PARIS QUE VIENNENT LES DIFFICULTÉS

Du moderne indiscutable

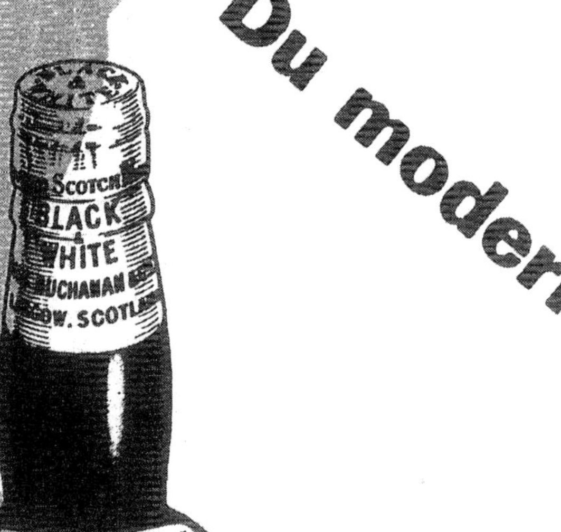

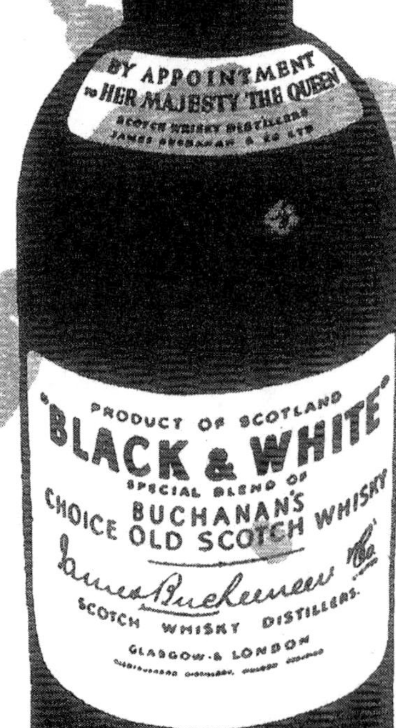

des années et des années d'usage

Bitter Victory

The Situationist International

De Sade liberated from the Bastille in 1789, Baudelaire on the barricades in 1848, Courbet tearing down the Vendome Column in 1870. French political history is distinguished by a series of glorious and legendary moments which serve to celebrate the convergence of popular revolution with art in revolt. In this century avant-garde artistic movements took up the banner of revolution consciously and enduringly. The political career of André Breton and the surrealists began with their manifestoes against the Moroccan war (the 'Riff' war) in 1925 and persisted through to the Manifesto of the 121, which Breton signed in 1960, shortly before his death, denouncing the Algerian war and justifying resistance. In May 1968 the same emblematic role was enacted once again by the militants of the Situationist International.

The SI was founded in 1957, at Cosio d'Arroscia in northern Italy, principally out of the union of two prior avant-garde groups, the Movement for an Imaginist Bauhaus (Asger Jorn, Pinot Gallizio and others) and the Lettrist International (led by Guy Debord). The Movement for an Imaginist Bauhaus itself originated from splits in the post-war Cobra group of artists, which Jorn had helped found, and the SI was soon joined by another key Cobra artist, Constant. The ancestry of both Cobra and Lettrism can be traced back to the International Surrealist movement, whose break-up after the war led to a proliferation of new splinter groups and an accompanying surge of new experimentation and position-taking. The SI brought together again many of the threads whose dispersal signalled the decay and eventual decomposition of surrealism. In many ways, its project was that of re-launching surrealism on a new foundation, stripped of some of its elements (emphasis on the unconscious, quasi-mystical and occultist thinking, cult of irrationalism) and enhanced by others, within the framework of cultural revolution.

In its first phase (1957–1962) the SI developed a number of ideas which had originated in the Lettrist International, of which the most significant were those of *urbanisme unitaire* (integrated city-creation, unitary urbanism), psychogeography, play as free and creative activity, *dérive* (drift) and *détournement* (diversion, semantic shift). The SI expounded its position in its journal, brought out books and embarked on a number of artistic activities. Artists were to break down the divisions between individual art-forms, to create *situations*, constructed encounters and creatively lived moments in specific urban settings, instances of a critically transformed everyday life. They were to produce settings for situations and experimental models of possible modes of transformation of the city, as well as to agitate against the sterility and oppression of the actual environment and ruling economic and political system.

During this period a number of prominent painters and artists from many European countries joined the group and became involved in the activities and publications of the SI. With members from Algeria, Belgium, England, France, Germany, Holland, Italy and Sweden, the SI became a genuinely international movement, held together organizationally by annual conferences (57-Cosio d'Arroscia, Italy; 58-Paris, France; 59-Munich, Germany; 60-London, England; 61-Goteborg, Sweden; 62-Antwerp, Belgium) and by the journal, which was published once or twice a year in Paris, with an editorial committee that changed over time and represented the different national sections.

From the point of view of art, 1959 was an especially productive (or should one say, dialectically destructive) year. These artists held major exhibitions of their work. Asger Jorn showed his 'Modifications' (*peintures détournées*, altered paintings) at the Rive Gauche gallery in Paris. These were over-paintings by Jorn on second-hand canvases by unknown painters, which he bought in flea-markets or the like, transforming them by this double inscription. The same year Pinot Gallizio held a show of his *caverna dell antimateria* (grotto of anti-matter) at the Galerie René Drouin. This was the culmination of his experiments with *pittura industriale* – rolls of canvas up to 145 metres in length, produced mainly by hand, but with the aid of painting machines and spray-guns with special resins devised by Pinot Gallizio himself. His painting of this period was both a 'diverted' parody of automation (which the SI viewed with hostile concern) and a prototype of vast rolls of 'urbanist' painting which could engulf whole cities. Later in 1959 Constant exhibited a number of his *ilots-maquettes* (model precincts) at the Stedelijk museum in Amsterdam.

Asger Jorn, *Fin de Copenhague* (excerpt), 1957

These were part of his ongoing 'New Babylon' project, inspired by unitary urbanism – the design of an experimental utopian city with changing zones for free play, whose nomadic inhabitants could collectively choose their own climate, sensory environment, organization of space and so on.

However, during this period a series of internal disagreements arose inside the organization which finally culminated in a number of expulsions and a split in 1962, when a rival Second Situationist International was set up around Jorgen Nash (Asger Jorn's younger brother) and joined by others from the Dutch, German and Scandinavian sections. In broad terms, this can be characterized as a split between 'artists' and 'political theorists' (or 'revolutionaries'). The main issue at stake was the insistence of the 'theoretical' group, based around Debord in Paris, that art could not be recognized as a separate activity, with its own legitimate specificity, but must be dissolved into a unitary revolutionary praxis. After the split the SI was reformed and centralized around a central office in Paris. The journal continued to appear annually, but the next conference was not held till 1966 – in Paris.

After 1962 Debord assumed an increasingly central role in the SI surrounded by a new generation of militants who were not professional artists. The earlier artistic goals and projects either fell away or were transposed into an overtly political (and revolutionary) register within a unitary theoretical system. In 1967 Debord published his *magnum opus*, 'The Society of the Spectacle', a lapidary totalization of situationist theory, which combined the situationist analysis of culture and society within the framework of a theoretical approach and terminology drawn from Lukács's 'History and Class Consciousness' and the political line of council communism, characteristic of the *Socialisme öu barbarie group*, but distinctively recast by Debord. In this book, Debord described how capitalist societies, east and west (state and market) complemented the increasing fragmentation of everyday life, including labour, with a nightmarish false unity of the 'spectacle', passively consumed by the alienated workers (in the broadest possible sense of non-capitalist and non-bureaucrats). Not until they became 'conscious' (in the totalizing Lukácsian sense) of their own alienation could and would they rise up to liberate themselves and institute an anti-statist dictatorship of the proletariat in which power was democratically exercised by autonomous workers' councils.

'The Society of the Spectacle' is composed in an aphoristic style, drawing on the philosophical writings of Hegel and the polemical tropes of the young Marx, and it continues to extol *détournement* (and the obligation to plagiarize) but, in general, it is a work of theory without artistic pretensions. This did not mean, however, that the situationists had retreated from any forms of action but the elaboration of theory. The previous winter a student uprising at the University of Strasbourg, one of a wave sweeping across the world, had been specifically inspired by the SI and based its political activity on situationist theory. The next year, of course, 1968, saw the great revolutionary uprising, first of students, then of workers, which threatened to topple the De Gaulle regime. Here again student groups were influenced by the SI, especially at Nanterre, where the uprising took shape, and the situationists themselves played an active role in the events, seeking to encourage and promote workers' councils, and a revolutionary line within them, without exercizing power of decision and execution or political control of any kind.

1968 was both the zenith of SI activity and success, and also the beginning of its rapid decline. One more issue of the journal was published, in 1969, and the same year the last conference was held, in Venice. Further splits followed and in 1972 the organization was dissolved. For the Situationists 1968 proved a 'Bitter Victory'. Indeed, ironically, their contribution to the revolutionary uprising was remembered mainly through the diffusion and spontaneous expression of situationist ideas and slogans, in graffiti and in posters using *détournement* (mainly of comic strips, a graphic technique pioneered after 1962), as well as in serried assaults on the routines of everyday life. In short, a cultural rather than a political contribution, in the sense that the Situationists had come to demand. Debord's political theory was more or less reduced to the title of his book, generalized as an isolated catch-phrase, separated from its theoretical project. Council communism was quickly forgotten by students and workers alike.

Thus the Situationist International was fated to be incorporated into the legendary series of avant-garde artists and groups whose path had intersected with popular revolutionary movements at emblematic moments. Its dissolution in 1972 brought to an end an epoch which began in Paris with the Futurist Manifesto of 1909 – the epoch of the historic avant-gardes with their typical apparatus of international congress, quarrels, scandals, indictments, expulsions, polemics, group photographs, little magazines, mysterious episodes, provocations, utopian theories and intense desires to transform art, society, the world and the pattern of everyday life.

This is a truth, but a partial truth. If we can see the SI as the summation of the historic avant-gardes, we can equally see it as the summation of 'western marxism' – and in neither case does the fact that a period has ended mean that it need no longer be understood or its lessons learned and valued. May '68 was both a curtain-call and a prologue, a turning-point in a drama we are all still blindly living. Western marxism developed in two phases. The first followed the 1914–1918 war and the Bolshevik revolution. In 1923 Lukács published his collection of essays 'History and Class Consciousness' and Korsch the first edition of his book, 'Marxism and Philosophy'.

The second phase of western marxism came after the Second World War and the victory over fascism of the Soviet Union (together, of course, with its American ally). Immediately after the war Sartre began his long process of interweaving existentialism with marxism, and Lefebvre published his 'Critique of Everyday Life' (1947). A decisive new impetus came when the Soviet Union suppressed the Hungarian revolution in 1956 and a wave of intellectuals left the western Communist parties. It is from this date especially that we can see the beginnings of the 'New Left' and the intellectual cross-currents which led to 1968.

Debord dates his own 'independent' life from 1950, when he first threw himself into the artistic and cultural scene of the Left Bank, its bars, its cinemas, its bookshops. His thought was marked in turn by Sartre (the concept of 'situation') and Lerebvre (the critique of everyday life), the 'Arguments' group and Lukács (the subject-object dialectic and the concept of 'reification'). In the first instance Debord envisaged Lefebvre's everyday life as a series of fortuitous Sartrean situations. Existence, Sartre had argued, is always existence within surroundings, within a given situation, which is both lived-in and lived-beyond, through the subject's choice of the manner of being in that situation, itself a given. Debord, following Lefebvre's injunction to transform everyday life, incorporated that as an injunction to construct situations, as an artistic and practical activity, rather than accept them as given, to impose a conscious order at least in enclaves of everyday life, an order which would permit fully free activity, play set consciously within the context of everyday life, not separated from it in the sphere of 'leisure'.

From situation, Debord enlarged his scope to city, and from city to society. This, in turn, involved an enlargement of the subject of transformation from the group (the affinity-group of Lettrists or Situationists with shared goals) to the mass of the proletariat, constructing the totality of social situations in which it lived. It is at this point that Debord was forced to think beyond the sphere of possible action of himself and his immediate associates and engage with classical revolutionary theory. This, in turn, radicalized him further and sent him back to western marxism to reinterpret it on a new basis. Instead of changing transient and brief periods, limited *ambiances*, the whole of social space and time was to be transformed and, if it was to be transformed, it must first be theorized.

Debord, reading Lukács many decades later, was able to relate Lukács' theory of the reification of labour in the commodity to the appearance of 'consumerism' in the long post-war boom of Keynesian capitalism. Just as Lukács was writing during the first period of Fordism, that of standardization and mass production, so Debord was writing in the second, that of variety marketing and mass consumption. Consumer society confronted producers with their products alienated not only in money form, quantitatively, but also in image form, qualitatively, in advertizing, publicity, media – instances of the general form of 'spectacle'.

He took from Lukács the ringing endorsement of the revolutionary workers' councils in *History and Class Consciousness* and transposed Lukács critique of the mensheviks to fit the contemporary western communist parties and the unions they controlled.

Debord had only to read 'communist' for 'menshevik' to fit a contemporary political analysis into the historic Lukácsian framework. But, for Debord, the fact that the communist party was bureaucratic in form and ideology, a force of order rather than revolution, meant, not that an alternative party should be built, but that the very idea of 'party' should be rejected. Instead of a party, necessarily separated from the working class, the revolution should be carried out by the workers themselves, organized in self-managing councils.

At the same time, the concept of revolution itself changed from the Leninist model. Instead of seeking state power, the councils should move directly to abolishing the state. The revolution meant the immediate realization of the realm of freedom, the abolition of all forms of reification and alienation in their totality, and their replacement by forms of untrammeled subjectivity. Thus the syndicalist spectre rose up again to haunt social democracy, fortified by the philosophical armoury of western marxism and carried, in accordance with Debord's temperament, to its extreme conclusion. Lukács had always assumed the existence of 'mediations' within the totality, forms of unity within difference, but Debord's maximalist vision sought to abolish all 'separation', to unite subject and object, practice and theory, structure and superstructure, politics and administration, in a single unmediated totality.

The impetus behind this maximalism came from the idea of the transformation of everyday life. This in turn derived from Lefebvre's idea of 'total (that is, unalienated) man'. Lefebvre was the first French marxist to revive the 'humanist' ideas of the young Marx and (though he never questioned the privileged role of economics in marxist theory) he began to argue that marxism had been wrongly restricted to the domain of the economic and the political, when its analysis should be extended to cover every aspect of life, wherever alienation existed – in private life, in leisure time, as well as at work. Marxism needed a topical sociology; it should be involved in cultural studies; it should not be afraid of the trivial; in the last analysis, marxism meant, not only the transformation of economic and political structures, but 'the transformation of life right down to its detail, right down to its everydayness', economics and politics were only means to the realization of an unalienated, 'total' humanity.

Lefebvre began his intellectual career in the 1920s in close association with Andre Breton and the Surrealists. As a member of the *Philosophies* group he co-signed the manifesto against the Riff war in 1924 and remained involved with the surrealists at least until his entry into the Communist party in 1928. In retrospect, personal and political quarrels aside, we can see how much Lefebvre owed to Breton – not only the idea of the transformation of everyday life, a fundamental surrealist concept, but even his introduction to Hegel and Marx.

Historians of western marxism have tended to discount Breton, seeing him as 'off-beat' or lacking in 'seriousness'. Yet, as did Lukács, Breton brought about an eruption of romanticism into marxism, and again as with Lukács, this both drew from a previous literary background and reflected a convert's enthusiasm for the drama of revolution.

For Breton, the transformation of everyday life moved on a different time scale from that of the Revolution. It could take place, for *individuals*, here and now, however transiently and imperfectly. In Breton's interpretation of Freud, we find that everyday 'reality' can satisfy us all too little. As a result we are forced to act out our desires as fantasies, thus compensating 'for the insufficiencies of our actual existence'. But anyone 'who has any artistic gift', rather than retreating into fantasy or displacing repressed desires into symptoms, can 'under certain favourable conditions' sublimate desires into artistic creation, thus putting the world of desire in positive contact with that of reality, even managing to 'turn these desire-fantasies into reality'. In his book 'Communicating Vessels' Breton describes how his dreams re-organize events of everyday life ('day's residues' in Freudian terms) into new patterns, just as everyday life presents him with strange constellations of material familiar from his dreams. The two supposedly distinct realms are in fact 'communicating vessels'. Thus Breton does not argue for dreams over everyday life, or vice versa, but for their reciprocal interpermeation, as value and goal. Debord's rejections of surrealism focussed mainly on the blind alleys and wrong turnings down which Breton's faith in the unconscious and belief in 'objective chance' (a phrase, incidentally, borrowed from Engels) came to lead him in his later years.

However, despite opting for Lettrism rather than Surrealism, Debord was still able to collaborate with the Belgian Surrealists around *'Les levres nues'*, in the late fifties, and he continued to recognize the legacy he had inherited from Surrealism, albeit in mutilated form, while also striving to supersede it, to go beyond the 'realization' of art to its 'suppression', that is, its integration into the totality through its own self-negation. What this meant in effect was the displacement of the surrealist notion of poetic freedom, as the uncompromising release of repressed desire, into the political register of council communism. This displacement also involved, of course, a semantic shift in the meaning of the word 'desire' (from unconscious to conscious) which enabled the SI to endorse the surrealist slogan 'Take your desires for reality', adopted by the Enragés at Nanterre. The poetic revolution *must be* the political revolution and vice versa, unconditionally and in full self-consciousness.

However, the Lettrist International around Debord was not the only channel by which surrealist, and marxist, thought reached the Situationist International. The artists from the Cobra movement brought with them their own revision of Surrealism and their own political positions and theories. Asger Jorn, in particular, was not only a prolific artist and dedicated organizer, but also a compulsive writer and theorist. The first phase of the SI was marked as much by Jorn as by Debord and though Jorn resigned from the group in 1961, his influence was lasting. He was never criticized or denounced by Debord, either through the period of the schism (when Jorn collaborated with both parties, under different false names) or during the highly politicized period before and after 1968. Debord paid a moving posthumous tribute to his old comrade (Jorn died in 1973) in his introductory essay to *'Le Jardin d'Albisola'* (1974), a book of photographs of the ceramic garden Jorn had built in Albisola, northern Italy, in the late fifties, the time of their first contact.

Cobra (the name originates from the initial letters of Copenhagen, Brussels, Amsterdam) was formed by a group of artists from Denmark, Holland and Belgium (including Jorn and Constant) in November, 1948. In broad terms, Cobra grew from the disenchantment with surrealism of artists whose political ideas were formed during the Resistance. After Breton returned to Paris, he took a militantly anti communist line politically and sought to re-impose his own views and tastes on surrealist groups which had flourished independently during his exile. These artists were unwilling to break with communist comrades with whom they had worked in the struggle against the German occupation and wanted to see Surrealism move forward on to new, experimental ground, rather than revive pre-war trends, especially towards abstraction in painting and 'super-naturalism' in ideology.

Jorn, Constant, and their friends had been formed by the Resistance and were active in small national avant-garde groups. At the end of the war, Jorn returned to Paris (where he had studied with Léger and worked with Le Corbusier in the late thirties). There he met members of the French surrealist movement who later joined the Revolutionary Surrealists, and also Constant, with whom he struck up a friendship. He even went on a pilgrimage to visit André Breton, who dubbed him 'Swedenborgian', but reportedly, 'got lost in the labyrinth of theories delivered sometimes rather abruptly in Jorn's gravelly French'.

Later the same year (December, 1946) Jorn went north to Lapland to spend time in retreat, reading and writing, developing the outline of a heterodox marxist theory of art.

Before the war, Jorn had been deeply influenced by the Danish syndicalist, Christian Christensen, and he continued to honour Christensen, paying homage to him in the pages of the 'Situationist International' many decades later. During the Resistance Jorn left syndicalism for communism, but he always retained the libertarian principles he had learned from Christensen, as well as a faith in direct action and collective work. The theoretical project Jorn set himself was massive and arduous. Essentially he wanted to recast elements from Surrealism (magic, child art, 'primitive' art, automatism) and combine these with strong strands of Scandinavian romanticism and libertarian activism within a materialist and marxist framework.

He began by defining materialism in relation to nature. Materialist art would express the natural being of humans as well as their social being. European art was vitiated by its classical heritage, its metaphysical over-valuation of reason and the ideal. The 'materialist attitude to life' must involve the expression of natural rhythms and passions, rather than seeking to subordinate activity to a sovereign reason or engage in the unnatural and slavish copying of nature. Materialist art, therefore, was on the side of festival and play – 'spontaneity, life, fertility and *movement*'. Jorn consistently attacked classicism (and its surrogate realism and functionalism) and favoured instead the 'oriental' and the 'nordic', which he associated with ornament and magical symbolism respectively. Jorn believed that the intensively local and the extensively cosmopolitan should mutually reinforce each other.

Constant, though rather more sparing in his prose, developed a line of thought similar to that of Jorn, but much simpler. For Constant Surrealism had been right in its struggle against constructivism ('objective formalism') but had become too intellectualized. It was necessary to find new ways of expressing the impulse that lay behind Surrealism in order to create a popular, libertarian art. In his painting, Constant, like Jorn, developed a style which was neither abstract nor realist, but used figurative forms that drew on child art and the motifs of magical symbolism, without effacing the differentiating trace of physical gestures.

Cobra thus brought together elements from Surrealism, a commitment to revolutionary politics, and an openess to experiment and new ideas, a determination to make art which was materialist, festive and vital. Cobra wanted to displace the three major contenders in the Paris art-world: the decomposing School of Paris (which sought to unite a refined Cubism with a pallid Fauvism), orthodox Bretonian Surrealism, and the various forms of abstract and non-figurative art. By the time the movement dissolved in 1951, after only three years of existence, it had both triumphed historically, but failed in its immediate aims, in that it proved impossible at that time either to set up alternative art centres to Paris or to conquer the Paris art-world from the outside. Although many of the Cobra artists stayed in loose touch, the group broke up organizationally and geographically. Jorn and Constant both ended up in the Situationist movement (which underwent the same problems between Paris and the Cobra capitals).

The immediate reasons for the break-up of the group were organizational and political, personal and material. The Danish group pursued a life of its own (like ostriches, Dotrémont complained, in contrast to the French, who were often more like giraffes, with their heads held high in the air); the Dutch and the Belgians began to drift to Paris, and Paris, in turn, began to absorb elements of Cobra back into the mainstream. Personal difficulties threatened to divide close friends. Dotrémont, Constant and Jorn reacted to their dilemma in different ways. Dotrémont in Belgium eventually became disenchanted with politics altogether and began to take the first steps towards de-politicizing the movement. Constant and Jorn disagreed. In a world in which 'politics are (not without our complicity) put between us and the Universe like barbed wire', it was all the more important to struggle to maintain a genuine and direct relationship between art and politics, to reject stultifying labels and ideological prejudices – 'Experimentation in these conditions has a historical role to play: to thwart prejudice, to unclog the senses, to unbutton the *uniforms of fear.*' However, Constant and Jorn interpreted that historical role differently. Constant began to move out of painting altogether, collaborating with the Dutch architect, Aldo van Eyck, and then, after the dissolution of Cobra, moving to London and devoting himself to research into experimental urbanism and city-planning. Constant sought an art that would be public and collective in a way that easel painting could never be, a transposition into contemporary terms of the ideas of the communal, festive use of space. Jorn persisted in painting, but eager to find a way of reviving the Cobra project in a purer, more advanced form: a hope realized with the foundation of the SI.

Looking back at the Cobra movement, it is possible now to see many points of similarity between Cobra attitudes and those of Jackson Pollock or De Kooning (who often looks like a displaced mutant of Dutch Cobra). Pollock, like Jorn, extolled the spontaneous, the vital, the ornamental (in Jorn's sense of the 'arabesque'). His background too was in political mural art, which he rejected for a new approach, indebted to Surrealism but departing from it. Like Jorn he was influenced by indigenous ritual art – Indian sand painting and totems, rather than Viking runes and ancient petroglyphs. Pollock's 'Blue Poles' can be measured with Jorn's great 'Stalingrad', now in Silkeborg. If Jorn always resisted the pull of abstraction, it was largely because of his political commitment, the quest for an art which would be neither bourgeois, Stalinist (social realist) or surrealist. Jorn's experience of the Resistance and the vicissitudes of the Cold War in Europe prevented the headlong slide into individualist abstraction of his American counterparts.

After leaving a Swiss sanitarium in 1954, Jorn began to visit Italy for his health, and because it was relatively a cheap place to live. Indefatigable as ever, he had founded the Movement for an Imaginist Bauhaus while still in the clinic, and soon he was able to combine some of the old Cobra artists with new Italian friends, drawn first from the Nuclear Painting movement, and then (after 1955) the group gathered around Pinot Gallizio in Alba. This new venture of Jorn's began after he was approached by the Swiss artist, Max Bill, who had been given the job of setting up the new *Hochschule für Gestallung* in Ulm, which was planned as a 'new Bauhaus'. At first, Jorn was enthusiastic about the project but he soon found himself in violent disagreement with Bill.

Jorn was in favour of an ideal Bauhaus which would bring together artists in a collective project, in the spirit of William Morris or the Belgian socialist, Van der Velde, who had inspired Gropius. But he was resolutely opposed to functionalism and what he regarded as a moralistic rationalism that threatened to exclude spontaneity, irregularity and ornament in the name of order, symmetry and puritanism. The polemic against the technological thinking of Bill brought Jorn to formulate a theoretical and polemical counterattack, on the grounds of general aesthetics and urbanism. At the 1954 Triennale of Industrial Design in Milan, Jorn engaged in public debate with Bill on the theme of 'Industrial Design in Society'. Jorn argued that the Bauhaus and Le Corbusier had been revolutionary in their day, but they had been wrong in subordinating aesthetics to technology and function, which had inevitably led towards standardization, automation, and a more regulated society. Thus Jorn began to venture into areas which brought him closer to Constant, as well as to the Lettrist International who were simultaneously developing their own theories of unitary urbanism, psychogeography and *dérive*. In 1955 Jorn met Pinot Gallizio, who had been a partisan during the war, was now an independent left councilman in his hometown of Alba and shared Jorn's interests in popular culture and archaeology. Together they set up an Experimental Laboratory as a prototype Imaginist Bauhaus, libertarian (without teachers or pupils, but only co-workers), aiming to unite all the arts and committed to an anti-productivist aesthetic. The next year, Pinot Gallizio and Jorn organized a conference in Alba, grandly entitled the 'First World Congress of Free Artists', which was attended by both Constant and Gil Wolman, representative of the Lettrist International (though Debord himself did not attend). The stage was now set for the foundation of the Situationist International.

Besides a common approach to urbanism, there were other issues that linked Jorn, Pinot-Gallizio and Constant with the Lettrist International: a revolutionary political position. Independent of both Stalinism and Trotskyism (and their artistic correlates, social realism and orthodox surrealism), a dedicated seriousness about the theory and goals of art combined with an unswerving avant-gardism, and a common interest in the transformation of everyday life, in festivity, in play and in waste or excess (as defined by the norms of a purposive rationalism). The journal of the Lettrist International was called 'Potlatch' after the great forests of the Northwest Coast Indians of Canada and Alaska, in which the entire wealth of a chief was given away or even 'wastefully' destroyed. Described by Boas (and his native informants) and then by Marcel Mauss in his classic 'The Gift', the idea had fascinated French intellectuals. Potlatch was taken to exemplify the opposite of an exchange or market economy – objects were treated as gifts rather than as commodities, in the setting of a popular feast. Generosity and waste rather than egotism and utility determined their disposal. The theme of festivity is linked, for Jorn, with that of play. In his 1948 'Magic and the Fine Arts' Jorn observed that 'if play is continued among adults in accordance with their natural life force, life, in retaining its creative spontaneity, then it is the content of ritual, its humanity and life, which remain the primary factor and the form changes uninterruptedly, therefore, with the living content. But if play lacks its vital purpose then ceremony fossilizes into an empty form which has no other purpose than its own formalism, the *observance of forms*'. Festivity is thus ritual vitalized by play in the same way, the formal motif of art must be vitalized by the creative figure, the play of calligraphy. This concept of play linked Jorn closely to Constant who was deeply influenced by Johan Mulzinga's *Homo Ludens*, published in Holland just before the war. Mulzinga argued that man should be seen not simply as *homo faber* (man as maker) or *homo sapiens* (man as thinker) but also as *homo ludens* (man as player). He traces the role of play both in popular festivities and in art – in the rhythms of music and dance, as well as masks, totems and 'the magical mazes of ornamental motifs'. Mulzinga's thought converged in France with that of Roger Caillois, who also made the link to festival and thence to leisure: '*Vacation* is the successor of the festival. Of course, this is still a time of expenditure and free activity, when regular work is interrupted, but it is a phase of *relaxation* and not of *paroxysm*'. Play too had a crucial place both in Breton's thought and to less extent Sartre's. In the background, of course, was Schiller's celebration of play in his 'On the Aesthetic Education of Man'.

In 1957 the Situationist International was proclaimed at Cosio d'Arroscia and the collaboration between Jorn and Debord was sealed by the publication of a jointly composed book. This work, '*Fin de Copenhague*', like '*Memoires*', was both a *détournement* of found images and words, and a piece of impromptu, spontaneous, collective work in the festive spirit. The common ground between the different currents in the Situationist International was reinforced and enriched by theoretical publication in the journal and by joint artistic projects. These established both an enlarged aesthetic scope and a clarified political direction, in which all the parties could contribute. The next task was to make a dramatic intervention in the art-world and this was achieved in 1959, when both Jorn and Pinot Gallizio held exhibitions in Paris in May, and Constant in Amsterdam later that year. Jorn's show of *Modifications* was intended, in a startlingly original manner, to position his work not only within the situationist context of *détournement*, but also between Jackson Pollock and kitsch, in a gesture which would transcend the duality of the two. In his catalogue notes Jorn stressed that an artwork was always simultaneously an object and an intersubjective communication, a sign. The danger for art was that of falling back into being simply an object, an end in itself. On the one hand, Pollock produced paintings which were objectified traces of an 'act in itself', through which he sought to realize his own self in matter for his own pleasure, rather than as the realization of an intersubjective link. The action of painting failed to be effective as an act of communication. On the other hand, the anonymous kitsch paintings which Jorn bought in the market were merely objects in themselves with no trace of subjective origin at all, simply free-floating in time and space. By overpainting them in his own mind, Jorn sought to resolve a subjectivity to them, to reintegrate them into a circuit of communication, a dialectic of subject and object.

Jorn characterized Pollock as an 'oriental' painter (on the side of abstract ornament) and the kitsch works as 'classical' (on the side of representation, both idealizing and naturalistic). In the past, Jorn had himself taken the side of the 'oriental' against the 'classical'. Thus he commented on the Laocoön, 'Laocoön's fate the fate of the upper class', identifying the snakes (the serpentine, oriental line) with the natural, the materialist, the revolutionary classes, and the representation of Laocoön (the classical form) with the ideal, with repression and sublimation. However, in the case of his own 'Modifications' Jorn characterized his own project as 'nordic' rather than 'oriental'. Here the 'nordic', separated out and set over and against the 'oriental', implied the use of 'symbolic' motifs rather than abstract ornament. Thus the paintings were magical actions which revitalized dead objects through subjective inscription, transforming them into living signs. The kitsch paintings were not simply *détournées* but were sacrificial objects in a festive fertility rite. Objectified beings were broken open, vandalized and mutilated to realise the 'becoming' latent within them.

At the same time, Jorn saw the 'Modifications' as a celebration of kitsch, it was only because kitsch was popular art, that a living kernel could still be found in it. In his very first contribution to the Danish art magazine *Helheston*, during the war, Jorn had written in praise of kitsch, in his essay, 'Intimate banalities' (1941). Jorn wanted to get beyond the distinction between 'high' and 'low' art, while his sympathies were always on the side of the 'low' in its struggle against the 'high'. Jorn also wanted to unite the two dialectically and supersede the split between the two, which deformed all human subjectivity. In this article he praised both the collective rage for celluloid flutes which swept a small Danish town (trivial, yet festive) and the work of a tatoo artist (an ornamental supplement, both mutilation and creation, like that of the 'modifications' themselves). Further, in combining 'high' with 'low', Jorn also wanted to deconstruct the antinomy of 'deep' and 'shallow'. In 'Magic and the Fine Arts', he had long previously remarked how 'today we are unable to create general artistic symbols as the expression of more than a single individual reality. Modern artists have made desperate attempts to do this. The basic problem is that a general concept must be created by the people themselves as a communal reality, and today we do not have that kind of fellowship among the people which would allow that. If the artist has plumbed the depths, like Klee, he has lost his contact with the people, and if he has found a popular means of expression, like Mayakovsky, he has, in a tragic way, betrayed the deeper side of himself, because a people's culture which combines the surface issues with the deeper things does not exist'. Thus, for Jorn, the deconstruction of antinomies could only be fully realized through social change, but in the meantime, artistic gestures like those of the 'Modifications' could symbolically enact their possibility and thus help form the missing fellowship.

Pinot Gallizio and Constant followed different paths. Rather than seeking, like Jorn, to re-inscribe unalienated creativity into easel painting itself, albeit in an original, dialectical form, they each began to push beyond the limits of easel painting. For Pinot Gallizio, the economy of standardization and quantity, of unending sameness, must be superseded by a civilization of 'standard-luxury', marked by unending diversity. Machines would be playful. In the service of *homo ludens* rather than *homo faber*. Free time, rather than being filled with banality and brain-washing, could be occupied in creating brightly painted *autostrade* (freeways), massive architectural and urbanistic constructions, fantastic palaces of synesthesia.

Constant's 'New Babylon' project was similar to Pinot Gallizio's in its conceptual basis, but very different in its style. In his essay 'The Great Game to come' (*'Le Grand Jeu a venir'*, published in 1959) Constant called for a playful rather than functional urbanism, a projection into the imaginary future of the discoveries made by the Lettrist method of *dérive*, drifting journeys through actually existing cities to experience rapid, aimless changes of environment (*'ambiance'*) and consequent changes of psychological state. Constant had been inspired by Pinot Gallizio, who had become the political representative of the gypsies who visited Alba, to build a model for a nomadic encampment. From this he developed to building architectural models of a visionary city ('New Babylon'), as well as making blueprints, plans and elevations, moving out of painting altogether. Sceptical of the prospect of immediate political change, Constant set about planning the urban framework for a possible post-revolutionary society of the future. New Babylon was devised on the assumption of a technologically advanced society in which, through the development of automation, alienated labour had been totally abolished and humanity could develop itself entirely to play. It would be the ceaselessly changing, endlessly dramatic habitat of *homo ludens*, a vast chain of megastructures each of which could be internally re-organized at will to satisfy the desires of its transient users and creators.

Thus the Situationist International launched itself into the artworld. In Paris and Amsterdam, with exceptional ambition and bravura. Not only were the works formally path-breaking, pushing up to and beyond the limits of painting, but their stakes, their theoretical engagement, went far beyond the contemporary discourse of art and aesthetics in its implications. There had not been such a fruitful interchange between art, theory and politics since the 1920s. Yet, despite this, the Situationist intervention in the art world hardly lasted a year. In the summer of 1960 Pinot Gallizio was expelled (he died in 1964) and Constant resigned, both as a result of disagreements and denunciations stemming from contacts they and/or their associates made in the art world, outside the framework of the SI. In April of the next year, 1961, Jorn resigned, as part of the upheaval which led to the schism of 1962, when Nash and the German *Spur* group of artists (who had joined in 1959) were ousted and set up the dissident Second Situationist International and Situationist Bauhaus, which have lasted up to today, maintaining the project of a situationist art, with vivid flares of provocation and festivity.

The refusal by Debord and his supporters of any separation between artistic and political activity, which precipitated the schism, led in effect, not to a new unity within situationist practice but to a total elimination of art, except in propagandist and agitational forms. In fact, the SI simply reappropriated the orthodox Marxist and Leninist triad of theory, propaganda, agitation, which structures Lenin's 'what is to be done'. Theory displaced art as the vanguard activity, and politics (for those who wished to retain absolutely clean hands) was postponed till the day when it would be placed on the agenda by the spontaneous revolt of those who executed rather than gave orders. Miraculously, that day duly came, to the surprise of the Situationists as much as anyone else, and the uprising was ignited, to an extent, by the impact of the preceding years of 'theoretical practice'. The problem remained that the revolutionary subjectivity that erupted into the objectified 'second nature' of the society of the spectacle came from nowhere and vanished again whence it came. In terms of situationist theory it represented a paroxystic expansion and collapse of consciousness, detached from the historical process which faced the subject, before, during and after, as an essentially undifferentiated negative totality.

In a strange way, the two legendary theoretical mentors of 1968, Debord and Althusser, form mirror images of each other, complementary halves of the ruptured unity of western Marxism. Thus Debord saw a decline in Marx's theory after the 'Communist Manifesto' and the defeats of 1848, while Althusser, conversely, rejected everything before 1845. (They could both agree to accept the Manifesto, but otherwise near-total breakdown!) For Debord, everything after 1848 was sullied by an incipient economism and mechanism; for Althusser everything before 1845 was ruined by idealism and subjectivism. For Debord, the revolution would be the result of the subjectivity of the proletariat, 'the class of consciousness'. 'Consciousness' had no place in Althusser's system, nor even subjectivity – he postulated a historical 'process without a subject'. When, after the defeat of 1968, both systems disintegrated, leftists abandoned the grand boulevards of Totality, for a myriad *dérives* and peregrinations in the winding lanes and labyrinthine back-streets.

The publication in France of Lukács 'History and Class Consciousness' (1960) and Levi-Strauss's 'The Savage Mind' (1962) provided the basis for two fundamentally opposed totalizing myths, to be combatted on the terrain of Marxism by two antagonistic crusades, one for a true revolutionary subjectivity (Debord) and the other for a true revolutionary objectivity (Althusser), each vitiated by the idealism and rationalism the other denounced. One was, so to speak, abstractly romantic, the other abstractly classical. The unfulfilled dialectical project that remains (one which Jorn would have relished) is evidently that of re-articulating the two halves, each a one-sided development to an extreme of one aspect of the truth.

In 1978 Debord returned to the cinema to make *'In Girum Imus Nocte et Consumimur Igni'*, like his previous work a collage of found footage, but with a soundtrack that is simultaneously an autobiographical, a theoretical and a political reflection. He remembers Ivan Chtcheglov (the first formulator of 'unitary urbanism') and pays tribute to his dead comrades, Jorn and Pinot Gallizio. He recapitulates the story of Lacenaire in 'Les Enfants du Paradis', long the object of his identification, like Dr Omar and Prince Valiant. He does not regret that an avant-garde was sacrificed in the shock of a charge. *'Je trouve qu'elle était faite pour cela'*. Avant-gardes have their day and then, 'after them operations are undertaken in a much vaster theatre'. The Situationist International left a legacy of great value. The wasteful luxury of utopian projects, however doomed, is no bad thing, we need not persist in seeking a unique condition for revolution, but neither need we forget the desire for liberation. We move from place to place and from time to time. This is true of art as well as politics.

Documents: Situationist International

Extracts from Situationist International Anthology
Edited and translated by Ken Knabb
Bureau of Public Secrets, 1981

Des souvenirs merveilleux surgissent soudain

certain de ne jamais être déçu

même à la fin

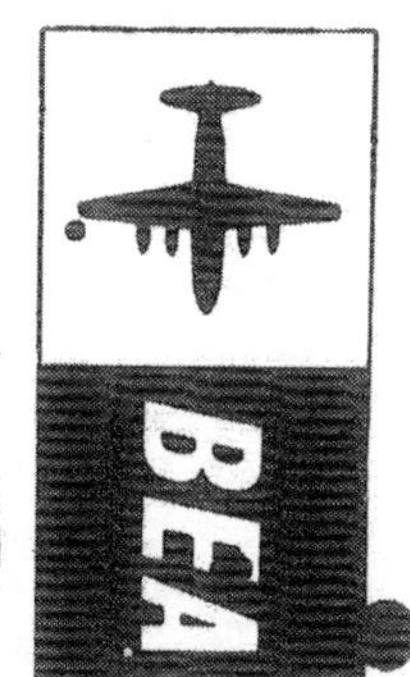

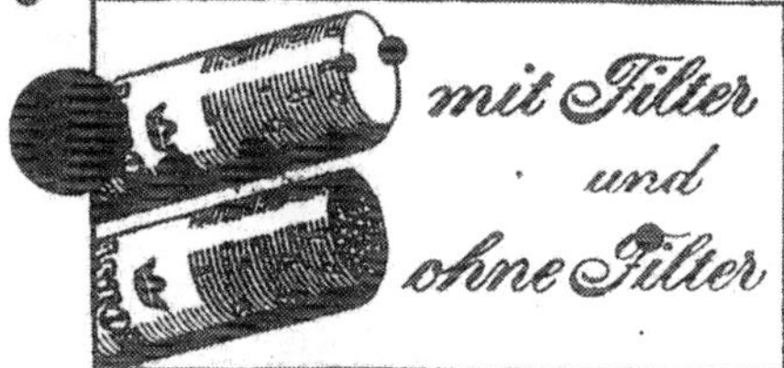

e tragikomische Geschichte – nicht ernst zu nehmen

lle a choisi

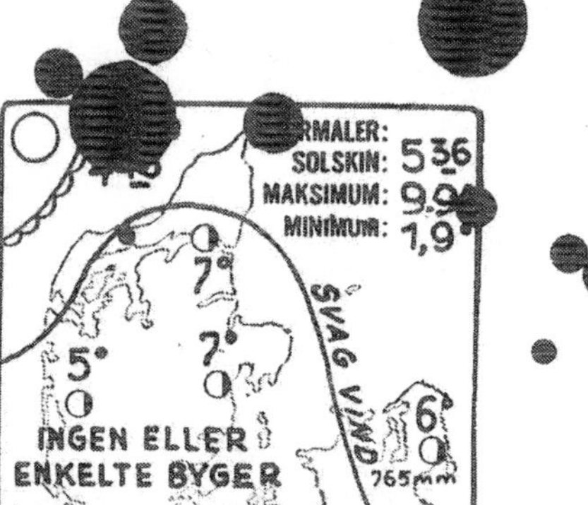

RENSEIGNEMENTS SITUATIONNISTES (CHRONOLOGIE)

DG : Der Deutsche Gedanke
SP : Spur
SR : Situationistik Rev.

A : article
B : brochure
C : conférence
E : exposition
F : film
L : livre
T : tract

La revue Internationale Situationniste sera le Bulletin central édité par les sections de l'Internationale Situationniste jusqu'au nº 8 inclus. Elle deviendra la *Revue de la section française* à partir du nº 12.

Référence à l'édition Van Gennep. nº / page	Dates	Revues (nº)	Publications	Conférences	Conseil central	Lieux	Participants	Démissions	Exclusions	
										1956
	Septembre					Alba (Congrès)	×			Gil J. Wolman (Internationale Lettriste/*Potlatch*); Asger Jorn, Giuseppe Pinot-Gallizio, Piero Simondo, Elena Verrone (Bauhaus Imaginiste); Constant (ex-Cobra); Sottsas et un ou deux inconnus (sans appartenance précise); Enrico Baj, exclu tout de suite du congrès sur l'exigence du délégué lettriste (Mouvement *Arte Nuclare* de Milan).
										1957
1/27	Juillet			1		Cosio d'Arroscia	×			**FONDATION. Rumney (Comité psychogéographique de Londres); Bernstein, Debord (Internationale Lettriste/*Potlatch*); Jorn, Olmo, Pinot-Gallizio, Simondo, Verrone (Mouvement pour un Bauhaus Imaginiste).**
										1958
1/27	25/26 janvier			2		Paris	×		×	Bernstein, Debord, Jorn, Khatib, Pinot-Gallizio. Olmo, Simondo, Verrone.
1/27	1er janvier		T			Munich				*Nervenruh! Keine experimente*, premier manifeste de la section allemande.
1/28	Mars								×	Rumney.
1/27	s. d.		T			Paris				*Nouveau théâtre d'opération dans la culture*, tract de la section française.
1/27	s. d.		T			Paris				*Aux producteurs de l'art moderne*, tract de la section française.
1/29	12 avril		T			Bruxelles				SCANDALE. Korun poursuivi. Tract : *Adresse de l'Internationale Situationniste à l'assemblée générale des critiques d'art.*
1/27	Mai		B			Turin				Édition italienne de *Rapport sur la construction des situations.*
2/27	30 mai		E			Turin	×			Exposition de peinture industrielle : Pinot-Gallizio, Melanotte.
2/27	Juin		T			Turin				Tract de Bernstein : *Elogio di Pinot-Gallizio.*
1/27	s. d.		A			Bruxelles				Article de Korun sur l'I.S. dans le nº 11 de *Gard Sivik.*
1/27	s. d.		B			Bruxelles				2e édition française de *Rapport sur la construction des situations.*
1/27	s. d.		A			Bruxelles				Article de Korun et Jorn dans *Kunst Meridiaan.*
	Juin	1				Paris				**Comité de rédaction : Dahou, Pinot-Gallizio, Wyckaert.**
1/27	Juin		B			Paris				Jorn publie *Pour la forme.*
2/29	4 juillet		T			Milan				SCANDALE van Guglielmi. Tract de la section italienne : *Difendete la liberta ovunque.*
2/29	7 juillet		T			Paris				Jorn publie : *Au secours de van Guglielmi.*
2/27	8 juillet		E			Milan	×			Exposition de peinture industrielle : Pinot-Gallizio, Melanotte.
2/27	Juillet		C			Turin				Déclaration de Jorn sur la peinture industrielle.
2/27	8 juillet		T			Milan				Réédition du texte de Bernstein : *Elogio di Pinot-Gallizio.*
2/12	Automne								×	Korun relevé de ses fonctions.
3/16	Novembre		T			Munich				*Erklärung von Amsterdam* de Constant et Debord. Document interne.
3/16	Novembre		T			Munich				*Thesen über die Kulturelle Revolution* de Debord. Idem.
	Décembre		L			Copenhague				Debord et Jorn publient *Mémoires.*
	Décembre	2				Paris				**Comité de rédaction : Dahou, Jorn, Wyckaert**
	s. d.		A			Amsterdam				Debord publie dans la revue du Stedelijk Museum : *Dix ans d'art expérimental : Jorn et son rôle dans l'invention théorique.*
										1959
3/17	Février								×	Platschek.
3/16	Mars		A			Amsterdam				*Résolution contre la restauration de la bourse d'Amsterdam.* Article de la section hollandaise.
3/19	17/20 avril			3		Munich	×			**Armando, Constant, Debord, Eisch, Höfl, Jorn, Melanotte, Oudejans, Pinot-Gallizio, Prem, Stadler, Sturm, Wyckaert, Zimmer.**
3/22	20 avril		T							***Ein Kultureller Putsch während Ihr Schlaft!*** **Tract.**
	Avril		F			Paris				Début du tournage de *Sur le passage de quelques personnes à travers une assez courte unité de temps.*
3/19	s.d.					Amsterdam				Fondation du bureau d'urbanisme unitaire à Amsterdam.
3/16	Avril		C			Amsterdam				Conférence sur magnétophone par la section hollandaise à l'Académie d'Architecture.
3/16	Juin		C			Amsterdam				Conférence sur magnétophone par la section hollandaise au Stedelijk Museum.
3/17	15 juillet	P				Amsterdam				Parution du premier numéro de *Potlatch* nouvelle série.
3/16	Août		A			Amsterdam				Article de la section hollandaise dans *Forum* nº 6.
3/18	Novembre		T			Alba				Tract dénonçant l'ignoble Cuixard, diffusé par le *Laboratorio Sperimentale* d'Alba.
3/35	Novembre		B			Turin				Pinot-Gallizio publie *Per un arte unitaria applicabile.*
	Décembre	3				Paris				**Comité de rédaction : Constant, Jorn, Sturm, Wyckaert.**
	Décembre		F			Paris				Montage de *Sur le passage de quelques personnes...*
	s. d.							×		Dahou.

Protagonistes, Chronologie, Bibliographie: Avec un index des noms insulté. Raspand & Voyer, *Editions Champs Libre*, 1972

1960

4/13	Mars		L			Copenhague				Jorn et Nash publient *Stavrim Soneter* chez Permild et Rosengreen.
4/13	Printemps								×	Alberts, Oudejans, Armando.
	Juin	**4**				**Paris**				**Comité de rédaction : Constant, Jorn, Sturm, Wyckaert.**
5/10	Eté								×	Pinot-Gallizio, Melanotte, Wuerich.
5/10	Eté							×		Constant.
5/11	20 juillet		B			Paris				Publication par Canjuers *(Socialisme ou Barbarie)* et Debord de *Préliminaires pour une définition de l'unité du programme révolutionnaire.*
5/10	Août	SP				Munich				Parution de *Spur* n° 1, revue de la section allemande.
5/19	**24/28 sept.**			**4**		**Londres**	×			**Debord, de Jong, Jorn, Kotanyi, Lindell, Nash, Prem, Sturm, Wyckaert, Zimmer.**
										Fondation du conseil central.
										Transfert du bureau d'urbanisme unitaire à Bruxelles. Directeur : Kotanyi.
5/14	**27 sept.**									***Resolution of the fourth conference of the S.I. concerning the imprisonment of Alexander Trocchi.***
5/26	**28 septembre**		C							**Déclaration faite au nom de la conférence de l'I. S. devant l'*Institut of Contemporary Art* par Wyckaert.**
	Septembre		F			Paris				Début du tournage de *Critique de la séparation.*
5/12	7 octobre		T							*Hands off Alexander Trocchi.* Tract.
5/12	**4/6 novembre**				**1**	**Bruxelles**	×			**Debord, (Jorn absent), Kotanyi, Nash, Sturm, Wyckaert.**
5/13										**Décision de boycott à l'encontre d'*Arguments*.**
5/10	Novembre	SP				Munich				Parution de *Spur* n° 2.
	Décembre	**5**				**Paris**				**Comité de rédaction (le conseil central) : Debord, Jorn, Kotanyi, Nash, Sturm, Wyckaert.**
6/39	Décembre		T			Munich				*Januar Manifest*, manifeste sur la fête par la section allemande.
5/11	s. d.		B			Paris				Jorn publie *Critique de la politique économique.*
5/11	s. d.					Silkeborg				Le musée d'art moderne de S. crée une bibliothèque situationniste.
	s. d.?	SP				Munich				Parution de *Spur* n° 3.
	s. d.							×		Höfl, Khatib.

1961

6/40	**6/8 janvier**				**2**	**Paris**	×			**Debord, Jorn, Kotanyi, Nash, Prem (qui remplace Sturm), Wyckaert.**
6/39	Janvier		T			Munich				*L'avant-garde est inacceptable*, tract des sections allemande et suédoise.
	Février		F			Paris				Montage de *Critique de la séparation.*
6/28	Février	SP				Munich				Parution de *Spur* n° 4.
7/50	Mars							×		Frankin.
6/41 7/53	s. d.									SCANDALE van de Loo. (Galerie van de Loo à Essen.)
6/40	**11/13 avril**				**3**	**Munich**	×			**Debord, Kotanyi, Nash, Sturm (Jorn démissionnaire, Wyckaert exclu).**
								×		Jorn.
									×	**Wyckaert.**
6/27	17 mai		C			Paris				Conférence sur magnétophone par Debord au C.N.R.S. : *Perspectives de modifications conscientes dans la vie quotidienne.*
7/51	Juin	SP				Munich				Parution de *Spur* n° 5. Menaces de saisie.
	Août	**6**				**Paris**				**Comité de rédaction (le conseil central) : Debord, Kotanyi, Nash, Sturm.**
7/25	**Août**			**5**		**Göteborg**	×			**Debord, Elde, de Jong, Kotanyi, Kunzelmann, Larsson, Martin, Nash, Prem, Stadler, Strid, Sturm, Vaneigem, Zimmer.**
										Election du nouveau conseil central.
										Zimmer détaché au bureau d'urbanisme unitaire à Bruxelles.
7/51	9 novembre	SP				Munich				Parution et saisie de *Spur* n° 6. Inculpation de Prem, Zimmer, Sturm, Kunzelmann.
7/51	10 novembre		T			Munich				Tract sur la saisie et les inculpations. Entraîne l'inculpation de Lausen.
	s.d.							×		Ovadia.

1962

	Janvier	SP				Munich				Parution de *Spur* n° 7.
7/49	**10/11 février**				**4**	**Paris**	×			**Debord, (Elde absent), Kotanyi, Kunzelmann, Lausen, Nash, Vaneigem. Ce sera la dernière réunion du conseil central.**
									×	**Kunzelmann, Prem, Sturm, Zimmer, Eisch, Nele, Fischer, Stadler (spuristes).**
			T							***Nicht hinauslehnen*, tract sur l'exclusion des spuristes.**
7/53 8/63	Mars					Stockholm		×	×	SCISSION : Nash, Elde, de Jong, Lindell, Larsson, Strid (nashistes).
	Avril	**7**				**Paris**				**Comité de rédaction (le conseil central) : Debord, Kotanyi, Lausen, Vaneigem.**
8/64	4 mai					Munich				Jugement des spuristes (5 mois ½ avec sursis).
8/64	25 juin		T			Munich				Tract sur le procès de Munich.
8/64	5 juillet					Munich				Jugement de Lausen. (Il fut emprisonné 3 semaines.)
8/64	16 juillet		T			Munich				*Das unbehagen in der Kultur*, tract sur la condamnation de Lausen.
8/56	Octobre	SR				Copenhague				Parution de *Situationistik Revolution* n° 1. Martin directeur. Revue de la section scandinave.
8/66	Octobre					Rome				Le *dernier* concile de l'Église catholique commence à Rome.
8/66	**12/16 novembre**			**6**		**Anvers**	×			**Bernstein, Debord, Kotanyi, Lausen, Martin, Strijbosch, Vaneigem.**
										Désignation du nouveau conseil central : Bernstein, Debord, Kotanyi, Lausen, Martin, Strijbosch, Trocchi, Vaneigem.
										Suppression de la division en sections. L'I.S. considérée comme un seul centre uni.
8/64	Novembre					Munich				Les spuristes font appel. Peines légèrement diminuées.
8/63	Novembre		C			Aarhus				Conférence de Martin à l'université d'Aarhus.

1963

	Janvier	8				Paris				Comité de rédaction (le conseil central) : Bernstein, Debord, Kotanyi, Lausen, Martin, Strijbosch, Trocchi, Vaneigem.
9/30 12/107	Février		T			Paris				*Aux poubelles de l'histoire*, tract contre Henri Lefebvre et la revue *Arguments*.
9/31	27 février		T			Anvers				*Pas de dialogue avec les suspects. Pas de dialogue avec les cons* (en néerlandais), tract contre une nuance de surréalistes staliniens.
9/31	Avril	DG				Bruxelles				Parution de *Der Deutsche Gedanke* nº 1, revue en allemand de l'I. S. Directeur : Vaneigem.
9/33	s. d.					Paris				L'I.S. rencontre deux délégués du Zengakuren : T. Kurokawa et Toru Tagaki.
9/31	Juin					Odense (Danemark)				SCANDALE : manifestation *Destruction RSG 6*, sous la direction de Martin.
			T							Réédition de *Danger! Official secret RSG 6*.
			B							Éditions en danois, français et anglais de la brochure : *Les situationnistes et les nouvelles formes d'action dans la politique et dans l'art*.
			E							Cartographies thermonucléaires de Martin et Bernstein.
										Rudi Renson refoulé à la frontière danoise.
9/33	27 octobre								×	Kotanyi, Laugesen.
9/34	Décembre		T			Paris				*Sur l'exclusion d'Attila Kotanyi* [illegible]act.

1964

9/36	12 février					Alba				Mort de Giuseppe Pinot-Gallizio.
9/37	Juillet		T			Paris				*España en el corazon*, texte sur de nouveaux tracts subversifs expérimentés en Espagne.
9/21 9/36	s.d.		T			Espagne/ Danemark				Comics érotico-politiques.
	Août	9				Paris				**Comité de rédaction : Bernstein, Martin, Strijbosch, Vaneigem.**
10/83	Septembre		A			Londres				Note de Bernstein dans le *Times Literary Supplement : About the S.I.*
10/83	Automne							×		Trocchi.
10/7	Décembre					Berkeley/ U.S.A.				SCANDALE : fête populaire à l'université.
10/83	s. d.		L			Paris/Aarhus				Debord publie *Contre le cinéma*, préface de Jorn, édité par l'*Institut Scandinave de Vandalisme Comparé*.

1965

10/22	s. d.					Danemark				Inculpation de Martin sur plainte du Réarmement Moral à propos de l'édition des comics espagnols et danois. L'inculpation fut abandonnée par la suite.
10/83	Février		T			Danemark				*Im Namen des Volkes*, tract de Martin sur le procès intenté par le Réarmement moral.
10/22	16 mars					Randers (Danemark)				SCANDALE anti-militariste orchestré par Martin.
10/24	18 mars									Explosion d'une bombe incendiaire déposée par le provocateur Kanstrup au domicile de Martin.
10/83	17 mars					Strasbourg				SCANDALE Moles/Schöffer avec tomates.
			T							*La tortue dans la vitrine*. Tract.
			T							Réédition de *Correspondance avec un cybernéticien*.
10/83	Mars								×	Lausen.
10/43	Juillet		T			Alger				*Adresse aux révolutionnaires d'Algérie et de tous les pays*.
10/3	13/16 août					Los Angeles				SCANDALE : grande fête populaire à Watts, avec pillages et incendies.
10/7	20 octobre					Edimburg				SCANDALE : grande fête populaire à l'université avec *teach-in*.
10/84	Novembre		B			Paris				Réédition en cinq langues de l'*Adresse aux révolutionnaires*...
10/84	Décembre		T			Paris/Alger				*La lutte des classes en Algérie*. Tract édité à Alger, imprimé à Paris, diffusé dans Alger et les principales villes d'Algérie.
10/84	Décembre		B			Paris/U.S.A.				*The decline and the fall*... Édité et imprimé à Paris. Diffusé aux U.S.A. Très vite réédité à New York puis un peu partout aux U.S.A.
10/84	s. d.									Vaneigem termine son *Traité*.

1966

	Mars	10				Paris				**Comité de rédaction : Bernstein, Frey, Khayati, Martin, Vaneigem.**
11/55	s. d.							×		Renson.
11/54	9/11 juillet			7		Paris	×			Bernstein, Debord, Frey, Edith Frey, Garnault, Hartstein, Holl, Khayati, Lungela, Martin, Nicholson-Smith, Vaneigem, Viénet.
11/55									×	Strijbosch.
11/55	Été								×	Hartstein.
11/23	Nov./décembre					Strasbourg				SCANDALE avec retour de la colonne Durruti.
11/33	Novembre		T			Strasbourg				*Le retour de la colonne Durruti*, très beau comics par A. Bertrand.
	Novembre		B			Strasbourg				*De la misère en milieu étudiant*.
	s. d.		B			Londres				Publication de *Totality for the Kids*, traduction par Ch. Gray de *Banalités de base* de Vaneigem.

1967

11/55 11/67	15 janvier					Paris			×	Frey, Garnault, Holl, Edith Frey (garnaultins).
11/62 11/28	22 janvier		T			Paris				*Attention! Trois provocateurs.* Tract sur l'exclusion des garnaultins.
	s. d.		T			France				*Sexologie de la misère. Misère de la sexologie.* Tract diffusé sur les résidences universitaires de Lyon, Nantes, Paris, Strasbourg, Toulouse.
11/62	Mars		B			Paris				Seconde édition de *De la misère.*
11/3	Août		B			Paris				*Le point d'explosion de l'idéologie en Chine.*
	Octobre	**11**				**Paris**				**Comité de rédaction : Khayati, Martin, Nicholson-Smith, Vaneigem.**
11/63	Novembre		L			Paris				*La société du spectacle.* Livre de Debord.
12/83	Novembre					Londres		×		Radcliffe.
12/83	21 décembre								×	Clarke, Gray, Nicholson-Smith.
11/63	Décembre		L			Paris				*Traité de savoir-vivre...* Livre de Vaneigem.
11/34	Décembre		T			Paris				Belles affiches-comics de Vaneigem-Bertrand et de Vaneigem-Joannès. Menaces d'inculpation (incitation au meurtre, au vol, à la débauche) par la suite abandonnée.
	s. d.		×			New York Londres				Nombreuses publications par les sections américaine et anglaise reconstituées.
	s. d.							×		Bernstein, Lungela.

1968

	10 mai					Paris				Les situationnistes participent à l'édification et à la défense des barricades de la rue Gay-Lussac.
	14 mai					Paris				Fondation du *Comité Enragés-Internationale Situationniste* où ils fusionnent avec l'élite des extrémistes de Nanterre.
	15 mai					Paris				Le *Comité Enragés-Internationale Situationniste* contrôle le comité d'occupation de la Sorbonne.
	16 mai 15 h					Paris				Le *Comité Enragés-Internationale Situationniste*, au nom de la Sorbonne occupée, appelle « à l'occupation immédiate de toutes les usines en France et à la formation de conseils ouvriers ». Un communiqué du premier ministre répond à 17 heures qu' « en présence de diverses tentatives annoncées ou amorcées par des groupes d'extrémistes pour provoquer une agitation généralisée... le gouvernement a le devoir de maintenir la paix publique ».
	17 mai 19 h					Paris				La majorité de l'assemblée générale réunie dans la Sorbonne n'ayant pas osé approuver l'appel de son comité d'occupation, les situationnistes annoncent qu'ils se retirent d'une assemblée déjà noyautée par des bureaucrates modérantistes. Ils regroupent les éléments révolutionnaires dans le C.M.D.O. *(Conseil pour le Maintien des Occupations)* qui dans les jours suivants s'empare des bâtiments de l'I.P.N.
	Pour les diverses publications, se reporter à la bibliographie de l'I.S.									
	Fin juin									Exil des situationnistes les plus compromis.
	Juillet					Bruxelles				Rédaction d'*Enragés et situationnistes dans le mouvement des occupations.*
	Octobre		L			Paris				Parution d'*Enragés et situationnistes...* de Viénet.
	Novembre	SR				Randers				Parution de *Situationistik Revolution* n° 2.

1969

12/103	Juin	×				New York				Parution de *Situationist International* n° 1. Revue de la section américaine. Comité de rédaction : Chasse, Elwell, Horelick, Verlaan.
12/103	Juillet	×				Milan				Parution de *Internazionale Situationista* n° 1. Revue de la section italienne. Comité de rédaction : Pavan, Salvadori, Sanguinetti. Directeur : Salvadori.
	Septembre	**12**				**Paris**				**Revue de la section française. Comité de rédaction: Khayati, Riesel, Sébastiani, Vaneigem, Viénet.**
12/105	Septembre			8		Venise	×			*Section américaine* : Chasse, Elwell, Horelick, Verlaan; *section scandinave* : Martin; *section italienne* : Pavan, Rothe, Salvadori, Sanguinetti; *section française* : de Beaulieu, Cheval, Chevalier, Debord, Khayati, Riesel, Sébastiani, Vaneigem, Viénet.
								×		Khayati.
	Octobre								×	Chevalier.
	19 décembre		T			Milan				*Il Reichstag brucia?* Tract dénonçant la provocation policière des bombes de Milan et de Rome du 12 décembre. Abusivement soupçonnés, les situationnistes italiens doivent fuir.

Nous nous sommes trouvés dans l'impossibilité de prolonger notre tableau au-delà du 31 décembre 1969, et nous considérons que la période qui débute alors n'est pas ouverte aux historiens. Les importantes archives de l'I. S. concernant cette période ne sont pas encore communiquées à l'Institut International d'Histoire Sociale d'Amsterdam, avec qui nous ne manquerons pas de poursuivre nos travaux, en collaboration, dès que cela s'avérera possible.
Nous croyons cependant devoir signaler que certains documents de l'I. S. qui ont déjà largement circulé, et que nous avons pu nous procurer, établissent que Raoul Vaneigem a été contraint de démissionner en novembre 1970, du fait de profondes contradictions relevées entre ses énoncés programmatiques et sa propre activité pratique; et aussi que René Riesel a été exclu en septembre 1971 pour mensonge et mesquinerie radicale dans l'intelligence et dans l'existence.

Definitions

Internationale Situationiste No1, June 1958

Constructed situation: A moment of life concretely and deliberately constructed by the collective organization of a unitary ambiance and a game of events.

Situationist: Having to do with the theory or practical activity of constructing situations. One who engages in the construction of situations. A member of the Situationist International.

Situationism: A meaningless term improperly derived from the above. There is no such thing as situationism, which would mean a doctrine of interpretation of existing facts. The notion of situationism is obviously devised by antisituationists.

Psychogeography: The study of the specific effects of the geographical environment, consciously organized or not, on the emotions and behaviour of individuals.

Psychogeographical: Relating to psychogeography. That which manifests the geographical environment's direct emotional effects.

Psychogeographer: One who explores and reports on psychogeographical phenomena.

Dérive: A mode of experimental behaviour linked to the conditions of urban society: a technique of transient passage through varied ambiances. Also used to designate a specific period of continuous dériving.

Unitary urbanism: The theory of the combined use of arts and techniques for the integral construction of a milieu in dynamic relation with experiments in behaviour.

Détournement: Short for: détournement of pre-existing aesthetic elements. The integration of present or past artistic production into a superior construction of a milieu. In this sense there can be no situationist painting or music, but only a situationist use of these means. In a more primitive sense, détournement within the old cultural spheres is a method of propaganda, a method which testifies to the wearing out and loss of importance of those spheres.

Culture: The reflection and prefiguration of the possibilities of organization of everyday life in a given historical moment; a complex of aesthetics, feelings and mores through which a collectivity reacts on the life that is objectively determined by its economy. (We are defining this term only in the perspective of the creation of values, not in that of the teaching of them.)

Decomposition: The process in which the traditional cultural forms have destroyed themselves as a result of the emergence of superior means of dominating nature which enable and require superior cultural constructions. We can distinguish between an active phase of the decomposition and effective demolition of the old superstructures – which came to an end around 1930 – and a phase of repetition which has prevailed since then. The delay in the transition from decomposition to new construction is linked to the delay in the revolutionary liquidation of capitalism.

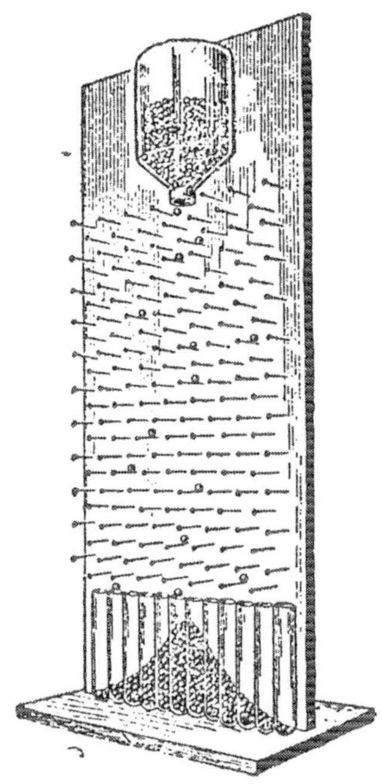

Cet appareil permet le tracé automatique de la courbe de Gauss (position des billes à l'arrivée). Les problèmes artistiques de la dérive se situent au niveau des trajets relativement imprévisibles de chaque bille.

Notes on the Formation of an Imaginist Bauhaus

Asger Jorn 1957

What was the Bauhaus?

The Bauhaus was an answer to the question: What 'education' do artists need in order to take their place in the machine age?

How was the Bauhaus idea realized?

It was realized with a 'school' in Germany; first at Weimar, then at Dessau; founded by the architect Walter Gropius in 1919 – destroyed by the Nazis in 1933.

What is the International Movement for an Imaginist Bauhaus?

It is the answer to the question **where and how** to find a justified place for artists in the machine age. This answer demonstrates that the education carried out by the old Bauhaus is false.

How has the idea of an International Movement for an Imaginist Bauhaus been realized?

The Movement was founded in Switzerland in 1953 as a tendency for the forming of a united organization capable of promoting an integral revolutionary cultural attitude. In 1954 the experience of the Albissola gathering demonstrated that experimental artists must get hold of industrial means and subject them to their own nonutilitarian ends. In 1955 an imaginist laboratory was founded at Alba. Conclusion of the Albissola experience: complete inflationary devaluation of modern values of decoration (cf. ceramics produced by children). In 1956 the Alba Congress dialectically defines unitary urbanism. In 1957 the Movement promulgates the watchword of psychogeographical action.

What we want.

We want the same economic and practical means and possibilities that are already at the disposal of scientific research, of whose great results everyone is aware.

Artistic research is identical to 'human science,' which for us means 'concerned' science, not purely historical science. This research should be carried out by artists with the assistance of scientists.

The first institute ever formed for this purpose is the experimental laboratory for free artistic research founded 29 September 1955 at Alba. Such a laboratory is not an instructional institution; it simply offers new possibilities for artistic experimentation.

The leaders of the old Bauhaus were great masters with exceptional talents, but they were bad teachers. The pupils' works were only pious imitations of their masters. The real influence of the latter was indirect, by force of example: Ruskin on Van de Velde, Van de Velde on Gropius.

This is not at all a critique, it is simply a statement of fact from which the following conclusions may be drawn. The direct transfer of artistic gifts is impossible, artistic adaptation takes place through a series of contradictory phases: Stupefaction – Wonder – Imitation – Rejection – Experience – Possession.

None of these phases can be avoided, although they need not all be gone through by any one individual.

Our practical conclusion is the following: we are abandoning all efforts at pedagogical action and moving toward experimental activity.

Formulary for a new urbanism

Sire, I am from the other country

Ivan Chtcheglov, October 1953

We are bored in the city, there is no longer any Temple of the Sun. Between the legs of the women walking by, the dadaists imagined a monkey wrench and the surrealists a crystal cup. That's lost. We know how to read every promise in faces – the latest stage of morphology. The poetry of the billboards lasted twenty years. We are bored in the city, we really have to strain still to discover mysteries on the sidewalk billboards, the latest state of humor and poetry:

Shower-Bath of the Patriarchs
Meat Cutting Machines
Notre-Dame Zoo
Sports Pharmacy
Martyrs Provisions
Translucent Concrete
Golden Touch Sawmill
Center for Functional Recuperation
Sainte-Anne Ambulance
Café Fifth Avenue
Prolonged Volunteers Street
Family Boarding House in the Garden
Hotel of Strangers
Wild Street

And the swimming pool on the Street of Little Girls. And the police station on Rendezvous Street. The medical-surgical clinic and the free placement center on the Quai des Orfèvres. The artificial flowers on Sun Street. The Castle Cellars Hotel, the Ocean Bar and the Coming and Going Café. The Hotel of the Epoch.

And the strange statue of Dr. Philippe Pinel, benefactor of the insane, in the last evenings of summer. To explore Paris.

And you, forgotten, your memories ravaged by all the consternations of two hemispheres, stranded in the Red Cellars of Pali-Kao, without music and without geography, no longer setting out for the hacienda *where the roots think of the child and where the wine is finished off with fables from an old almanac.* Now that's finished. You'll never see the hacienda. It doesn't exist.

The hacienda must be built.

All cities are geological; you cannot take three steps without encountering ghosts bearing all the prestige of their legends. We move within a *closed* landscape whose landmarks constantly draw us toward the past. Certain *shifting angles,* certain *receding* perspectives, allow us to glimpse original conceptions of space, but this vision remains fragmentary. It must be sought in the magical locales of fairy tales and surrealist writings: castles, endless walls, little forgotten bars, mammoth caverns, casino mirrors.

These dated images retain a small catalyzing power, but it is almost impossible to use them in a *symbolic urbanism* without rejuvenating them by giving them a new meaning. Our imaginations, haunted by the old archetypes, have remained far behind the sophistication of the machines. The various attempts to integrate modern science into new myths remain inadequate. Meanwhile abstraction has invaded all the arts, contemporary architecture in particular. Pure plasticity, inanimate, storyless, soothes the eye. Elsewhere other fragmentary beauties can be found – while the promised land of syntheses continually recedes into the distance. Everyone wavers between the emotionally still-alive past and the already dead future.

We will not work to prolong the mechanical civilizations and frigid architecture that ultimately lead to boring leisure.

We propose to invent new, changeable decors . . .

Darkness and obscurity are banished by artificial lighting, and the seasons by air conditioning; night and summer are losing their charm and dawn is disappearing. The man of the cities thinks he has escaped from cosmic reality, but there is no corresponding expansion of his dream life. The reason is clear: dreams spring from reality and are realized in it.

The latest technological developments would make possible the individual's unbroken contact with cosmic reality while eliminating its disagreeable aspects. Stars and rain can be seen through glass ceilings. The mobile house turns with the sun. Its sliding walls enable vegetation to invade life. Mounted on tracks, it can go down to the sea in the morning and return to the forest in the evening.

Architecture is the simplest means of *articulating* time and space, of *modulating* reality, of engendering dreams. It is a matter not only of plastic articulation and modulation expressing an ephemeral beauty, but of a modulation producing influences in accordance with the eternal spectrum of human desires and the progress in realizing them.

The architecture of tomorrow will be a means of modifying present conceptions of time and space. It will be a means of *knowledge* and a *means of action.*

The architectural complex will be modifiable. Its aspect will change totally or partially in accordance with the will of its inhabitants . . .

Past collectives offered the masses an absolute truth and incontrovertible mythical exemplars. The appearance of the notion of *relativity* in the modern mind allows one to surmise the **Experimental** aspect of the next civilisation (although I'm not satisfied with that word; say, more supple, more 'fun'). On the bases of this mobile civilization, architecture will, at least initially, be a means of experimenting with a thousand ways of modifying life, with a view to a mythic synthesis.

A mental disease has swept the planet: banalization. Everyone is hypnotized by production and conveniences – sewage system, elevator, bathroom, washing machine.

This state of affairs, arising out of a struggle against poverty, has overshot its ultimate goal – the liberation of man from material cares – and become an obsessive image hanging over the present. Presented with the alternative of love or a garbage disposal unit, young people of all countries have chosen the garbage disposal unit. It has become essential to bring about a complete spiritual transformation by bringing to light forgotten desires and by creating entirely new ones. And by carrying out an *intensive propaganda* in favour of these desires.

We have already pointed out the need of constructing situations as being one of the fundamental desires on which the next civilization will be founded. This need for *absolute* creation has always been intimately associated with the need to *play* with architecture, time and space . . .

Chirico remains one of the most remarkable architectural precursors. He was grappling with the problems of absences and presences in time and space.

We know that an object that is not consciously noticed at the time of a first *visit* can, by its absence during subsequent visits, provoke an indefinable impression: as a result of this sighting backward in time, *the absence of the object becomes a presence one can feel.* More precisely: although the quality of the impression generally remains indefinite, it nevertheless varies with the nature of the removed object and the importance accorded it by the visitor, ranging from serene joy to terror. (It is of no particular significance that in this specific case memory is the vehicle of these feelings. I only selected this example for its convenience.)

In Chirico's paintings (during his Arcade period) an *empty space* creates a *full-filled time.* It is easy to imagine the fantastic future possibilities of such architecture and its influence on the masses. Today we can have nothing but contempt for a century that relegates such *blueprints* to its so-called museums.

This new vision of time and space, which will be the theoretical basis of future constructions, is still imprecise and will remain so until experimentation with patterns of behaviour has taken place in cities specifically established for this purpose, cities assembling – in addition to the facilities necessary for a minimum of comfort and security – buildings charged with evocative power, symbolic edifices representing desires, forces, events past, present and to come. A rational extension of the old religious systems, of old tales, and above all of psychoanalysis, into architectural expression becomes more and more urgent as all the reasons for becoming impassioned disappear.

Everyone will live in his own personal 'cathedral', so to speak. There will be rooms more conducive to dreams than any drug, and houses where one cannot help but love. Others will be irresistibly alluring to travellers . . .

This project could be compared with the Chinese and Japanese gardens of illusory perspectives [*en trompe-l'oeil*] – with the difference that those gardens are not designed to be lived in at all times – or with the ridiculous labyrinth in the Jardin des Plantes, at the entry to which is written (height of absurdity, Ariadne unemployed): *Games are forbidden in the labyrinth.*

This city could be envisaged in the form of an arbitrary assemblage of castles, grottos, lakes, etc. It would be the baroque stage of urbanism considered as a means of knowledge. But this theoretical phase is already outdated. We know that a modern building could be constructed which would have no resemblance to a medieval castle but which would preserve and enhance the *Castle* poetic power (by the conservation of a strict minimum of lines, the transposition of certain others, the positioning of openings, the topographical location, etc.).

The districts of this city could correspond to the whole spectrum of diverse feelings that one encounters *by chance* in everyday life.

Bizarre Quarter – Happy Quarter (specially reserved for habitation) – Noble and Tragic Quarter (for good children) – Historical Quarter (museums, schools) – Useful Quarter (hospital, tool shops) – Sinister Quarter, etc. And an *Astrolaire* which would group plant species in accordance with the relations they manifest with the stellar rhythm, a planetary garden comparable to that which the astronomer Thomas wants to establish at Laaer Berg in Vienna. Indispensable for giving the inhabitants a consciousness of the cosmic. Perhaps also a Death Quarter, not for dying in but so as to have somewhere to *live in peace,* and I think here of Mexico and of a principle of cruelty in innocence that appeals more to me every day.

The Sinister Quarter, for example, would be a good replacement for those hellholes that many people once possessed in their capitals: they symbolized all the evil forces of life. The Sinister Quarter would have no need to harbor real dangers, such as traps, dungeons or mines. It would be difficult to get into, with a hideous decor (piercing whistles, alarm bells, sirens wailing intermittently, grotesque sculptures, power-driven mobiles, called *Auto-Mobiles*), and as poorly lit at night as it is blindingly lit during the day by an intensive use of reflection. At the center, the 'Square of the Appalling Mobile.' Saturation of the market with a product causes the product's market value to fall: thus, as they explored the Sinister Quarter, the child and the adult would learn not to fear the anguishing occasions of life, but to be amused by them.

The principle activity of the inhabitants will be the *Continuous Dérive.* The changing of landscapes from one hour to the next will result in complete disorientation . . .

Later, as the gestures inevitably grow stale, this dérive will partially leave the realm of direct experience for that of representation . . .

The economic obstacles are only apparent. We know that the more a place is *set apart for free play,* the more it influences people's behaviour and the greater is its force of attraction. This is demonstrated by the immense prestige of Monaco and Las Vegas – and Reno, that caricature of free love – although they are mere gambling places. Our first experimental city would live largely off tolerated and controlled tourism. Future avant-garde activities and productions would naturally tend to gravitate there. In a few years it would become the intellectual capital of the world and would be universally recognized as such.

Toward a Situationist International

Excerpt from report on the construction of Situations and on the International Situationist tendency's conditions of organization and action.

Guy Debord, June 1957

Our central idea is that of the construction of situations, that is to say, the concrete construction of momentary ambiances of life and their transformation into a superior passional quality. We must develop a methodical intervention based on the complex factors of two components in perpetual interaction: the material environment of life and the comportments which it gives rise to and which radically transform it.

Our perspectives of action on the environment ultimately lead us to the notion of unitary urbanism. Unitary urbanism is defined first of all by the use of the ensemble of arts and technics as means contributing to an integral composition of the milieu. This ensemble must be envisaged as infinitely more far-reaching than the old domination of architecture over the traditional arts, or than the present sporadic application to anarchic urbanism of specialized technology or of scientific investigations such as ecology. Unitary urbanism must, for example, dominate the acoustic environment as well as the distribution of different varieties of food and drink. It must include the creation of new forms and the detournement of previous forms of architecture, urbanism, poetry and cinema. Integral art, which has been talked about so much, can only be realized at the level of urbanism. But it can no longer correspond to any of the traditional aesthetic categories. In each of its experimental cities unitary urbanism will act by way of a certain number of force fields, which we can temporarily designate by the classic term 'quarter.' Each quarter will tend toward a specific harmony, divided from neighbouring harmonies, or else will play on a maximum breaking-up of internal harmony.

Secondly, unitary urbanism is dynamic, that is, in close relation to styles of behaviour. The most elementary unit of unitary urbanism is not the house, but the architectural complex, which combines all the factors conditioning an ambiance, or a series of clashing ambiances, on the scale of the constructed situation. The spatial development must take into account the emotional effects that the experimental city will determine. One of our comrades has advanced a theory of states-of-mind quarters according to which each quarter of a city would be designed to provoke a specific basic sentiment to which the subject would knowingly expose himself. It seems that such a project draws opportune conclusions from the current tendency of depreciation of the randomly encountered primary sentiments, and that its realization could contribute to accelerating that depreciation. The comrades who call for a new, free architecture must understand that this new architecture will primarily be based not on free, poetic lines and forms – in the sense that today's 'lyrical abstract' painting uses those words – but rather on the atmospheric effects of rooms, hallways, streets, atmospheres linked to the gestures they contain. Architecture must advance by taking emotionally moving situations, rather than emotionally moving forms, as the material it works with. And the experiments conducted with this material will lead to unknown forms. Psychogeographical research, 'the study of the exact laws and specific effects of the action of the geographical environment, consciously organized or not, on the emotions and behaviour of individuals,' thus takes on a double meaning: active observation of present-day urban agglomerations and development of hypotheses on the structure of a situationist city. The progress of psychogeography depends to a great extent on the statistical extension of its methods of observation, but above all on experimentation by means of concrete interventions in urbanism. Before this stage is attained we cannot be certain of the objective truth of the first psychogeographical findings. But even if these findings should turn out to be false, they would still be false solutions to what is certainly a real problem.

Our action on behaviour, linked with other desirable aspects of a revolution in mores, can be briefly defined as the invention of games of an essentially new type. The most general goal must be to extend the non-mediocre part of life, to reduce the empty moments of life as much as possible. One could thus speak of our action as an enterprise of quantitatively increasing human life, an enterprise more serious than the biological methods currently being investigated. This automatically implies a qualitative increase whose developments are unpredictable. The situationist game is distinguished from the classic conception of the game by its radical negation of the element of competition and of separation from everyday life. The situationist game is not distinct from a moral choice, the taking of one's stand in favour of what will ensure the future reign of freedom and play. This perspective is obviously linked to the inevitable, continual and rapid increase of leisure time resulting from the level of productive forces our era has attained. It is also linked to the recognition of the fact that a battle of leisure is taking place before our eyes whose importance in the class struggle has not been sufficiently analyzed. So far, the ruling class has succeeded in using the leisure the revolutionary proletariat wrested from it by developing a vast industrial sector of leisure activities that is an incomparable instrument for stupefying the proletariat with by-products of mystifying ideology and bourgeois tastes. The abundance of televised imbecilities is probably one of the reasons for the American working classes' inability to develop any political consciousness. By obtaining by collective pressure a slight rise in the price of its labor above the minimum necessary for the production of that labor, the proletariat not only extends its power of struggle, it also extends the terrain of the struggle. New forms of this struggle then arise alongside directly economic and political conflicts. It can be said that revolutionary propaganda has so far been constantly overcome in these new forms of struggle in all the countries where advanced industrial development has introduced them. That the necessary changing of the infrastructure can be delayed by errors and weaknesses at the level of superstructures has unfortunately been demonstrated by several experiences of the twentieth century. It is necessary to throw new forces into the battle of leisure, and we will take up our position there.

A rough experimentation toward a new mode of behaviour has already been made with what we have termed the *dérive*, which is the practice of a passional journey out of the ordinary through rapid changing of ambiances, as well as a means of study of psychogeography and of situationist psychology. But the application of this will to playful creation must be extended to all known forms of human relationships, so as to influence, for example, the historical evolution of sentiments like friendship and love. Everything leads us to believe that the essential elements of our research lie in our hypotheses of constructions of situations.

The life of a person is a succession of fortuitous situations, and even if none of them is exactly the same as another the immense majority of them are so undifferentiated and so dull that they give a perfect impression of similitude. The corollary of this state of things is that the rare intensely engaging situations found in life strictly confine and limit this life. We must try to construct situations, that is to say, collective ambiances, ensembles of impressions determining the quality of a moment. If we take the simple example of a gathering of a group of individuals for a given time, it would be desirable, while taking into account the knowledge and material means we have at our disposal, to study what organization of the place, what selection of participants and what provocation of events produce the desired ambiance. The powers of a situation will certainly expand considerably in both time and space with the realization of unitary urbanism or the education of a situationist generation. The construction of situations begins on the ruins of the modern spectacle. It is easy to see to what extent the very principle of the spectacle – nonintervention – is linked to the alienation of the old world. Conversely, the most pertinent revolutionary experiments in culture have sought to break the spectator's psychological identification with the hero so as to draw him into activity by provoking his capacities to revolutionize his own life. The situation is thus made to be lived by its constructors. The role played by a passive or merely bit-part playing 'public' must constantly diminish, while that played by those who cannot be called actors but rather, in a new sense of the term, 'livers,' must steadily increase.

So to speak, we have to multiply poetic subjects and objects – which are now unfortunately so rare that the slightest ones take on an exaggerated emotional importance – and we have to organize games of these poetic objects among these poetic subjects. This is our entire program, which is essentially transitory. Our situations will be ephemeral, without a future; passageways. The permanence of art or anything else does not enter into our considerations, which are serious. Eternity is the grossest idea a person can conceive of in connection with his acts. [. . .]

The situationist minority first constituted itself as a tendency in the lettrist left wing, then in the Lettrist International which it ended up controlling. The same objective movement has led several avant-garde groups of the recent period to similar conclusions. Together we must eliminate all the relics of the recent past. We consider today that an accord for a united action of the revolutionary avant-garde in culture must be carried out on the basis of such a program. We have neither guaranteed recipes nor definitive results. We only propose an experimental research to be collectively led in a few directions that we are presently defining and toward others that have yet to be defined. The very difficulty of succeeding in the first situationist projects is a proof of the newness of the domain we are penetrating. That which changes our way of seeing the streets is more important than what changes our way of seeing painting. Our working hypotheses will be reexamined at each future upheaval, wherever it comes from. [. . .]

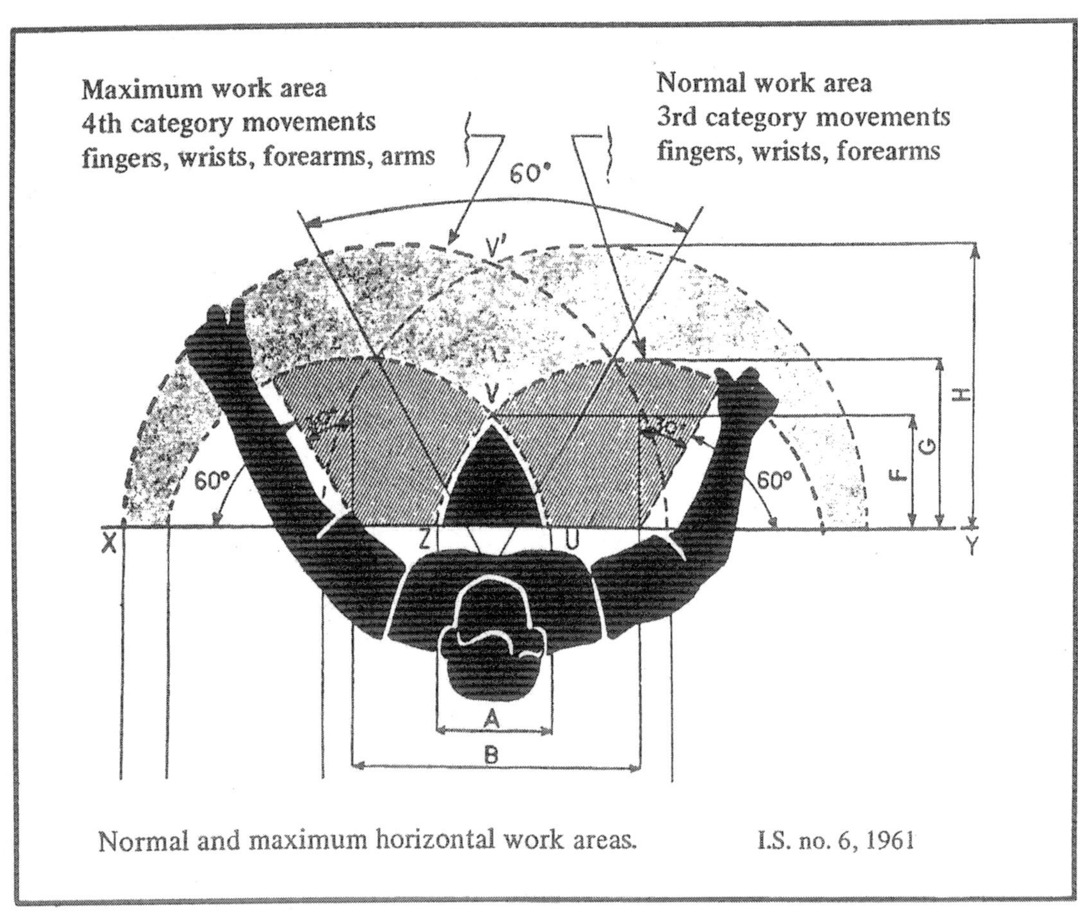

Normal and maximum horizontal work areas. I.S. no. 6, 1961

Détournement as negation and prelude

Guy Debord

Internationale Situationniste, No 3, December 1959

Détournement, the reuse of preexisting artistic elements in a new ensemble, has been a constantly present tendency of the contemporary avant-garde both before and since the establishment of the SI. The two fundamental laws of détournement are the loss of importance of each détourned autonomous element – which may go so far as to lose its original sense completely – and at the same time the organization of another meaningful ensemble that confers on each element its new scope and effect.

Détournement has a peculiar power which obviously stems from the double meaning, from the enrichment of most of the terms by the coexistence within them of their old senses and their new, immediate senses. Détournement is practical because it is so easy to use and because of its inexhaustible potential for reuse. Concerning the negligible effort required for détournement, we have already said, 'The cheapness of its products is the heavy artillery that breaks through all the Chinese walls of understanding' (*Methods of Détournement*, May 1956). But these points would not by themselves justify recourse to this method, which the same text describes as 'clashing head-on against all social and legal conventions.' Détournement has a historical significance. What is it?

'Détournement is a game made possible by the capacity of *devaluation*,' writes Jorn in his study *Détourned Painting* (May 1959), and he goes on to say that all the elements of the cultural past must be 'reinvested' or disappear. Détournement is thus first of all a negation of the value of the previous organization of expression. It arises and grows increasingly stronger in the historical period of the decomposition of artistic expression. But at the same time, the attempts to reuse the 'détournable bloc' as material for other ensembles express the search for a vaster construction, a new genre of creation at a higher level.

The SI is a very special kind of movement, of a nature different from preceding artistic avant-gardes. Within culture the SI can be likened to a research laboratory, for example, or to a party in which we are situationists but nothing that we do is situationist. This is not a disavowal for anyone. We are partisans of a certain future of culture, of life. Situationist activity is a definite craft which we are not yet practicing.

Thus the signature of the situationist movement, the sign of its presence and contestation in contemporary cultural reality (since we cannot represent any common style whatsoever), is first of all the use of détournement. We may mention, on the level of détourned expression, Jorn's altered paintings; Debord and Jorn's book *Mémoires*, 'composed entirely of prefabricated elements,' in which the writing on each page runs in all directions and the reciprocal relations of the phrases are invariably uncompleted; Constant's projects for détourned sculptures; and Debord's détourned documentary film, *On the Passage of a Few Persons Through a Rather Brief Period of Time*. On the level of what *Methods of Détournement* calls 'ultradétournement, that is, the tendencies for détournement to operate in everyday social life' (e.g. passwords or the wearing of disguises, belonging to the sphere of play), we might mention, at different levels, Gallizio's industrial painting; Wyckaert's 'orchestral' project for assembly-line painting with a division of labor based on color; and numerous détournements of buildings that were at the original of unitary urbanism. But we should also mention in this context the SI's very forms of 'organization' and propaganda.

At this point in the world's development all forms of expression are losing all grip on reality and being reduced to self-parody. As the readers of this journal can frequently verify, present-day writing always has an element of parody. 'It is necessary,' states *Methods of Détournement*, 'to conceive of a parodic-serious stage where the accumulation of détourned elements, far from aiming at arousing indignation or laughter by alluding to some original work, will express our indifference toward a meaningless and forgotten original, and concern itself with rendering a certain sublimity.'

The parodic-serious expresses the contradictions of an era in which we find ourselves confronted with both the urgent necessity and the near impossibility of bringing together and carrying out a totally innovative collective action. An era in which the greatest seriousness advances masked in the ambiguous interplay between art and its negation; in which the essential voyages of discovery have been undertaken by such astonishingly incapable people.

Basic banalities (II)

Summary of preceding sections

Raoul Vaneigem

Internationale Situationiste, No 8, January 1963

The vast majority of people have always devoted all their energy to *Survival*, thereby denying themselves any chance to *Live*. They continue to do so today as the *Welfare State* imposes the elements of this survival in the form of technological conveniences (appliances, preserved food, prefabricated cities, Mozart for the masses).

The organization controlling the material equipment of our everyday life is such that what in itself would enable us to construct it richly plunges us instead into a poverty of abundance, making alienation all the more intolerable as each convenience promises liberation and turns out to be only one more burden. We are condemned to slavery to the means of liberation.

To be understood, this problem must be seen in the clear light of hierarchical power. But perhaps it isn't enough to say that hierarchical power has preserved humanity for thousands of years like alchohol preserves a foetus – by arresting either growth or decay. It should also be specified that hierarchical power represents the highest stage of privative appropriation, and historically is its alpha and omega. Privative appropriation itself can be defined as appropriation of things by means of appropriation of people, the struggle against natural alienation engendering social alienation.

Privative appropriation entails an *Organization of Appearance* by which its radical contradictions can be dissimulated: the servants must see themselves as degraded reflections of the master, thus reinforcing, through the looking glass of an illusory freedom, everything that reinforces their submission and passivity; while the master must identify himself with the mythical and perfect servant of a god or of a transcendence which is nothing other than the sacred and abstract representation of the *Totality* of people and things over which he wields power – a power all the more real and less contested as he is universally credited with the virtue of his renunciation. The mythical sacrifice of the director corresponds to the real sacrifice of the executant; each negates himself in the other, the strange becomes familiar and the familiar strange, each fulfills himself by being the inversion of the other. From this common alienation a harmony is born, a negative harmony whose fundamental unity lies in the notion of sacrifice. This objective (and perverted) harmony is sustained by myth – this term being used to designate the organization of appearance in unitary societies, that is, in societies where slave, tribal or feudal power is officially consecrated by a divine authority and where the sacred allows power to seize the totality.

The harmony originally based on the '*Gift* of oneself' contains a form of relationship that was to develop, become autonomous and destroy it. This relationship is based on partial *Exchange* (commodity, money, product, labor power . . .), the exchange of a part of oneself, which underlies the bourgeois notion of freedom. It arises as commerce and technology become preponderant within agrarian-type economies.

When the bourgeoisie seized power the unity of power was destroyed. Sacred privative appropriation became secularized in capitalist mechanisms. Freed from the grip of power, the totality once again became concrete and immediate. The era of fragmentation has been nothing but a succession of attempts to recapture an inaccessible unity, to reconstitute some ersatz sacred behind which to shelter power.

A revolutionary moment is when 'everything reality presents' finds its immediate *Representation*. All the rest of the time hierarchical power, increasingly deprived of its magical and mystical regalia, strives to make everyone forget that the totality (which has never been anything other than reality!) is exposing its imposture.

14

By directly attacking the mythical organization of appearance, the bourgeois revolutions, in spite of themselves, attacked the weak point not only of unitary power but of any hierarchical power whatsoever. Does this unavoidable mistake explain the guilt complex that is one of the dominant traits of bourgeois mentality? In any case, the mistake was undoubtedly inevitable.

It was a mistake because once the cloud of lies dissimulating privative appropriation was pierced, myth was shattered, leaving a vacuum that could be filled only by a delirious freedom and a splendid poetry. Orgiastic poetry, to be sure, has not yet destroyed power. Its failure is easily explained and its ambiguous signs reveal the blows struck at the same time as they heal the wounds. And yet – let us leave the historians and aesthetes to their collections – one has only to pick at the scab of memory and the cries, words and gestures of the past make the whole body of power bleed again. The whole organization of the survival of memories will not prevent them from dissolving into oblivion as they come to life; just as our survival will dissolve in the construction of our everyday life.

And it was an inevitable process: as Marx showed, the appearance of exchange-value and its symbolic representation by money opened a profound latent crisis in the heart of the unitary world. The commodity introduced into human relationships a universality (a 1000-franc note represents anything I can obtain for that sum) and an egalitarianism (equal things are exchanged). This 'egalitarian universality' partially escapes both the exploiter and the exploited, but they recognize each other through it. They find themselves face to face, confronting each other no longer within the mystery of divine birth and ancestry, as was the case with the nobility, but within an intelligible transcendence, the Logos, a body of laws that can be *understood by everyone*, even if such understanding remains cloaked in mystery. A mystery with its initiates: first of all priests struggling to maintain the Logos in the limbo of divine mysticism, but soon yielding to philosophers and then to technicians both their positions and the dignity of their sacred mission. From Plato's Republic to the Cybernetic State.

Thus, under the pressure of exchange-value and technology (generally available mediation), myth was gradually secularized. Two facts should be noted, however.

a) As the Logos frees itself from mystical unity, it affirms itself both within it and against it. Upon magical and analogical structures of behaviour are superimposed rational and logic ones which negate the former while preserving them (mathematics, poetics, economics, aesthetics, psychology, etc.).

b) Each time the Logos, the 'organization of intelligible appearance,' becomes more autonomous, it tends to break away from the sacred and become fragmented. In this way it presents a double danger for unitary power. We have already seen that the sacred expresses power's seizure of the totality, and that anyone wanting to accede to the totality must do so through the mediation of power: the interdict against mystics, alchemists and gnostics is sufficient proof of this. This also explains why present-day power 'protects' specialists (though without completely trusting them): it vaguely senses that they are the missionaries of a resacralized Logos. There are historical signs that testify to the attempts made within mystical unitary power to found a rival power asserting its unity in the name of the Logos – Christian syncretism (which makes God psychologically explainable), the Renaissance, the Reformation and the Enlightenment.

The masters who strove to maintain the unity of the Logos were well aware that only unity can stabilize power. Examined more closely their efforts can be seen not to have been as vain as the fragmentation of the Logos in the nineteenth and twentieth centuries would seem to prove. In the general movements of atomization the Logos has been broken down into specialized techniques (physics, biology, sociology, papyrology, etc.), but at the same time the need to re-establish the totality has become more imperative. It should not be forgotten that all it would take would be an all-powerful technocratic power in order for there to be a totalitarian domination of the totality, for the Logos to succeed myth as the seizure of the totality by a future unitary (cybernetic) power. In such an event the vision of the Encyclopédistes (strictly rationalized progress stretching indefinitely into the future) would have known only a two-century postponement before being realized. This is the direction in which the Stalino-cyberneticians are preparing the future. In this perspective, peaceful coexistence should be seen as a preliminary step towards a totalitarian unity. It is time everyone realized that they are already resisting it.

15

We know the battlefield. The problem now is to prepare for battle before the pataphysician, armed with his totality without technique, and the cybernetician, armed with his technique without totality, consummate their political coitus.

From the standpoint of hierarchical power, myth could be desacralized only if the Logos, or at least its desacralizing elements, were resacralized. To attack the sacred was at the same time supposed to liberate the totality and thus destroy power (we've heard that one before!). But the power of the bourgeoisie – fragmented, impoverished, constantly contested – maintains a relative stability by relying on this ambiguity: Technology, which objectively desacralizes, subjectively appears as an instrument of liberation. Not a real liberation, which could be attained only by desacralization – that is, by the end of the spectacle – but a caricature, an imitation, an induced hallucination. What the unitary vision of the world transferred into the beyond (above), fragmentary power pro-jects ('throws forward') into a state of future well-being, of brighter tomorrows proclaimed from atop the dunghill of today – tomorrows that are nothing more than the present multiplied by the number of gadgets to be produced. From the slogan 'Live in God' we have gone on to the humanistic motto 'Survive until you are old,' euphemistically expressed as: 'Stay young at heart and you'll live a long time.'

Once desacralized and fragmented, myth loses its grandeur and its spirituality. It becomes an impoverished form, retaining its former characteristics but revealing them in a concrete, harsh, tangible fashion. God doesn't run the show anymore, and until the day the Logos takes over with its arms of technology and science, the phantoms of alienation will continue to materialize and sow disorder everywhere. Watch for them: they are the first symptoms of a future order. We must start to *play* right now if the future is not to become impossible (the hypothesis of humanity destroying itself – and with it, obviously, the whole experiment of constructing everyday life). The vital objectives of a struggle for the construction of everyday life are the sensitive key points of all hierarchical power. To build one is to destroy the other. Caught in the vortex of desacralization and resacralization, we stand essentially for the negation of the following elements: the organization of appearance as a *spectacle* in which everyone denies himself; the *separation* on which private life is based, since it is there that the objective separation between owners and dispossessed is lived and reflected on every level; and *sacrifice*. These three elements are obviously interdependent, just as are their opposites: participation, communication, realization. The same applies to their context: nontotality (a bankrupt world, a controlled totality) and totality.

16

The human relationships that were formerly dissolved in divine transcendence (the totality crowned by the sacred) settled out and solidified as soon as the sacred stopped acting as a catalyst. Their materiality was revealed and, as the capricious laws of the economy succeed those of Providence, the power of men began to appear behind the power of gods. Today a multitude of roles corresponds to the mythical role everyone once played under the divine spotlight. Though their masks are now human faces, these roles still require both actors and extras to deny their real lives in accordance with the dialectic of real and mythical sacrifice. The spectacle is nothing but desacralized and fragmented myth. It forms the armor of a power (which could also be called essential mediation) that becomes vulnerable *to every blow* once it no longer succeeds in dissimulating (in the cacophony where all cries drown out each other and form an overall harmony) its nature as privative appropriation, and the greater or lesser dose of misery it allots to everyone.

Roles have become impoverished within the context of a fragmentary power eaten away by desacralization, just as the spectacle represents an impoverishment in comparison with myth. They betray its mechanisms and artifices so clumsily that power, to defend itself against popular denunciation of the spectacle, has no other alternative than to itself take the initiative in this denunciation by even more clumsily changing actors or ministers, or by organizing pogroms of supposed or prefabricated scapegoat agents (agents of Moscow, Wall Street, the Judeocracy or the Two Hundred Families). Which also means that the whole cast has been forced to become hams, that style has been replaced by manner.

Myth, as an immobile totality, encompassed all movement (consider pilgrimage, for example, as fulfillment and adventure within immobility). On the one hand, the spectacle can seize the totality only by reducing it to a fragment and to a series of fragments (psychological, sociological, biological, philological and mythological world-views), while on the other hand, it is situated at the point where the movement of desacralization converges with the efforts at resacralization. Thus it can succeed in imposing immobility only within the real movement, the movement that changes it despite its resistance. In the era of fragmentation the organization of appearance makes movement a linear succession of immobile instants (this notch-to-notch progression is perfectly exemplified by Stalinist 'Dialectical Materialism'). Under what we have called 'the colonization of everyday life', the only possible changes are changes of fragmentary roles. In terms of more or less inflexible conventions, one is successively citizen, head of family, sexual partner, politician, specialist, professional, producer, consumer. Yet what boss doesn't himself feel bossed? The proverb applies to everyone: You sometimes get a fuck, but you always get fucked!

The era of fragmentation has at least eliminated all doubt on one point: everyday life is the battlefield where the war between power and the totality takes place, with power using all its strength to control the totality.

What do we demand in backing the power of everyday life against hierarchical power? We demand *everything*. We are taking our stand in the generalized conflict stretching from domestic squabbles to revolutionary war, and we have gambled on the will to live. This means that we must survive as antisurvivors. Fundamentally we are concerned only with the moments when life breaks through the glaciation of survival (whether these moments are unconscious or theorized, historical – like revolution – or personal). But we must recognize that we are *also* prevented from freely following the course of such moments (except for the moment of revolution itself) not only by the general repression exerted by power, but also by the exigencies of our own struggle, our own tactics, etc. It is also important to find the means of compensating for this additional 'margin of error' by widening the scope of these moments and demonstrating their qualitative significance. What prevents what we say on the construction of everyday life from being recuperated by the cultural establishment (*Arguments*, academic thinkers with paid vacations) is the fact that all situationist ideas are nothing other than faithful developments of acts attempted constantly by thousands of people to try and prevent another day from being no more than twenty-four hours of wasted time. Are we an avant-garde? If so, to be avant-garde means to move in step with reality.

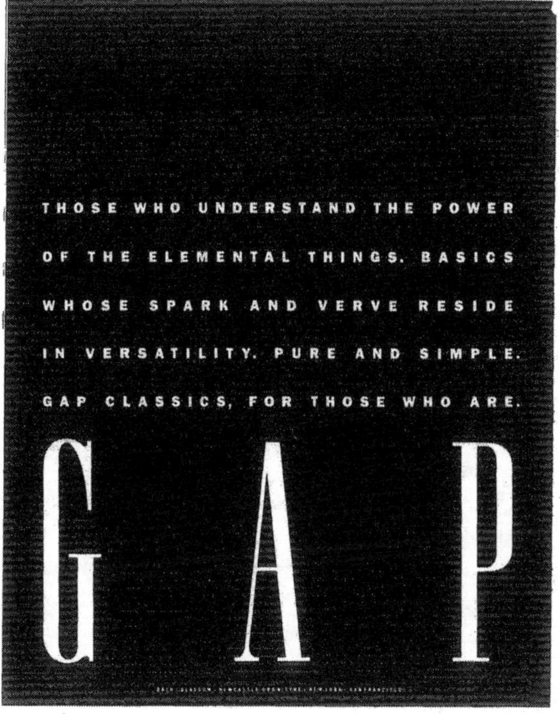

17

It's not the monopoly of intelligence that we hold, but that of its use. Our position is strategic, we are at the heart of every conflict. The qualitative is our striking force. People who half understand this journal ask us for an explanatory monograph thanks to which they will be able to convince themselves that they are intelligent and cultured – that is to say, idiots. Someone who gets exasperated and chucks it in the gutter is making a more meaningful gesture. Sooner or later it will have to be understood that the words and phrases we use are still lagging behind reality. The distortion and clumsiness in the way we express ourselves (which a man of taste called, not inaccurately, 'a rather irritating kind of hermetic terrorism') comes from our central position, our position on the ill-defined and shifting frontier where language captured by power (conditioning) and free language (poetry) fight out their infinitely complex war. To those who follow behind us we prefer those who reject us impatiently because our language is not yet authentic poetry – the free construction of everyday life.

Everything related to thought is related to the spectacle. Almost everyone lives in a state of terror at the possibility that they might awake to themselves, and their fear is deliberately fostered by power. Conditioning, the special poetry of power, has extended its dominion so far (all material equipment belongs to it: press, television, stereotypes, magic, tradition, economy, technology – what we call captured language) that it has almost succeeded in dissolving what Marx called the undominated sector, replacing it with another dominated one (see below our composite portrait of 'the survivor'). But lived experience cannot so easily be reduced to a succession of empty configurations. Resistance to the external organization of life, to the organization of life as survival, contains more poetry than any volume of verse or prose, and the poet, in the literary sense of the word, is one who has at least understood or felt this. But such poetry is in a most dangerous situation. Certainly poetry in the situationist sense of the word is irreducible and cannot be recuperated by power (as soon as an act is recuperated it becomes a stereotype, conditioning, language of power). But it is encircled by power. Power encircles the irreducible and holds it by isolating it; yet such isolation is impracticable. The two pincers are, first, the threat of disintegration (insanity, illness, destitution, suicide), and second, remote-controlled therapeutics. The first grants death, the second grants no more than survival (empty communication, the company of family or friendship, psychoanalysis in the service of alienation, medical care, ergotherapy). Sooner or later the SI must define itself as a therapy: we are ready to defend the poetry made by all against the false poetry rigged up by power (conditioning). Doctors and psychoanalysts better get it straight too, or they may one day, along with architects and other apostles of survival, have to take the consequences for what they have done.

18

All unresolved, unsuperseded antagonisms weaken. Such antagonisms can evolve only by remaining imprisoned in previous unsuperseded forms (anticultural art in the cultural spectacle, for example). Any radical opposition that fails or is partially successful (which amounts to the same thing) gradually degenerates into reformist opposition. Fragmentary oppositions are like the teeth on cogwheels, they mesh with each other and make the machine go round, the machine of the spectacle, the machine of power.

Myth maintained all antagonisms within the archetype of Manicheanism. But what can function as an archetype in a fragmented society? In fact, the memory of previous antagonisms, presented in their obviously devalued and unaggressive form, appears today as the last attempt to bring some coherence into the organization of appearance, so great is the extent to which the spectacle has become a spectacle of confusion and equivalences. We are ready to wipe out all trace of these memories by harnessing all the energy contained in previous antagonisms for a radical struggle soon to come. All the springs blocked by power will one day burst through to form a torrent that will change the face of the world.

In a caricature of antagonisms, power urges everyone to be for or against Brigitte Bardot, the *nouveau roman*, the 4-horse Citroën, spaghetti, mescal, miniskirts, the UN, the classics, nationalization, thermonuclear war and hitchhiking. Everyone is asked their opinion about every detail in order to prevent them from having one about the totality. However clumsy this maneouvre may be, it might have worked if the salesmen in charge of peddling it from door to door were not themselves waking up to their own alienation. To the passivity imposed on the dispossessed masses is added the growing passivity of the directors and actors subjected to the abstract laws of the market and the spectacle and exercising less and less real power over the world. Already signs of revolt are appearing among the actors – stars who try to escape publicity or rulers who criticize their own power; Brigitte Bardot or Fidel Castro. The tools of power are wearing out; their desire for their own freedom should be taken into account.

19

At the very moment when slave revolt threatened to overthrow the structure of power and to reveal the relationship between transcendence and the mechanism of privative appropriation, Christianity appeared with its grandiose reformism, whose central democratic demand was for the slaves to accede not to the reality of a human life – which would have been impossible without denouncing the exclusionary aspect of privative appropriation – but rather to the unreality of an existence whose source of happiness is mythical (the imitation of Christ as the price of the hereafter). What has changed? Anticipation of the hereafter has become anticipation of a brighter tomorrow; the sacrifice of real, immediate life is the price paid for the illusory freedom of an apparent life. The spectacle is the sphere when forced labor is transformed into voluntary sacrifice. Nothing is more suspect than the formula 'To each according to his work' in a world where work is the blackmail of survival; to say nothing of the formula 'To each according to his needs' in a world where needs are determined by power. Any construction that attempts to define itself autonomously, and thus partially, and does not take into account that it is in fact defined by the negativity in which everything is suspended, enters into the reformist project: It is trying to build on quicksand as though it were rock. Contempt and misunderstanding of the context fixed by hierarchical power can only end up reinforcing that context. On the other hand, the spontaneous acts we can see everywhere forming against power and its spectacle must be warned of all the obstacles in their path and must find a tactic taking into account the strength of the enemy and its means of recuperation. This tactic, which we are going to popularize, is *détournement*.

20

Sacrifice must be rewarded. In exchange for their real sacrifice the workers receive the instruments of their liberation (comforts, gadgets), but this liberation is purely fictitious since power controls the ways in which all the material equipment can be used; since power uses to its own ends both the instruments and those who use them. The Christian and bourgeois revolutions democratized mythical sacrifice, the 'sacrifice of the master.' Today there are countless initiates who receive crumbs of power for putting to public service the totality of their partial knowledge. They are no longer called 'initiates' and not yet 'priests of the Logos'; they are simply known as specialists.

On the level of the spectacle their power is undeniable: the contestant on 'Double Your Money' and the postal clerk running on all day about all the mechanical details of his car both identify with the specialist, and we know how production managers use such identification to bring unskilled workers to heel. Essentially the true mission of the technocrats would be to unify the Logos; if only – because of one of the contradictions of fragmentary power – they weren't so absurdly compartmentalized and isolated. Each one is alienated in being out of phase with the others; he knows the whole of one fragment and knows no realization. What real control can the atomic technician, the strategist or the political specialist exercise over a nuclear weapon? What ultimate control can power hope to impose on all the gestures developing against it? The stage is so crowded that only chaos reigns as master. 'Order reigns and doesn't govern' (*IS # 6*).

To the extent that the specialist takes part in the development of the instruments that condition and transform the world, he is preparing the way for the *revolt of the privileged*. Until now such revolt has been called fascism. It is essentially an operatic revolt – didn't

Nietzsche see Wagner as a precursor? – in which actors who have been pushed aside for a long time and see themselves as less and less free suddenly demand to play the leading roles. Clinically speaking, fascism is the hysteria of the spectacular world pushed to the point of paroxysm. In this paroxysm the spectacle momentarily ensures its unity while at the same time revealing its radical inhumanity. Through fascism and Stalinism, which constitute its romantic crises, the spectacle reveals its true nature: it is a disease.

We are poisoned by the spectacle. All the elements necessary for a detoxification (that is, for the construction of our everyday lives) are in the hands of specialists. We are thus highly interested in all these specialists, but in different ways. Some are hopeless cases: we are not, for example, going to try and show the specialists of power, the rulers, the extent of their delirium. On the other hand, we are ready to take into account the bitterness of specialists imprisoned in roles that are constricted, absurd or ignominious. We must confess, however, that our indulgence has its limits. If, in spite of all our efforts, they persist in putting their guilty conscience and their bitterness in the service of power by fabricating the conditioning that colonizes their own everyday lives; if they prefer an illusory representation in the hierarchy to true realization; if they persist in ostentatiously brandishing their specializations (their painting, their novels, their equations, their sociometry, their psychoanalysis, their ballistics); finally, if, knowing perfectly well – and soon *ignorance of this fact will be no excuse* – that only power and the SI hold the key to using their specialization, they nevertheless still choose to serve power because power, battening on their inertia, has chosen them to serve it, then fuck them! No one could be more generous. They should understand all this and above all the fact that henceforth the revolt of nonruling actors is linked to the revolt against the spectacle (see below the thesis on the SI and power).

21

The generalized anathematization of the lumpenproletariat stems from the use to which it was put by the bourgeoisie, which it served both as a regulating mechanism for power and as a source of recruits for the more dubious forces of order: cops, informers, hired thugs, artists . . . Nevertheless, the lumpenproletariat embodies a remarkably radical implicit critique of the *society of work*. Its open contempt for both lackeys and bosses contains a good critique of work as alienation, a critique that has not been taken into consideration until now because the lumpenproletariat was the sector of ambiguities, but also because during the nineteenth century and the beginning of the twentieth the struggle against natural alienation and the production of well-being still appeared as valid justifications for work.

Once it became known that the abundance of consumer goods was nothing but the flip side of alienation in production, the lumpenproletariat acquired a new dimension: it liberated a contempt for organized work which, in the age of the Welfare State, is gradually taking on the proportions of a demand that only the rulers still refuse to acknowledge. In spite of the constant attempts of power to recuperate it, every experiment carried out on everyday life, that is, every attempt to construct it (an illegal activity since the destruction of feudal power, where it was limited and restricted to a minority), is concretized today through the critique of alienating work and the refusal to submit to forced labor. So much so that the new proletariat tends to define itself negatively as a 'Front Against Forced Labor' bringing together all those who resist recuperation by power. This defines our field of action; it is here that we are gambling on the ruse of history against the ruse of power; it is here that we back the worker (whether steelworker or artist) who – consciously or not – rejects organized work and life, against the worker who – consciously or not – accepts working at the dictates of power. In this perspective, it is not unreasonable to foresee a transitional period during which automation and the will of the new proletariat leave work solely to specialists, reducing managers and bureaucrats to the rank of temporary slaves. In a generalized automation the 'workers,' instead of supervising machines, could devote their attention to watching over the cybernetic specialists, whose sole task would be to increase a production which, through a reversal of perspective, will have ceased to be the priority sector, in order to serve the priority of life over survival.

22

Unitary power strove to dissolve individual existence in a collective consciousness so that each social unit subjectively defined itself as a particle with a clearly determined weight suspended as though in oil. Everyone had to feel overwhelmed by the omnipresent evidence that everything was merely raw material in the hands of God, who used it for his own purposes, which were naturally beyond individual human comprehension. All phenomena were seen as emanations of a supreme will; any abnormal divergence signified some hidden meaning (any perturbation was merely an ascending or descending path toward harmony: the Four Reigns, the Wheel of Fortune, trials sent by the gods). One can speak of a collective consciousness in the sense that it was simultaneously for each individual and for everyone: consciousness of myth and consciousness of particular-existence-within-myth.

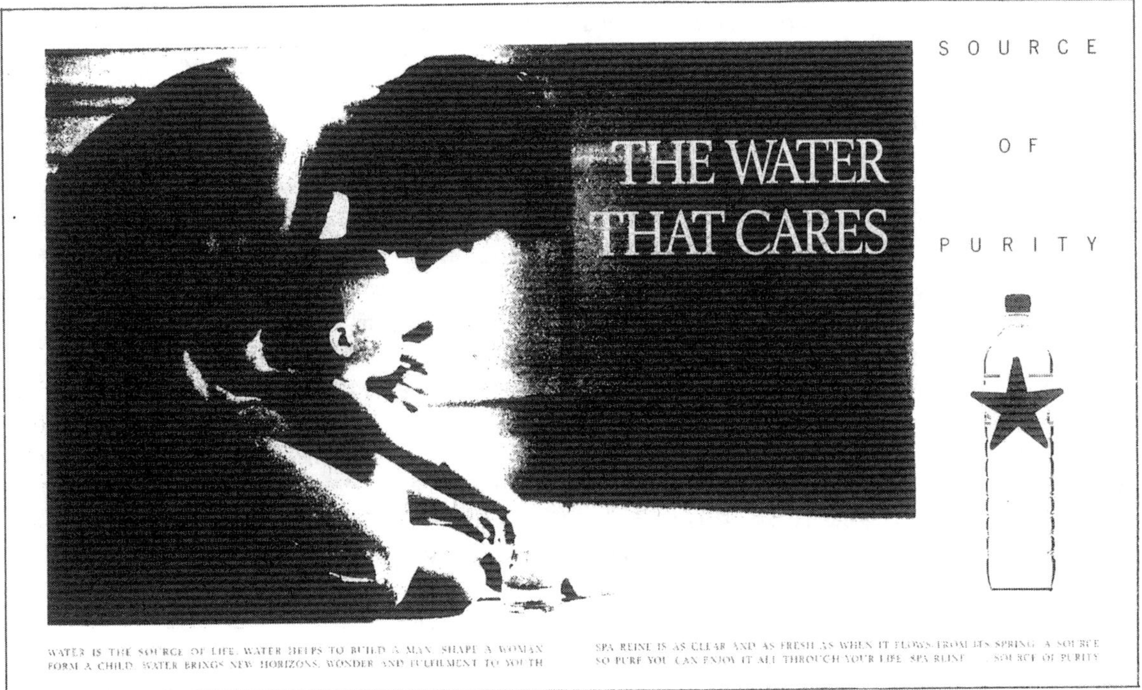

The power of the illusion was such that authentically lived life drew its meaning from what was not authentically lived; from this stems that priestly condemnation of life, the reduction of life to pure contingency, to sordid materiality, to vain appearance and to the lowest state of a transcendence that became increasingly degraded as it escaped mythical organization.

God was the guarantor of space and time, whose coordinates defined unitary society. He was the common reference point for all men; space and time came together in him just as in him all beings became one with their destiny. In the era of fragmentation, man is torn between a time and a space that no transcendence can unify through the mediation of any centralized power. We are living in a space and time that are out of joint, deprived of any reference point or coordinate, as though we were never going to be able to come into contact with ourselves, although everything invites us to.

There is a place where you create yourself and a time in which you play yourself. The space of everyday life, that of one's true realization, is encircled by every form of conditioning. The narrow space of our true realization defines us, yet we define ourselves in the time of the spectacle. Or put another way: our consciousness is no longer consciousness of myth and of particular-*being*-in-myth, but rather consciousness of the spectacle and of particular-*role*-in-the-spectacle. (I pointed out above the relationship between all ontology and unitary power; it should be recalled here that the crisis of ontology appears with the movement toward fragmentation.) Or to put it still another way: in the space-time relation in which everyone and everything is situated, time has become the imaginary (the field of identifications); space defines us, although we define ourselves in the imaginary and although the imaginary defines us *qua* subjectivities.

Our freedom is that of an abstract temporality in which we are *named* in the language of power (these names are the roles assigned to us), with a choice left to us to find officially recognized *synonyms* for ourselves. In contrast, the space of our authentic realization (the space of our everyday life) is under the dominion of silence. There is no name to name the space of lived experience except in poetry, in language liberating itself from the domination of power.

23

By desacralizing and fragmenting myth, the bourgeoisie was led to demand first of all independence of consciousness (demands for freedom of thought, freedom of the press, freedom of research, rejection of dogma). Consciousness thus ceased being more or less consciousness-reflecting-myth. It became consciousness of successive roles played within the spectacle. What the bourgeoisie demanded above all was the freedom of actors and extras in a spectacle no longer organized by God, his cops and his priests, but by natural and economic laws, 'capricious and inexorable laws' defended by a new team of cops and specialists.

God has been torn off like a useless bandage and the wound has stayed raw. The bandage may have prevented the wound from healing, but it justified suffering, it gave it a meaning well worth a few shots of morphine. Now suffering has no justification whatsoever and morphine is far from cheap. Separation has become concrete. Anyone at all can put their finger on it, and the only answer cybernetic society has to offer us is to become spectators of the gangrene and decay, spectators of survival.

The drama of consciousness to which Hegel referred is actually the consciousness of drama. Romanticism resounds like the cry of the soul torn from the body, a suffering all the more acute as each of us finds himself alone in facing the fall of the sacred totality and of all the Houses of Usher.

24

The totality is objective reality, in the movement of which subjectivity can participate only in the form of realization. Anything separate from the realization of everyday life rejoins the spectacle where survival is frozen (hibernation) and served out in slices. There can be no authentic realization except in objective reality, in the totality. All the rest is caricature. The objective realization that functions in the mechanism of the spectacle is nothing but the success of power-manipulated objects (the 'objective realization in subjectivity' of famous artists, stars, celebrities of *Who's Who*). On the level of the organization of appearance, every success – and every failure – is inflated until it becomes a stereotype, and is broadcast as though it were the only possible success or failure. So far power has been the only judge, though its judgement has been subjected to various pressures. Its criteria are the only valid ones for those who accept the spectacle and are satisfied to play a role in it. But there are no more artists on that stage, there are only extras.

25

The space-time of private life was harmonized in the space-time of myth. Fourier's harmony responds to this perverted harmony. As soon as myth no longer encompasses the individual and the partial in a totality dominated by the sacred, each fragment sets itself up as a totality. The fragment set up as a totality is, in fact, the *totalitarian*. In the dissociated space-time that constitutes private life, time – made absolute in the form of abstract freedom, the freedom of the spectacle – consolidates by its very dissociation the spatial absolute of private life, its isolation and constriction. The mechanism of the alienating spectacle wields such force that private life reaches the point of being defined as that which is deprived of spectacle; the fact that one escapes roles and spectacular categories is experienced as an additional privation, as a malaise which power uses as a pretext to reduce everyday life to insignificant gestures (sitting down, washing, opening a door).

26

The spectacle that imposes its norms on lived experience itself arises out of lived experience. The time of the spectacle, lived in the form of successive roles, makes the space of authentic experience the area of objective impotence, while at the same time the objective impotence that stems from the conditioning of privative appropriation makes the spectacle the ultimate of potential freedom.

Elements born of lived experience are acknowledged only on the level of the spectacle, where they are expressed in the form of stereotypes, although such expression is constantly contested and refuted in and by lived experience. The *composite portrait of the survivors* – whom Nietzsche referred to as the 'little people' or the 'last men' – can be conceived only in terms of the following dialectic of possibility/impossibility:

a) possibility on the level of the spectacle (variety of abstract roles) reinforces impossibility on the level of authentic experience;

b) impossibility (that is, limits imposed on real experience by privative appropriation) determines the field of abstract possibilities.

Survival is two-dimensional. Against such a reduction, what forces can bring out what constitutes the daily problem of all human beings: the dialectic of survival and life? Either the specific forces the SI has counted on will make possible the supersession of these contraries, reuniting space and time in the construction of everyday life; or life and survival will become locked in an antagonism growing weaker and weaker until the point of ultimate confusion and ultimate poverty is reached.

27

Lived reality is spectacularly fragmented and labeled in biological, sociological or other categories which, while being related to the communicable, never communicate anything but facts emptied of their authentically lived content. It is in this sense that hierarchical power, imprisoning everyone in the objective mechanism of privative appropriation, is also a dictatorship over subjectivity. It is as a dictator over subjectivity that it strives, with limited chances of success, to force each individual subjectivity to become objectivized, that is, to become an object it can manipulate. This extremely interesting dialectic should be analyzed in greater detail (objective realization in subjectivity – the realization of power – and objective realization in objectivity – which enters into the praxis of constructing everyday life and destroying power).

Facts are deprived of content in the name of the communicable, in the name of an abstract universality, in the name of a perverted harmony in which everyone realizes himself in an inverted perspective. In this context the SI is in the line of contestation that runs through Sade, Fourier, Lewis Carroll, Lautréamont, surrealism, lettrism – at least in its least known currents, which were the most extreme.

Within a fragment set up as a totality, each further fragment is itself totalitarian. Sensitivity, desire, will, intelligence, good taste, the subconscious and all the categories of the ego were treated as absolutes by individualism. Today sociology is enriching the categories of psychology, but the introduction of variety into the roles merely accentuates the monotony of the identification reflex. The freedom of the 'survivor' will be to assume the abstract constituent to which he has 'chosen' to reduce himself. Once any real realization has been put out of the picture, all that remains is a psychosociological dramaturgy in which interiority functions as a safety-valve, as an overflow to drain off the effects one has worn for the daily exhibition. Survival becomes the ultimate stage of life organized as the mechanical reproduction of memory.

28

Until now the approach to the totality has been falsified. Power has parasitically interposed itself as an indispensable mediation between man and nature. But the relation between man and nature is based only on praxis. It is praxis which constantly breaks through the coherent veneer of lies that myth and its substitutes try to maintain. It is praxis, even alienated praxis, which maintains contact with the totality. By revealing its own fragmentary character, praxis at the same time reveals the real totality (reality): it is the totality being realized by way of its opposite, the fragment.

In the perspective of praxis, every fragment is totality. In the perspective of power, which alienates praxis, every fragment is totalitarian. This should be enough to wreck the attempts cybernetic power will make to envelop praxis in a mystique, although the seriousness of these attempts should not be underestimated.

All praxis enters into our project; it enters with its share of alienation, with the impurities of power: but we are capable of filtering them out. We will elucidate the force and purity of acts of refusal as well as the manipulative maneouvres of power, not in a Manichean perspective, but as a means of developing, through our own strategy, this combat in which everywhere, at every moment, the adversaries are seeking one another but only clashing accidentally, lost in irremediable darkness and uncertainty.

29

Everyday life has always been drained to the advantage of apparent life, but appearance, in its mythical cohesion, was powerful enough to repress any mention of everyday life. The poverty and emptiness of the spectacle, revealed by all the varieties of capitalism and all the varieties of bourgeoisie, has revealed both the existence of everyday life (a shelter life, but a shelter for what and from what?) and the poverty of everyday life. As reification and bureaucratization grow stronger, the debility of the spectacle and of everyday life is the only thing that remains clear. The conflict between the human and the inhuman has also been transferred to the plane of appearance. As soon as Marxism became an ideology, Marx's struggle against ideology in the name of the richness of life was transformed into an ideological anti-ideology, as antispectacle spectacle (just as in avant-garde culture the antispectacular spectacle is restricted to actors alone, antiartistic art being created and understood only by artists, so the relationship between this ideological anti-ideology and the function of the professional revolutionary in Leninism should be examined). Thus Manicheanism has found itself momentarily revived. Why did St Augustine attack the Manicheans so relentlessly? It was because he recognized the danger of a myth offering only one solution, the victory of good over evil; he saw that this impossibility threatened to provoke the collapse of all mythical structures and bring into the open the contradiction between mythical and authentic life. Christianity offered the third way, the way of sacred confusion. What Christianity accomplished through the force of myth is accomplished today through the force of *things*. There can no longer be any antagonism between Soviet workers and capitalist workers or between the bomb of the Stalinist bureaucrats and the bomb of the non-Stalinist bureaucrats; there is no longer anything but unity in the chaos of reified beings.

Who is responsible? Who should be shot? We are dominated by a system, by an abstract form. Degrees of humanity and inhumanity are measured by purely quantitative variations of passivity. The quality is the same everywhere: we are all proletarianized or well on the way to becoming so. What are the traditional 'revolutionaries' doing? They are eliminating certain distinctions, making sure that no proletarians are any more proletarian than all the others. But what party is working for the end of the proletariat?

The perspective of survival has become intolerable. What is weighing us down is the *weight of things in a vacuum*. That's what reification is: everyone and everything falling at an equal speed, everyone and everything stigmatized with their equal value. The reign of equal values has realized the Christian project, but it has realized it outside Christianity (as Pascal had supposed) and, above all, it has realized it over God's dead body, contrary to Pascal's expectations.

The spectacle and everyday life coexist in the reign of equal values. People and things are interchangeable. The world of reification is a world without a center, like the new prefabricated cities that are its decor. The present fades away before the promise of an eternal future that is nothing but a mechanical extension of the past. Time itself is deprived of a center. In this concentration-camp world, victims and torturers wear the same mask and only the torture is real. No new ideology can soothe the pain, neither the ideology of the totality (Logos) nor that of nihilism – which will be the two crutches of the cybernetic society. The tortures condemn all hierarchical power, however organized or dissimulated it may be. The antagonism the SI is going to revive is the oldest of all, it is radical antagonism and that is why it is taking up again and assimilating all that has been left by the insurrectionary movements and great individuals in the course of history.

30

So many other banalities could be taken up and reversed. The best things never come to an end. Before rereading the above – which even the most mediocre intelligence will be able to understand by the third attempt – the reader would be well-advised to concentrate carefully on the following text, for these notes, as fragmentary as the preceding ones, must be discussed in detail and implemented. It concerns a central question: the SI and revolutionary power.

Being aware of the crises of both mass parties and 'elites,' the SI must embody the supersession of both the Bolshevik Central Committee (supersession of the mass party) and of the Nietzschean project (supersession of the intelligentsia).

a) Every time a power has presented itself as directing a revolutionary upsurge, it has automatically undermined the power of the revolution. The Bolshevik C.C. defined itself simultaneously as concentration and as representation. Concentration of a power antagonistic to bourgeois power and representation of the will of the masses. This duality led it rapidly to become no more than an empty power, a power of empty representation, and consequently to rejoin, in a common form (bureaucracy), a bourgeois power that was being forced (in response to the very existence of the Bolshevik power) to follow a similar evolution. The conditions for a concentrated power and mass representation exist potentially in the SI when it states that it holds the qualitative and that its ideas are in everyone's mind. Nevertheless we refuse both concentrated power and the right of representation, conscious that we are now taking the only *public attitude* (for we cannot avoid being known to some extent in a spectacular manner) enabling those who find that they share our theoretical and practical positions to accede to revolutionary power: power without mediation, power entailing the direct action of everyone. Our guiding image could be the Durruti Column, moving from town to village, liquidating the bourgeois elements and leaving the workers to see to their own self-organization.

b) The intelligentsia is power's hall of mirrors. Contesting power, it never offers anything but passive cathartic identification to those whose every gesture gropingly expresses real contestation. The radicalism – not of theory, obviously, but of gesture – that could be glimpsed in the 'Declaration of the 121,' however, suggests some different possibilities. We are capable of precipitating this crisis, but we can do so only by entering the intelligentsia as a power against the intelligentsia. This phase – which must precede and be contained within the phase described in point a) – will put us in the perspective of the Nietzschean project. We will form a small, almost alchemical, experimental group within which the realization of the total man can be started. Nietzsche could conceive of such an undertaking only within the framework of the hierarchical principle. It is, in fact, within such a framework that we find ourselves. It is therefore of the utmost importance that we present ourselves without the slightest ambiguity (on the level of the group, the purification of the nucleus and the elimination of residues now seems to be completed). We accept the hierarchical framework in which we are placed only while impatiently working to abolish our domination over those whom we cannot avoid dominating on the basis of our criteria for mutual recognition.

c) Tactically our communication should be a diffusion emanating from a more or less hidden center. We will establish nonmaterialized networks (direct relationships, episodic ones, contacts without ties, development of embryonic relations based on sympathy and understanding, in the manner of the red agitators before the arrival of the revolutionary armies). We will claim radical gestures (actions, writings, political attitudes, works) as our own by analyzing them, and we will consider that our own acts and analyses are supported by the majority of people.

Just as God constituted the reference point of past unitary society, we are preparing to create the central reference point for a unitary society now possible. But this point cannot be fixed. As opposed to the ever-renewed confusion that cybernetic power draws from the past of inhumanity, it stands for the game that everyone will play, 'the moving order of the future.'

On the passage of a few persons through a rather brief period of time

Soundtrack of a film by Guy Debord (1959)

Voice 1 *(male 'announcer')*: This neighborhood was made for the wretched dignity of the petty bourgeoisie, for respectable occupations and intellectual tourism. The sedentary population of the upper floors was sheltered from the influences of the street. This neighborhood has remained the same. It was the strange setting of our story. Here a systematic questioning of all the diversions and works of a society, a total critique of its idea of happiness, was expressed in acts.

These people also scorned 'subjective profundity'. They were interested in nothing but an adequate and concrete expression of themselves.

Voice 2 *(Debord, monotone)*: Human beings are not fully conscious of their real life . . . usually groping in the dark; overwhelmed by the consequences of their acts; at every moment groups and individuals find themselves confronted with results they have not wished.

Voice 1: They said that oblivion was their ruling passion. They wanted to reinvent everything each day; to become the masters and possessors of their own lives.

Just as one does not judge a man according to the conception he has of himself, one cannot judge such periods of transition according to their own consciousness on the contrary, one must explain the consciousness through the contradictions of material life, through the conflict between social conditions and the forces of social production.

The progress achieved in the domination of nature was not yet matched by a corresponding liberation of everyday life. Youth passed away among the various controls of resignation.

Our camera has captured for you a few aspects of a provisional microsociety.

The knowledge of empirical facts remains abstract and superficial as long as it is not concretized by its integration into the whole – which alone permits the supersession of partial and abstract problems so as to arrive at their *concrete essence*, and implicitly as their meaning.

This group was on the margins of the economy. It tended toward a role of pure consumption, and first of all the free consumption of its time. It thus found itself directly engaged in qualitative variations of daily life but deprived of any means to intervene in them.

The group ranged over a very small area. The same times brought them back to the same places. No one went to bed early. Discussion on the meaning of all this continued . . .

Voice 2: 'Our life is a journey – In the winter and the night. – We seek our passage . . .'

Voice 1: The abandoned literature nevertheless exerted a delaying action on new affective formulations.

Voice 2: There was the fatigue and the cold of the morning in this much-traversed labyrinth, like an enigma that we had to resolve. It was a looking-glass reality through which we had to discover the possible richness of reality. On the bank of the river evening began once again; and caresses; and the importance of a world without importance. Just as the eyes have blurred vision of many things and can see only one clearly, so the will can strive only incompletely toward diverse objects and can completely love only one at a time.

Voice 3 *(young girl)*: No one counted on the future. It would never be possible to be together later, or anywhere else. There would never be a greater freedom.

Voice 1: The refusal of time and of growing old automatically limited encounters in this narrow, contingent zone, where what was lacking was felt as irreparable. The extreme precariousness of the means of getting by without working was at the root of this impatience which made excesses necessary and breaks definitive.

Voice 2: One never really contests an organization of existence without contesting all of that organization's forms of language.

Voice 1: When freedom is practiced in a closed circle, it faded into a dream, becomes a mere representation of itself. The ambiance of play is by nature unstable. At any moment 'ordinary life' can prevail once again. The geographical limitation of play is even more striking than its temporal limitation. Any game takes place within the contours of its spatial domain. Around the neighborhood, around its fleeting and threatened immobility, stretched a half-known city where people met only by chance, losing their way forever. The girls there, because they were legally under the control of their families until the age of eighteen, were often recaptured by the defenders of that detestable institution. They were generally confined under the guard of those creatures who among all the bad products of a bad society are the most ugly and repugnant: nuns.

What usually makes documentaries so easy to understand is the arbitrary limitation of their subject matter. They describe the atomization of social functions and the isolation of their products. One can, in contrast, envisage the entire complexity of a moment which is not resolved into a work, a moment whose movement indissolubly contains facts and values and whose meaning does not yet appear. The subject matter of the documentary would then be this confused totality.

Voice 2: The epoch had arrived at a level of knowledge and technical means that made possible, and increasingly necessary, a *direct* construction of all aspects of a liberated affective and practical existence. The appearance of these superior means of action, still unused because of the delays in the project of liquidating the commodity economy, had already condemned aesthetic activity, whose ambitions and powers were both outdated. The decay of art and of all the values of former mores had formed our sociological background. The ruling classes' monopoly over the instruments we had to control in order to realize the collective art of our time has excluded us from a cultural production officially devoted to illustrating and repeating the past. An art film on this generation can only be a film on its absence of real works.

Everyone unthinkingly followed the paths learned once and for all, to their work and their homes, to their predictable future. For them duty had already become a habit, and habit a duty. They did not see the deficiency of their city. They thought the deficiency of their life was natural. We wanted to break out of this conditioning, in quest of another use of the urban landscape, in quest of new passions. The atmosphere of a few places gave us intimations of the future powers of an architecture it would be necessary to create to be the support and framework for less mediocre games. We could expect nothing of anything we had not ourselves altered. The urban environment proclaimed the orders and tastes of the ruling society just as violently as the newspapers. It is man who makes the unity of the world, but man has extended himself everywhere. Men can see nothing around them that is not their own image; everything speaks to them of themselves. Their very landscape is alive. There were obstacles everywhere. There was a coherence in the obstacles of all types. They maintained the coherent reign of poverty. Everything being connected, it was necessary to *change everything* by a unitary struggle, or nothing. It was necessary to link up with the masses, but we were surrounded by sleep.

Voice 3: The dictatorship of the proletariat is a desperate struggle, bloody and bloodless, violent and peaceful, military and economic, educational and administrative, against the forces and traditions of the old world.

Voice 1: In this country it is once again the men of order who have rebelled. They have reinforced their power. They have been able to aggravate the grotesqueness of the ruling conditions according to their will. They have embellished their system with the funereal ceremonies of the past.

Voice 2: Years, like a single instant prolonged to this point, come to an end.

Voice 1: That which was directly lived reappears frozen in the distance, fitted into the tastes and illusions of an era carried away with it.

Voice 2: The appearance of events that we have not made, that others have made against us, obliges us from now on to be aware of the passage of time, its results, the transformation of our own desires into events. What differentiates the past from the present is precisely its out-of-reach objectivity; there is no more should-be; being is so consumed that it has ceased to exist. The details are already lost in the dust of time. Who was afraid of life, afraid of the night, afraid of being taken, afraid of being kept?

Voice 3: That which should be abolished continues, and we continue to wear away with it. We are engulfed. We are separated. The years pass and we have not changed anything.

Voice 2: Once again morning in the same streets. Once again the fatigue of so many similarly passed nights. It is a walk that has lasted a long time.

Voice 1: Really hard to drink more.

Voice 2: Of course one might make a film of it. But even if such a film succeeds in being as fundamentally incoherent and unsatisfying as the reality it deals with, it will never be more than a re-creation – poor and false like this botched traveling shot.

Voice 3: There are now people who flatter themselves that they are authors of films, as others were authors of novels. They are even more backward than the novelists because they are ignorant of the decomposition and exhaustion of individual expression in our time, ignorant of the end of the arts of passivity. They are praised for their sincerity since they dramatize, with more personal depth, the conventions of which their life consists. There is talk of the liberation of the cinema. But what does it matter to us if one more art is liberated through which Pierre or Jacques or François can joyously express their slave sentiments? The only interesting venture is the liberation of everyday life, not only in the perspectives of history but for us and right away. This entails the withering away of alienated forms of communication. The cinema, too, has to be destroyed.

Voice 2: In the final analysis, stars are created by the need we have for them, and not by talent or absence of talent or even by the film industry or advertising. Miserable need, dismal, anonymous life that would like to expand itself to the dimensions of cinema life. The imaginary life on the screen is the product of this real need. The star is the projection of this need.

The images of the advertisements during the intermissions are more suited than any others for evoking an intermission of life.

To really describe this era it would no doubt be necessary to show many other things. But what would be the point? Better to grasp the totality of what has been done and what remains to be done than to add more ruins to the old world of the spectacle and of memories.

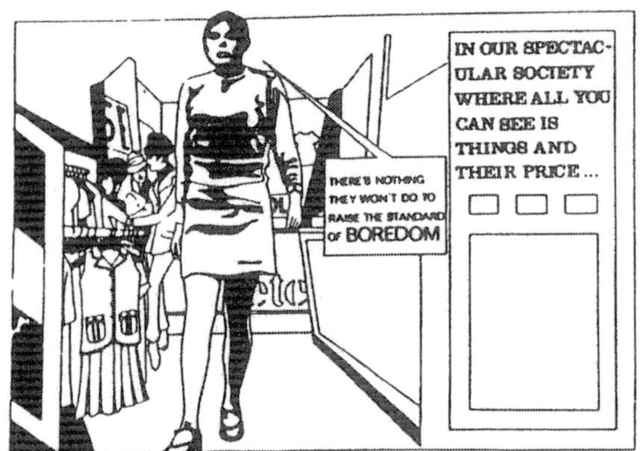

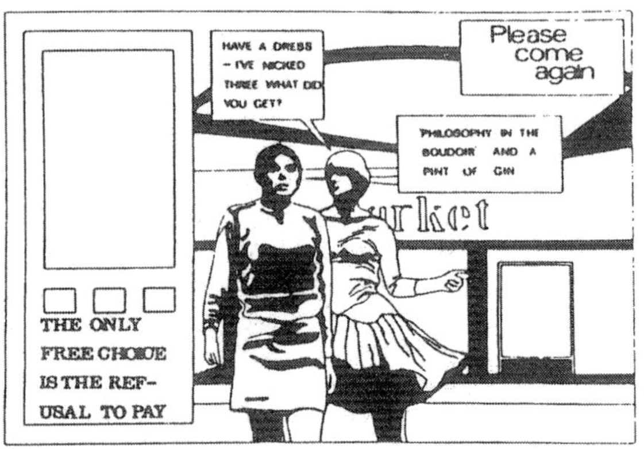

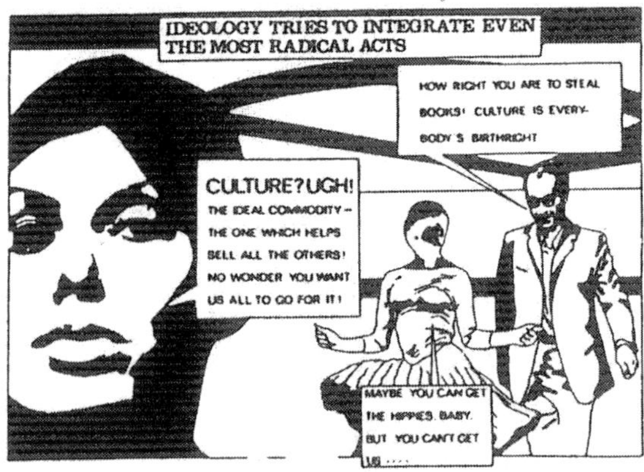

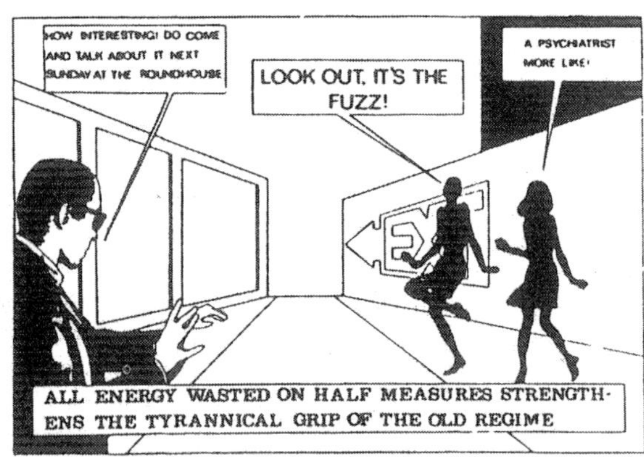

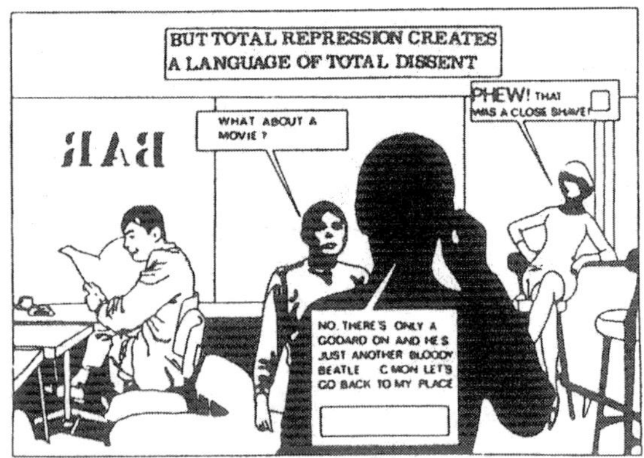

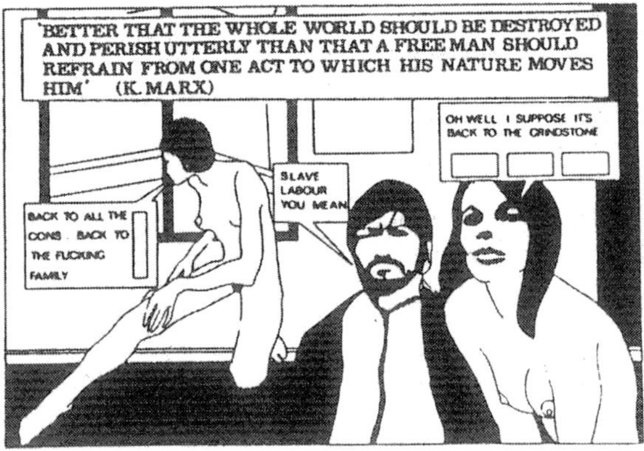

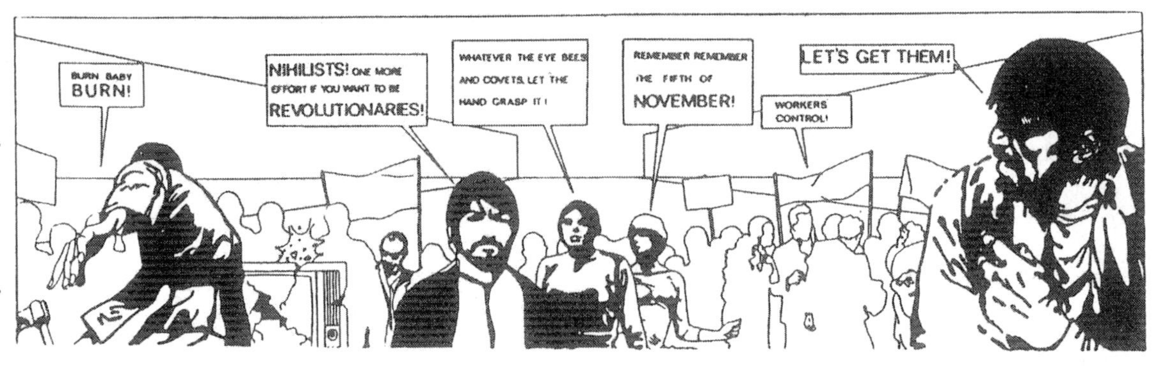

In our spectacular society, anon.

Documents: The SI in Britain

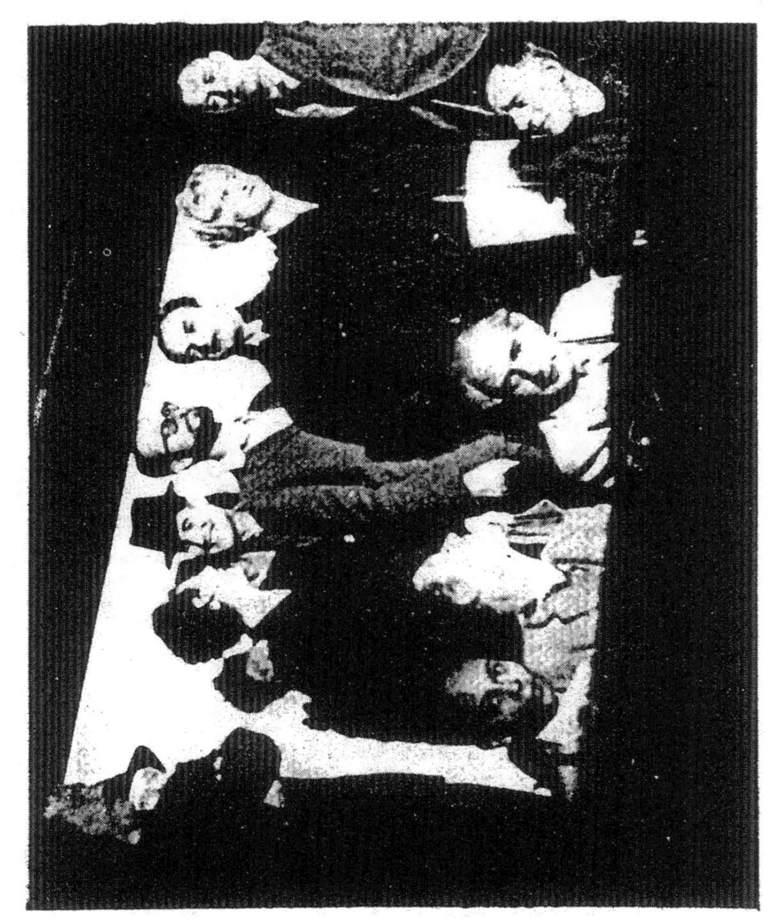

HURRY! HURRY! HURRY!

TELL US IN NOT MORE THAN 250 WORDS WHY YOUR GIRL IS THE SWEETEST GIRL IN TOWN

State in your letter her name, occupation and age (remember she must be single, and from sixteen to nineteen, inclusive), and pop a recent picture of her in the envelope. And please write her name and address clearly on the back of the picture as well.

Address your entry to:

Psychogeografical Comitee of Lon

(especially Debord and Jorn)

c/o Institute of Contemporary Art

17-18, Dover Street LONDON W 1

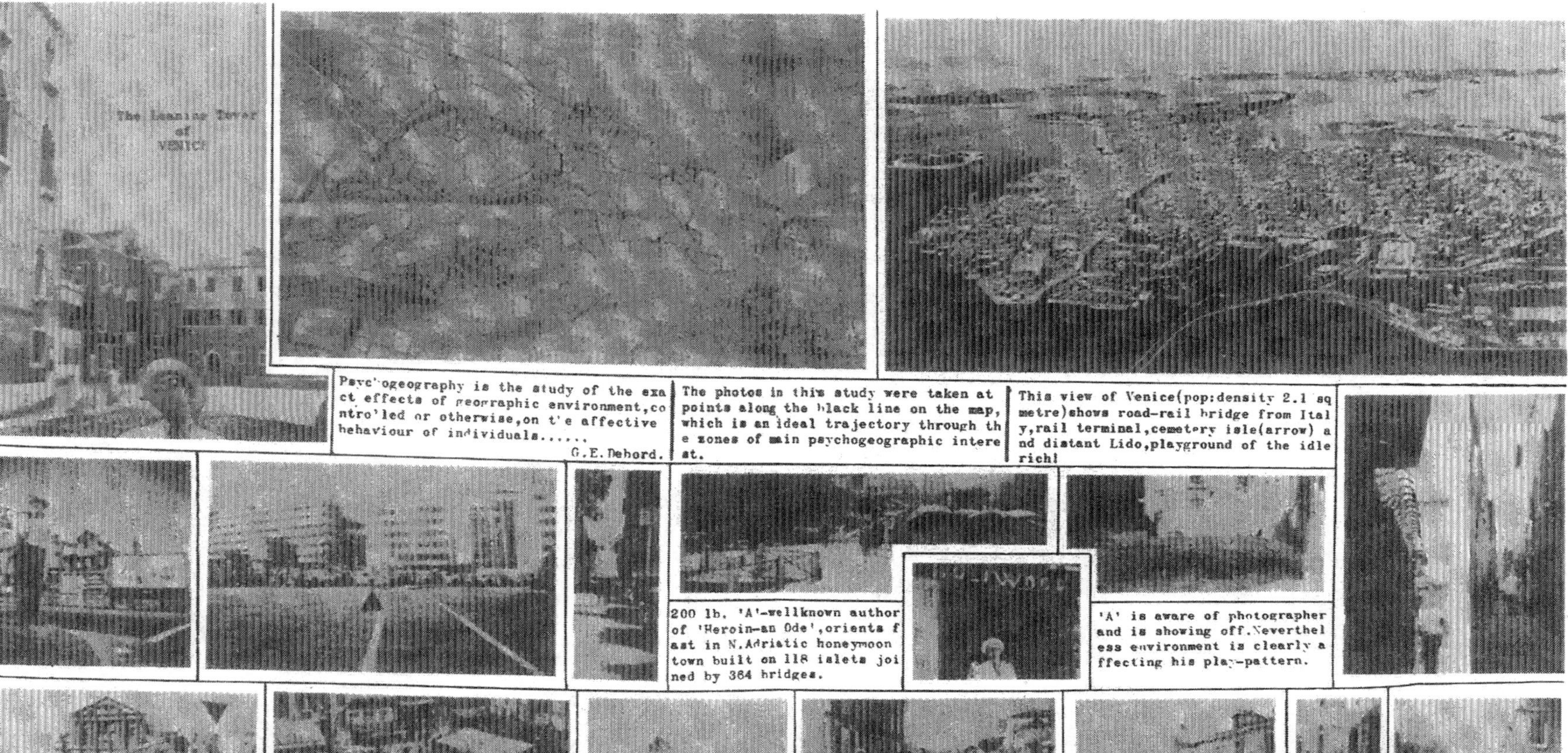

Psychogeographic maps of Venice Ralph Rumney, 1957

Asger Jorn, *Fin de Copenhague* (excerpt), 1957

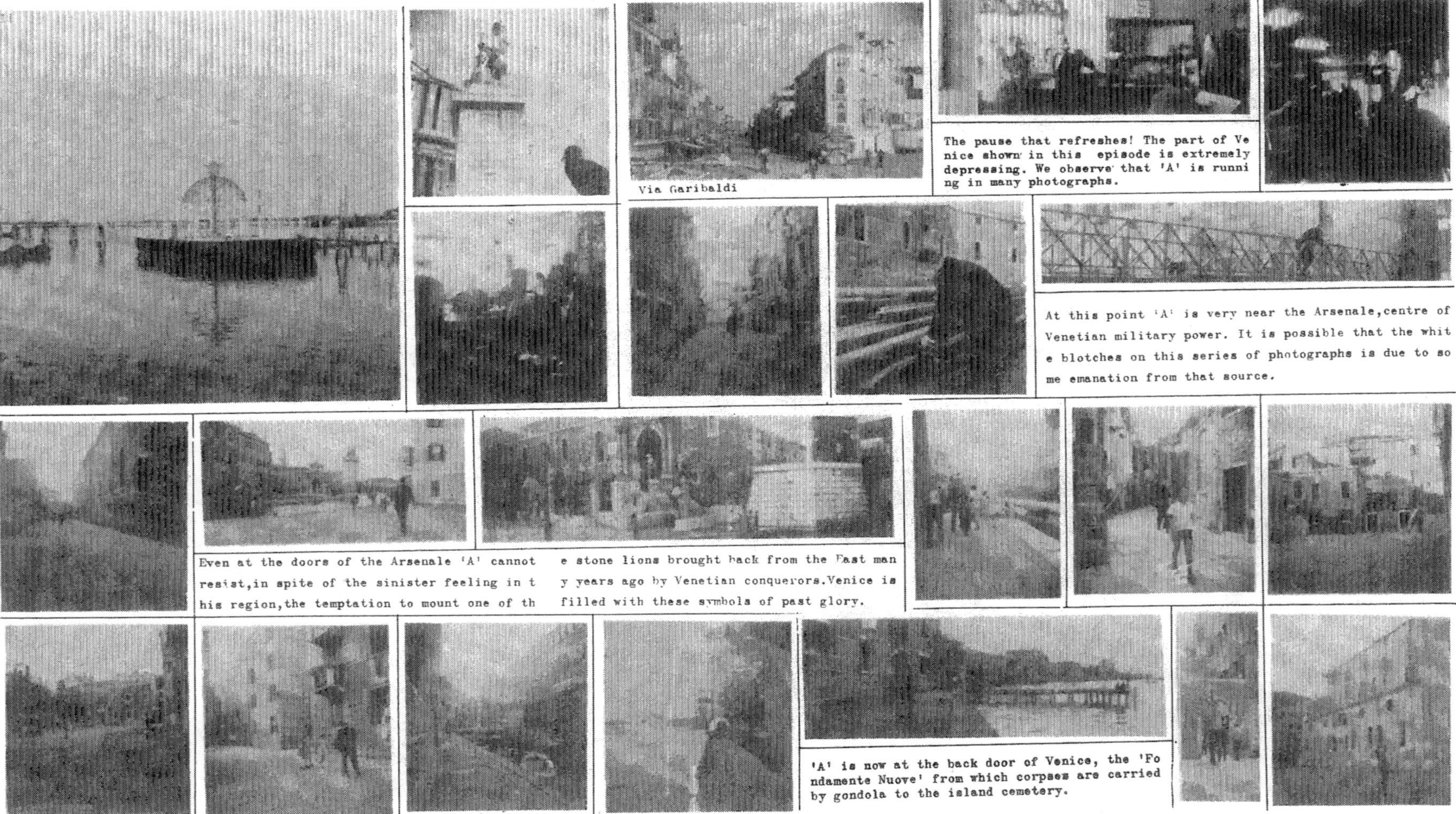
Via Garibaldi
The pause that refreshes! The part of Ve
nice shown in this episode is extremely
depressing. We observe that 'A' is runni
ng in many photographs.
At this point 'A' is very near the Arsenale, centre of
Venetian military power. It is possible that the whit
e blotches on this series of photographs is due to so
me emanation from that source.
Even at the doors of the Arsenale 'A' cannot
resist, in spite of the sinister feeling in t
his region, the temptation to mount one of th
e stone lions brought back from the East man
y years ago by Venetian conquerors. Venice is
filled with these symbols of past glory.
'A' is now at the back door of Venice, the 'Fo
ndamente Nuove' from which corpses are carried
by gondola to the island cemetery.

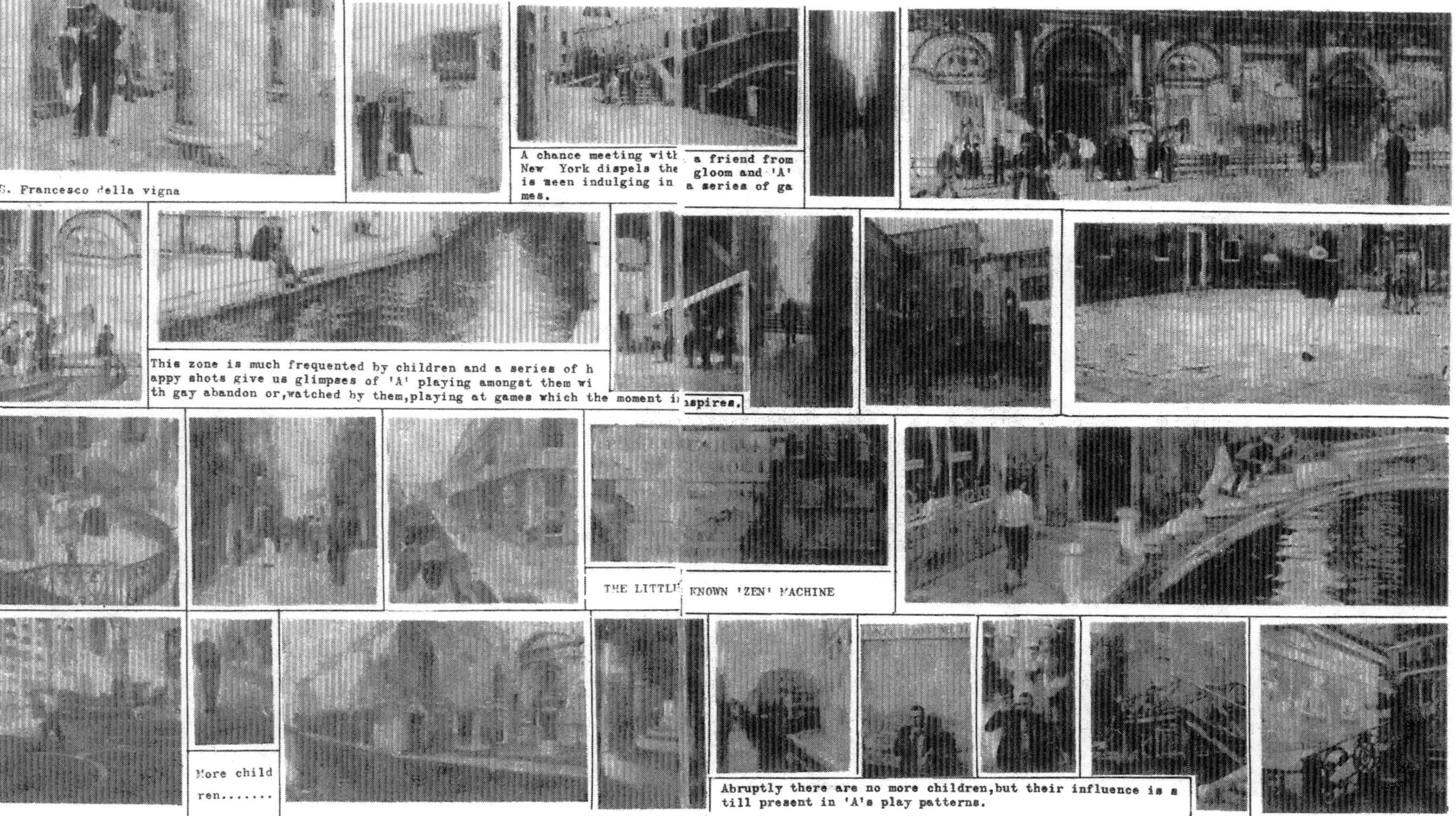
S. Francesco della vigna
A chance meeting with a friend from
New York dispels the gloom and 'A'
is seen indulging in a series of ga
mes.
This zone is much frequented by children and a series of h
appy shots give us glimpses of 'A' playing amongst them wi
th gay abandon or,watched by them,playing at games which the moment inspires.
THE LITTLE KNOWN 'ZEN' MACHINE
More child
ren.......
Abruptly there are no more children,but their influence is s
till present in 'A's play patterns.

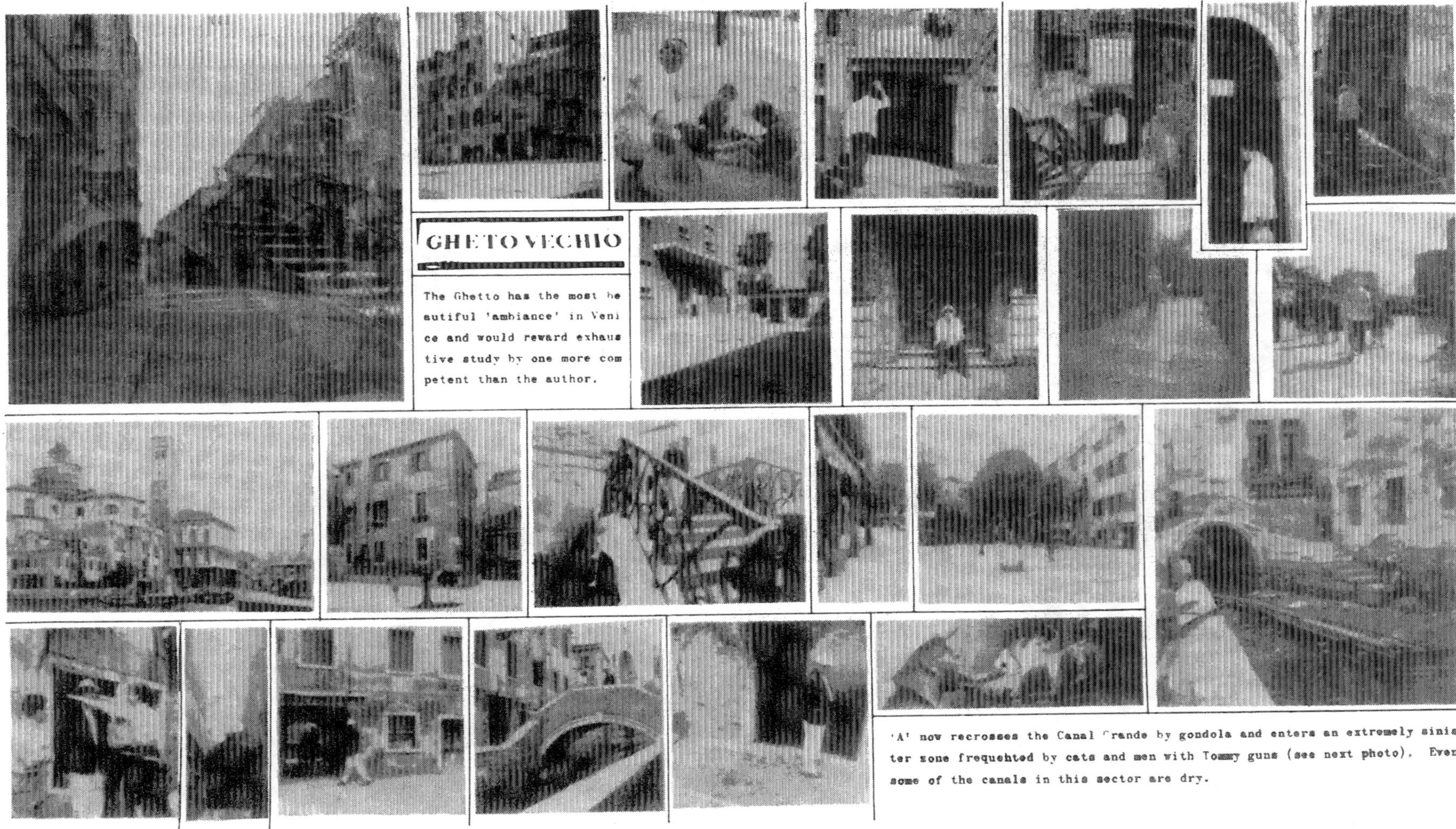

GHETO VECHIO

The Ghetto has the most beautiful 'ambiance' in Venice and would reward exhaustive study by one more competent than the author.

'A' now recrosses the Canal Grande by gondola and enters an extremely sinister zone frequented by cats and men with Tommy guns (see next photo). Even some of the canals in this sector are dry.

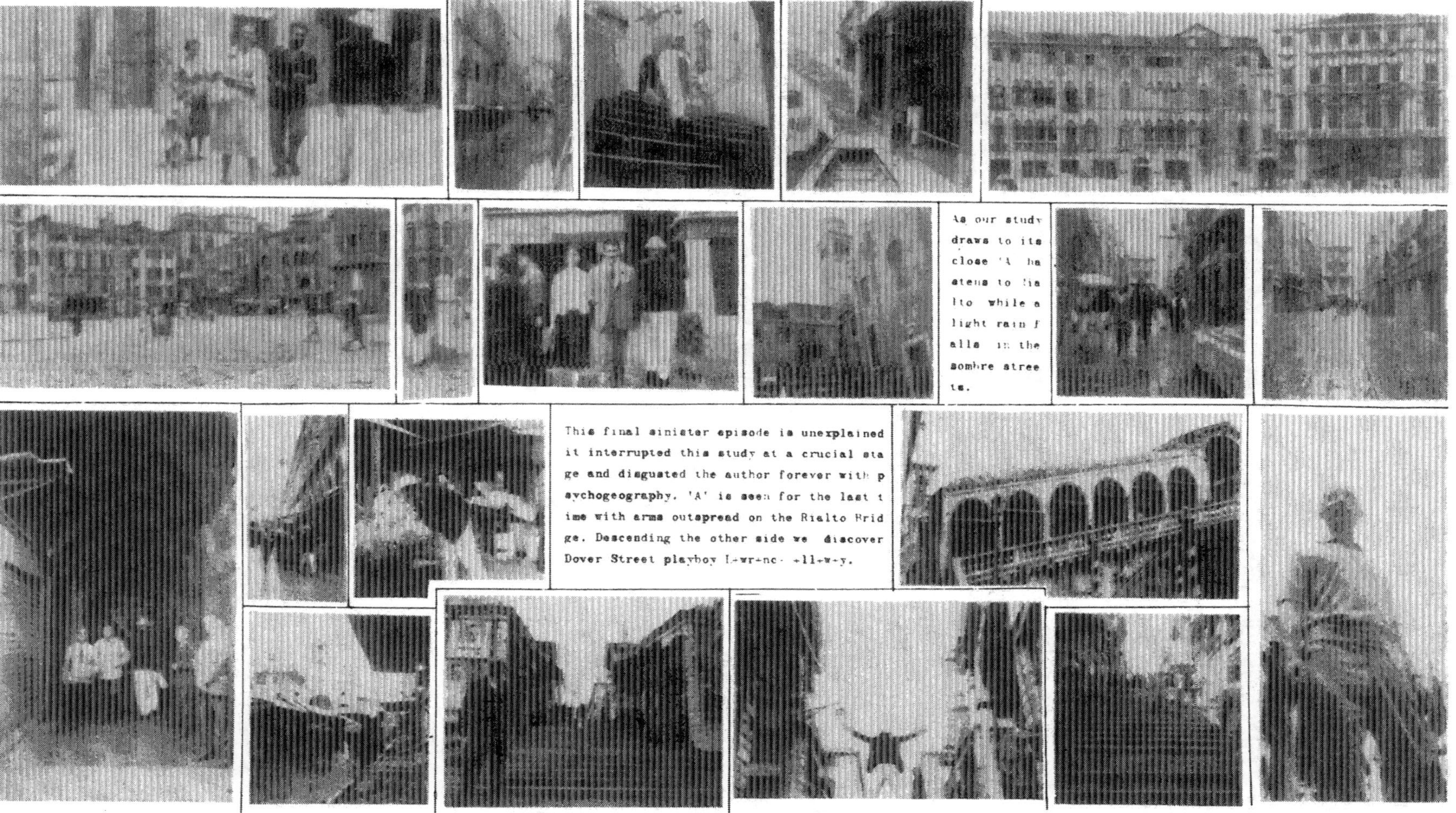
As our study
draws to its
close 'A' ha
stens to Ria
lto while a
light rain f
alls in the
sombre stree
ts.
This final sinister episode is unexplained
it interrupted this study at a crucial sta
ge and disgusted the author forever with p
sychogeography. 'A' is seen for the last t
ime with arms outspread on the Rialto Brid
ge. Descending the other side we discover
Dover Street playboy L-wr-nc- -ll-w-y.

Letter to the Times re Chinatown, Michèle Benstein, Guy Debord, Gil J Wolman *Potlatch*, October 1955

LETTRISTISCHE INTERVENTION

Brief an die Redaktion der „Times"

Sir,

The *Times* has just announced the projected demolition of the Chinese quarter in London.

We protest against such moral ideas in town-planning, ideas which must obviously make England more boring than it has in recent years already become.

The only pageants you have left are a coronation from time to time, an occasional royal marriage which seldom bears fruit; nothing else. The disappearance of pretty girls, of good family especially, will become rarer and rarer after the razing of Limehouse. Do you honestly believe that a gentleman can amuse himself in Soho?

We hold that the so-called modern town-planning which you recommend is fatuously idealistic and reactionary. The sole end of architecture is to serve the passions of men.

Anyway, it is inconvenient that this Chinese quarter of London should be destroyed before we have the opportunity to visit it and carry out certain psycho-geographical experiments we are at present undertaking.

Finally, if modernisation appears to you, as it does to us, to be historically necessary, we would counsel you to carry your enthusiasm into areas more urgently in need of it, that is to say, to your political and moral institutions.

Yours faithfully,

Michèle Bernstein, G.-E. Debord, Gil J. Wolman,
13. October 1955
POTLATCH

The Fourth SI Conference in London

Translated by Ken Knabb
Excerpts

The 4th Conference of the Situationist International was held in London, at a secret address in the East End, 24–28 September 1960, seventeen months after the Munich Conference (April 1959). The Situationists assembled in London were: Debord, Jaqueline de Jong, Jorn Kotányi, Katja Lindell, Jørgen Nash, Prem, Sturm, Maurice Wyckaert and HP Zimmer. [. . .]

The discussion of these perspective leads to posing the question: To what extent is the SI a political movement? Various responses state that the SI is political, but not in the ordinary sense. The discussion becomes somewhat confused. Debord proposes, in order to bring out clearly the opinion of the Conference, that each person respond in writing to a questionnaire asking if he considers that there are 'forces in the society that the SI can count on? What forces? In what conditions?' This questionnaire is agreed upon and filled out. The first responses express the view that the SI aims to establish a program of overall liberation and to act in accord with other forces on a social scale. (Kotányi: 'To rely on what we call free.' Jorn: 'We are against specialization and rationalization, but not against them as means. . . . The movements of social groups are determined by the character of their desires. We can accept other social movements only to the extent that they are moving in our direction. We are the new revolution . . . we should act with other organizations that seek the same path.') The session is then adjourned.

At the beginning of the second session, 26 September, Heimrad Prem reads a declaration of the German section in response to the questionnaire. This very long declaration attacks the tendency in the responses read the day before to count on the existence of a revolutionary proletariat, for the signers strongly doubt the revolutionary capacities of the workers against the bureaucratic institutions that have dominated their movement. The German section considers that the SI should prepare to realize its program on its own by mobilizing the avant-garde artists, who are placed by the present society in intolerable conditions and can count only on themselves to take over the weapons of conditioning. Debord responds with a sharp critique of these positions. [. . .] Kotányi reminds the German delegates that even if since 1945 they have seen apparently passive and satisfied workers in Germany and legal strikes organized with music to divert union members, in other advanced capitalist countries 'wildcat' strikes have multiplied. He adds that in his opinion they vastly underestimate the German workers themselves. [. . .] Debord proposes that the majority openly declare that it rejects the German theses. It is agreed that the two tendencies separately decide on their positions. The German minority withdraws to an adjoining room to deliberate. When it returns Zimmer announces, in the name of his group, that they retract the preceding declaration, not because they think it unimportant, but in order not to impede present situationist activity. He concludes: 'We declare that we are in complete agreement with all the acts already done by the SI, with or without us, and with those that will be done in the foreseeable future. We are also in agreement with all the ideas published by the SI. We consider the question debated today as secondary in relation to the SI's overall development, and propose to reserve further discussion of it for the future.' Everyone agrees to this. Kotányi and Debord, however, ask that it be noted in the minutes that they do not consider that the question discussed today is secondary. The German situationists agree to delete their reference to it as such. The session is adjourned, very late at night. [. . .]

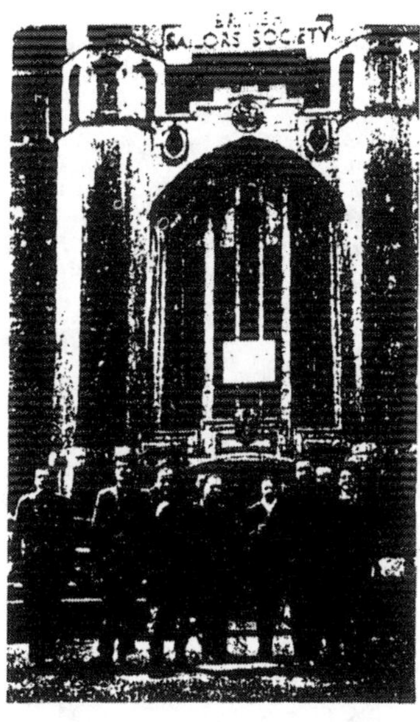

RESOLUTION

OF THE FOURTH CONFERENCE OF THE SITUATIONIST INTERNATIONAL

CONCERNING THE IMPRISONMENT OF ALEXANDER TROCCHI

The delegates to the fourth conference of the Situationist International, being informed of the arrest in the United States of their friend Alexander Trocchi, and of his charge of use of, and traffic in drugs, declare that the Situationist International retains full confidence in Alexander Trocchi.

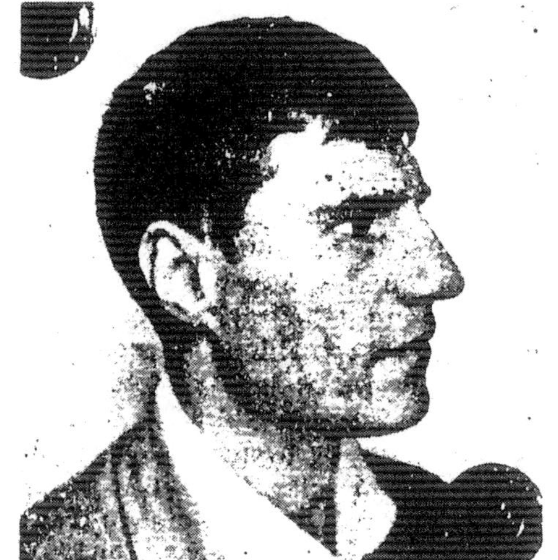

The conference DECLARES that Trocchi could not have, in any case, traffic in drugs ; this is clearly a police provocation by which the situationist will not allow themselves to be intimidated ;

AFFIRMS that drug taking is without importance ;

APPOINTS Asger Jorn, Jacqueline de Jong and Guy Debord to take immediate action on behalf of Alexander Trocchi and to report upon such action to the Situationist International at the earliest moment ;

CALLS in particular upon the cultural authorities of Britain and on all British intellectuals who value liberty to demand the setting free of Alexander Trocchi, who is beyond all doubt England's most intelligent creative artist today.

London, 27th september 1960.

Hands off Alexander Trocchi, Resolution of the 4th Conference of the SI, London, 1960

PROJECT SIGMA PAMPHLETS ALEXANDER TROCCHI

The Invisible Insurrection by A. T. 1/-d

Sigma: a tactical blueprint by A. T. 1/-d

Martin's Folly by William Burroughs 1/-d

Post Paid U. K.

from TROCCHI 7 Princes Square London W. 2

Invisible insurrection of a million minds

Alexander Trocchi

And if there is still one hellish, truly accursed thing in our time, it is our artistic dallying with forms, instead of being like victims burnt at the stake, signalling through the flames.
Antonin Artaud.[1]

Revolt is understandably unpopular. As soon as it is defined it has provoked the measures for its containment. The prudent man will avoid this definition which is in effect his death-sentence. Besides, it is a limit.

We are concerned not with the *coup-d'etat* of Trotsky and Lenin, but with the *coup-du-monde*, a transition of necessity more complex, more diffuse than the other, and so more gradual, less spectacular. Our methods will vary with the empirical facts pertaining here and now, there and then.

Political revolt is and must be ineffectual precisely because it must come to grips at the prevailing level of political process. Beyond the back-waters of civilisation it is an anachronism. Meanwhile, with the world at the edge of extinction, we cannot afford to wait for the mass. Nor to brawl with it.

The *coup-du-monde* must be in the broad sense cultural. With his thousand technicians Trotsky seized the viaducts and the bridges and the telephone exchanges and the power stations. The police, victims of convention, contributed to his brilliant enterprise by guarding the old men in the Kremlin. The latter hadn't the elasticity of mind to grasp that their own presence there at the traditional seat of government was irrelevant. History outflanked them. Trotsky had the railway stations and the powerhouses, and the 'government' was effectively locked out of history by its own guards.

So the cultural revolt must seize the grids of expression and the powerhouses of the mind. Intelligence must become self-conscious, realise its own power, and, on a global scale, transcending functions that are no longer appropriate, dare to exercise it. History will not overthrow national governments; it will outflank them. The cultural revolt is the necessary underpinning, the passionate substructure of a new order of things.

What is to be seized has no physical dimensions nor relevant temporal colour. It is not an arsenal, not a capital city, not an island, nor an isthmus visible from a peak in Darien. Finally, it is all these things too, of course, all that there is, but only by the way, and inevitably. What is to be seized – and I address that one million (say) here and there who are capable of perceiving at once just what it is I am about, a million potential 'technicians' – is ourselves. What must occur, now, today, tomorrow, in those widely dispersed but vital centres of experience, is a revelation. At the present time, in what is often thought of as the age of the mass, we tend to fall into the habit of regarding history and evolution as something which goes relentlessly on, quite out of our control. The individual has a profound sense of his own impotence as he realises the immensity of the forces involved. We, the creative ones everywhere, must discard this paralytic posture and seize control of the human process by assuming control of ourselves. We must reject the conventional fiction of 'unchanging human nature'. There is in fact no such permanence anywhere. There is only *becoming*.[2]

Organisation, control, revolution: each of the million individuals to whom I speak will be wary of such concepts, will find it all but impossible with a quiet conscience to identify himself with any group whatsoever, no matter what it calls itself. That is as it should be. But it is at the same time the reason for the importance of intelligence everywhere in the face of events, for which no one in particular can be said to be responsible, a yawning tide of bloody disasters, the natural outcome of that complex of processes, for the most part unconscious and uncontrolled, which constitute the history of man. Without organisation concerted action is impossible; the energy of individuals and small groups is dissipated in a hundred and one unconnected little acts of protest . . . a manifesto here, a hunger strike there. Such protests, moreover, are commonly based on the assumption that social behaviour is intelligent; the hallmark of their futility. If change is to be purposive, men must somehow function together in the social situation. And it is our contention that there already exists a nucleus of men who, if they will get themselves gradually and tentatively to the task, are capable of imposing a new and seminal idea: the world waits for them to show their hand.

We have already rejected any idea of a frontal attack. Mind cannot withstand matter (brute force) in open battle. It is rather a question of perceiving clearly and without prejudice what are the forces that are at work in the world and out of whose interaction tomorrow *must* come to be; and then, calmly, without indignation, by a kind of mental ju-jitsu that is ours by virtue of intelligence, of modifying, correcting, polluting, deflecting, corrupting, eroding, outflanking . . . inspiring what we might call *the invisible insurrection*. It will come on the mass of men, if it comes at all, not as something they have voted for, struck for, fought for, but like the changing season; they will find themselves in and stimulated by the *situation* consciously at last to recreate it within and without as their own.

Clearly, there is in principle no problem of production in the modern world. The urgent problem of the future is that of distribution which is presently (dis)ordered in terms of the economic system prevailing in this or that area. This problem on a global scale is an administrative one and it will not finally be solved until existing political and economic rivalries are outgrown. Nevertheless, it is becoming widely recognised that distributive problems are most efficiently and economically handled on a global scale by an international organisation like the United Nations (food, medicine, etc.) and this organisation has already relieved the various national governments of some of their functions. No great imagination is required to see in this kind of transference the beginning of the end for the nation-state. We should at all times do everything in our power to speed up the process.

Meanwhile, our anonymous million can focus their attention on the problem of 'leisure'. A great deal of what is pompously called 'juvenile delinquency' is the inarticulate response of youth incapable of coming to terms with leisure. The violence associated with it is a direct consequence of the alienation of man from himself brought about by the Industrial Revolution. Man has forgotten how to play. And if one thinks of the soulless tasks accorded each man in the industrial milieu, of the fact that education has become increasingly technological, and for the ordinary man no more than a means of fitting him for a 'job', one can hardly be surprised that man is lost. He is almost afraid of more leisure. He demands 'overtime' and has a latent hostility towards automation. His creativity stunted, he is orientated outwards entirely. He has to be amused. The forms that dominate his working life are carried over into leisure which becomes more and more mechanised; thus he is equipped with machines to contend with leisure which machines have accorded him. And to offset all this, to alleviate the psychological wear and tear of our technological age, there is, in a word, **Entertainment**.

When our man after the day's work comes twitching, tired, off the assembly-line into what are called without a shred of irony his 'leisure hours', with what is he confronted? In the bus on the way home he reads a newspaper which is identical to yesterday's newspaper, in the sense that it is a reshake of identical elements . . . four murders, thirteen disasters, two revolutions, and 'something approaching a rape' . . . which in turn is identical to the newspaper of the day before that . . . three murders, nineteen disasters, one counter-revolution, and something approaching an abomination . . . and unless he is a very exceptional man, one of our million potential technicians, the vicarious pleasure he derives from paddling in all this violence and disorder obscures from him the fact that there is nothing new in all this 'news' and that his daily perusal of it leads not to a widening of his consciousness of reality but to a dangerous contraction of consciousness, to a species of mental process that has more in common with the salivations of Pavlov's dogs than with the subtleties of human intelligence.

Contemporary man expects to be entertained. His active participation is almost non-existent. Art, whatever it is, is something of which the majority seldom thinks, something almost derisible towards which it is sometimes even proud to flaunt an attitude of invincible ignorance. This sorry state of affairs is unconsciously sanctioned by the stubborn philistines of our cultural institutions. Museums have approximately the same hours of business as churches, the same sanctimonius odours and silences, and a snobbish presumption in direct spiritual apposition to the vital man whose works are closeted there. What have those silent corridors to do with Rembrandt and the 'no smoking' signs to do with Van Gogh? Beyond the museum, the man in the street is effectively cut off from art's naturally tonic influence by the fashionable brokerage system which, incidentally, but of economic necessity, has more to do with the emergence and establishment of so-called 'art-forms' than is generally realised. Art can have no existential significance for a civilisation which draws a line between life and art and collects artifacts like ancestral bones for reverence. Art must inform the living; we envisage a situation in which life is continually renewed by art, a situation imaginatively and passionately constructed to inspire each individual to respond creatively, to bring to whatever act a creative comportment. We envisage it. But it is we, now, who must create it. For it does not exist.

The actual situation could not be in sharper contrast. Art anaesthetises the living; we witness a situation in which life is continually devitalised by art, a situation sensationally and venally misrepresented to inspire each individual to respond in a stock and passive way, to bring to whatever act a banal and automatic consent. For the average man, dispirited, restless, with no power of concentration, a work of art to be noticed at all must compete at the level of spectacle. It must contain nothing that is in principle unfamiliar or surprising; the audience must be able easily and without reservation to identify with the protagonist, to plant itself firmly in the 'driving-seat' of the emotional roller-coaster and switch over to remote control. What takes place is empathy at a very obvious level, blind and uncritical. To the best of my knowledge it was Brecht who first drew attention to the danger of that method of acting which aims to provoke the state of empathy in an audience at the expense of judgement. It was to counter this promiscuous tendency on the part of the modern audience to identify that he formulated his 'distance theory' of acting, a method calculated to inspire a more active and critical kind of participation. Unfortunately, Brecht's theory has had no impact whatsoever on popular entertainment. The zombies remain; the spectacle grows more spectacular. To adapt an epigram of a friend of mine: *Si nous ne voulons pas assister au spectacle de la fin du monde, il nous faut travailler a la fin du monde du spectacle . . .*[3]

For a long time now the best artists and fine minds everywhere have deplored the gulf that has come to exist between art and life. The same people have usually been in revolt during their youth and have been rendered harmless by 'success' somewhere around middle age. The individual is powerless. It is inevitable. And the artist has a profound sense of his own impotence. He is frustrated, even confounded. As in the writings of Kafka, this fearful sense of alienation pervades his work. Certainly the most uncompromising attack on conventional culture was launched by Dada at the end of the First World War. But the usual defence mechanisms were soon operating: the turds of 'anti-art' were solemnly framed and hung alongside 'the School of Athens'; Dada thereby underwent castration by card-index and was soon safely entombed in the histories as just another school of art. The fact is that while Tristan Tzara *et al* could point deftly to the chancre on the body politic, could turn the spotlight of satire on the hypocrisies that had to be swept away, they produced no creative alternative to the existing social order. What were we to do after we had painted a moustache on the *Mona Lisa*? Did we really wish Genghis Khan to stable his horses in the Louvre? And then? . . .

'The question is not who will patronise the arts, but what forms are possible in which artists will have control of their own means of expression, in such ways that they will have relation to a community rather than to a market or a patron.' (Raymond Williams) . . .

For myself and for my associates in Europe and America the key phrase in the above sentence is: *'artists will have control of their own means of expression'*. When they achieve that control, their 'relation to a community' will become a meaningful problem, that is, a problem amenable to formulation and solution at a creative and intelligent level. Thus we must concern ourselves forthwith with the question of how to seize and within the social fabric exercise that control. Our first move must be *to eliminate the brokers*.

At the beginning of these reflections I said that methods will vary with the empirical facts pertaining here and now, there and then. I was referring to the tentative, essentially tactical nature of our every act in relation to the given situation, and also to the international constitution of what we might call the new underground.

Obviously, all our operations must be adapted to the society in which they take place. Methods used effectively in London might be suicidal or simply impracticable in Moscow or Peking. Always, the tactics are for here and now; never are they in the narrow sense political. Again, these reflections themselves must be regarded as an act of the new underground, a prescriptive document which, in so far as it refers for the most part to what is yet to happen, awaits baptism by fire.

How to begin? At a chosen moment in a vacant country house (mill, abbey, church, or castle) not too far from the City of London, we shall forment a kind of cultural 'jam session': out of this will evolve the prototype of our *spontaneous university.*

The original building will stand deep within its own grounds, preferably on a river bank. It should be large enough for a pilot-group (astronauts of inner space) to situate itself, orgasm and genius, and their tonic and dream-machines and amazing apparatus and apportenances; with outhouses for 'workshops' large as could accommodate light industry; the entire site to allow for spontaneous architecture and eventual *town planning.* I underline the last because we cannot place too much emphasis on the fact that *'l'art integral ne pouvait se realiser qu'au niveau de l'urbanisme.'*[6] In the 1920s, Diaghilev, Picasso, Stravinski and Nijinsky acted in concert to produce a ballet; surely it does not strain our credulity to imagine a far larger group of our contemporaries acting in concert to create a town. We envisage the whole as a vital laboratory for the creation (and evaluation) of conscious *situations*; it goes without saying that it is not only the environment which is in question, plastic, subject to change, but men also . . .

In considering ways and means to establish our pilot project we have never lost sight of the fact that in a capitalist society any successful organization must be able to sustain itself in capitalist terms. The venture must pay. Thus we have conceived the idea of setting up a general agency to handle, as far as possible, all the work of the individuals associated with the university. Art, the products of all the expressive media of civilisation, its applications in industrial and commercial design, all this is fantastically profitable (consider the Musical Corporation of America). But, as in the world of science, it is not the creators themselves who reap most of the benefit. An agency founded by the creators themselves and operated by highly-paid professionals would be in an impregnable position. Such an agency, guided by the critical acumen of the artists themselves, could profitably harvest new cultural talent long before the purely professional agencies were aware it existed. Our own experience in the recognition of contemporary talent during the past fifteen years has provided us with evidence that is decisive. The first years would be the hardest. In time, granting that the agency functioned efficiently from the point of view of the individual artists represented by it, it would have first option on all new talent. This would happen not only because it would be likely to recognise that talent before its competitors, but because of the fact and fame of the university. It would be as though some ordinary agency were to spend 100 per cent of its profits on advertising itself. Other things being equal, why should a young writer, for example, not prefer to be handled by an agency controlled by his (better-known) peers, an agency which will apply whatever profit it makes out of him as an associate towards the extention of his influence and audience, an agency, finally, which at once offers him membership in the experimental university (which governs it) and all that that implies? And, before elaborating further on the economics of our project, it is perhaps time to describe briefly just what that membership does imply.

We envisage an international organisation with branch universities near the capital cities of every country in the world. It will be autonomous, un-political, economically independent. Membership of one branch (as teacher or student) will entitle one to membership of all branches, and travel to and residence in foreign branches will be energetically encouraged. It will be the object of each branch university to participate in and 'supercharge' the cultural life of the respective capital city at the same time as it promotes cultural exchange internationally and functions in itself as a non-specialised experimental school and creative workshop. Resident professors will be themselves creators. The staff at each university will be purposively international; as far as practicable, the students also. Each branch of the spontaneous university will be the nucleus of an experimental town to which all kinds of people will be attracted for shorter or longer periods and from which, if we are successful, they will derive a renewed and infectious sense of life. We envisage an organisation whose structure and mechanisms are infinitely elastic; we see it as the gradual crystallisation of a regenerative cultural force, a perpetual brainwave, creative intelligence everywhere recognizing and affirming its own involvement.

It is impossible in the present context to describe in precise detail the day-to-day functioning of the university. In the first place, it is not possible for one individual writing a brief introductory essay. The pilot project does not exist in the physical sense, and from the very beginning, like the Israeli kibbutzes, it must be a communal affair, tactics decided *in situ*, depending upon just what is available when. My associates and I during the past decade have been amazed at possibilities arising out of the spontaneous interplay of ideas within a group in constructed situations. It is on the basis of such experiences that we have imagined an international experiment. Secondly, and consequently, any detailed preconceptions of my own would be so much excess baggage in the spontaneous generation of the group situation.

Nevertheless, it is possible to make a tentative outline of the economic structure.

We envisage a limited liability company (International Cultural Enterprises Ltd) whose profits are invested in expansion and research. Its income will derive from:

1 Commissions earned by the Agency on sales of all original work of the associates.

2 Money earned from 'patents' or by subsidiaries exploiting applications (industrial and commercial) evolving out of 'pure studies'. Anyone who has spent time in an art workshop will know what I mean. The field is unlimited, ranging from publishing to interior decorating.

3 Retail income. The university will house a 'living museum', perhaps a fine restaurant. A showroom will be rented in the city for retail and as an advertisement.

4 Such income as derives from 'shows', cinematic, theatrical, or *situationist.*

5 Fees.

6 Subsidies, gifts, etc., which in no way threaten the autonomy of the project.

The cultural possibilities of this movement are immense and the time is ripe for it. The world is awfully near the brink of disaster. Scientists, artists, teachers, creative men of goodwill everywhere are in suspense. Waiting. Remembering that it is our kind even now who operate, if they don't control, the grids of expression, we should have no difficulty in recognising the spontaneous university as the possible detonator of the invisible insurrection.

Footnotes

1 **The Theatre and its Double**, Grove Press, New York, 1958.

2 The *prise de pouvoir* by an avant garde is obviously only an early stage in a larger, more universal movement, and it must not be forgotten that our group of originators 'ne pourra realiser son projet qu'en se supprimant . . . ne peut effectivement exister qu'en tant que parti se depasse lui-meme'. (Added to French version).

3 *Notes editoriales d'internationale Situationniste*, 3 December, 1959. Freely adapted from the original.

6 **Documents Situationnistes**, Guy-Ernest Debord. At present, town planning is determined by and tends to reinforce conventional functions, conventional attitudes. You sleep here, eat there, work there, die there. A revolutionary architecture will take no account of functions to be transcended. (cf Essay No 2)

E SIGMA FOLIO–THE SIGMA FOLIO–THE SIGMA FOLIO–THE SIGMA FOLIO–THE SIGMA FOLIO–THE SIGMA

The sigma folio is an entirely new dimension in publishing, through which the writer reaches his public immediately, outflanking the traditional trap of publishing-house policy, and by means of which the reader gets it, so to speak, "hot" from the writer's pen, from the photographer's lens, etc. In a sense you might be said to be subscribing to an encyclopaedia in the making: in another sense you will be participating in a tactical histurigem, to coin a word. In subscribing to the sigma folio, you are stimulating the growth of an interpersonal log constructing itself to alert, sustain, inform, inspire, and make vividly conscious of itself all intelligence everywhere from now on. You will receive various future informations and tactical objects and can judge for yourself at what points you can participate. Again, the folio is what we call a "futique"(what will be prized as an antique tomorrow); you will possess a first edition in this new dimension of publishing, a cover containing the expanding file of our activities. It should be understood there is no minimum and no maximum subscription fee, that if the whole venture is to retain its existential posture, we who originate it can enter into no legal contract to do any specific thing which tomorrow may have to be "transcended". Subscriptions, in short, are to sigma unlimited, and a reasonable sum seems to us to be one guinea (21/-), or three dollars ($3.00). We are most anxious that the sigma experiment should develop quickly so that the tendency on the part of the general public to associate it with particular names will be corrected. When the inspired mechanisms that are sigma are really "happening", one well-known individual more or less, here or there, will be of little significance. Come the day.

I wish to receive the sigma folio for one year.

I enclose..........

Name and address: ....

....

Notice to contributors, Alexander Trocchi, *The Sigma Portfolio*, 1964

The Situationists in London

Guy Atkins

Asger Jorn, 1964
Excerpt

One of the most successful conferences of SI was that held in London in the autumn of 1960. As the conference date drew near the participants arrived in ones and twos from their various countries. When they reached London they were set the 'psychogeographical' task of finding their way to 'The British Sailors Society' in the heart of the East End. A room had been booked there for the conference. The gist of the conference is reported in IS, V, pp.19–23, but one of the main events took place outside the conference room. This was the public meeting held at the Institute of Contemporary Arts, which was then in Dover Street. This meeting was a triumphant success for the Situationists, but the audience was merely bewildered.

The following description is based on some notes I made at the time. The meeting had been advertised to start at 8.15 pm, but shortly before 9 o'clock the group of Situationists who occupied the anteroom and bar of the ICA were still wrangling over the English translation of their 'declaration'. At this point Mrs Dorothy Morland, the director of the ICA, asked me to tell Guy Debord (who doesn't speak English), that she would cancel the meeting if he was not ready to begin by 9 o'clock. I thought that such an ultimatum would be counterproductive, so I reversed the message. I told Guy Debord that the *directrice* was most anxious that the text of the statement should be as authentic as possible and that the audience was quite willing to wait as long as necessary. At this Debord immediately gathered up his papers and the group filed into the auditorium. Jaqueline de Jong went out to fetch Jorn who was having dinner with his American dealer, Jon Streep, in a restaurant across the road.

The meeting from beginning to end, was a parody of a normal ICA evening. Toni del Renzio was the ICA's chairman that night. He opened the meeting by giving some of the historical background of the Situationist movement. When he mentioned the conference in Alba there was loud applause from the Situationists. At the mention of the 'unification conference' at Cosio d'Arroscia the clapping was terrific, accompanied by loud footstamping. The ICA audience was clearly baffled by this senseless display of euphoria. Del Renzio then introduced the SI spokesman Maurice Wyckaert.

Instead of beginning with the usual compliments, Wyckaert scolded the ICA for using the word 'Situationism' in its Bulletin. 'Situationism', Wyckaert explained, 'doesn't exist. There is no doctrine of this name.' He went on to tell the audience 'If you've now understood that there is no such thing as "Situationism" you've not wasted your evening.'

After a tribute to Alexander Trocchi, who had recently been arrested for drug trafficking in the United States, Wyckaert launched into a criticism of UNESCO. We were told that UNESCO had failed in its cultural mission. Therefore the Situationist International would seize the UNESCO building by 'the hammer blow of a *putsch*'. This remark was greeted with a few polite murmurs of approval.

Wyckaert ended as he had begun, with a gibe at the ICA. 'The Situationists, whose judges you perhaps imagine yourselves to be, will one day judge you. We are waiting for you at the turning.' There was a moment's silence before people realized that the speaker had finished. The first and only question came from a man who asked 'Can you explain what exactly Situationism is all about?' Wyckaert gave the questioner a severe look. Guy Debord stood up and said in French 'We're not here to answer cuntish questions'. At this he and the other Situationists walked out.

One of the interesting features of the evening had been the remarkable consistency of the play-acting by the Situationist audience in an unrehearsed situation.

This meeting was the second time that the ICA had let itself in for a Situationist hoax. Some months earlier *Hurlements en faveur de Sade* had been shown there. This film is Debord's masterpiece, made in 1952 while he was a Lettrist. It was first screened at the Musée de l'Homme in Paris, where it caused an uproar. After the performance several people showed their disapproval by 'desolidarifying' themselves from the Lettrist movement.

Hurlements . . . is a completely blank film in which nothing at all is shown on the screen. The sound track comes on occasionally and consists of odds and ends of prose spoken in a deadpan voice. The film is black-and-white in the sense that the screen is black during the silences, white for the sound track. Four of the spoken passages are random extracts from the Civil Code. Other utterances are bits of chit-chat such as 'Il est amusant, le téléphone'; 'Veux-tu une orange?'; 'Paris était très agréable à cause de la grève des transports'.

During a final silence of twenty-four minutes, when the only sound in the room was the turning of the reel, a member of the audience got up, thanked Mrs Morland for an interesting evening and apologized for having to leave early. Everyone else stayed to the end, hoping that a sensational titbit might still be coming. When the lights went up there was an immediate babble of protest. People stood around and some made angry speeches. One man threatened to resign from the ICA unless the money for his ticket was refunded. Another complained that he and his wife had come all the way from Wimbledon and had paid for a babysitter, because neither of them wanted to miss the film. These protests were so odd that it was as if Guy Debord himself were present, in his role of Mephistopheles, hypnotizing these ordinary English people into making fools of themselves in public.

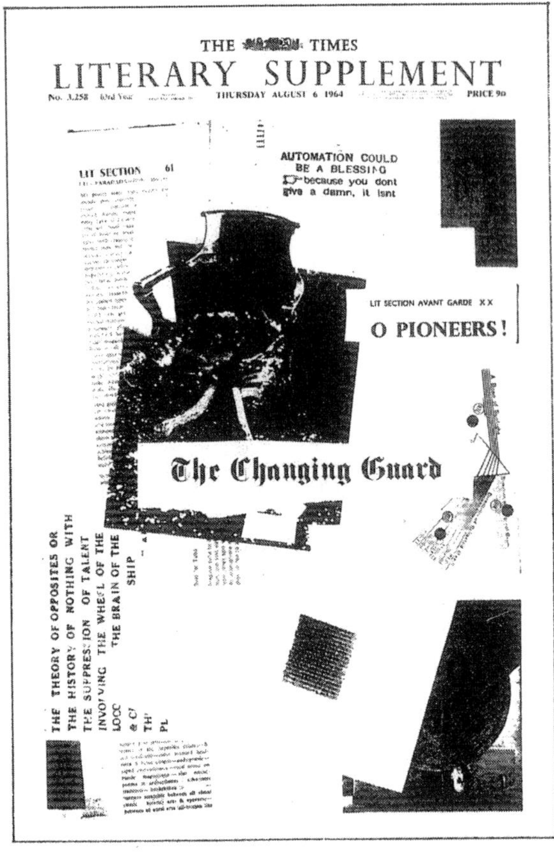
THE TIMES
LITERARY SUPPLEMENT
No. 3,258 63rd Year THURSDAY AUGUST 6 1964 PRICE 9d
LIT SECTION 61
AUTOMATION COULD BE A BLESSING because you dont give a damn, it isnt
LIT SECTION AVANT GARDE XX
O PIONEERS!
The Changing Guard
THE THEORY OF OPPOSITES OR THE HISTORY OF NOTHING WITH THE SUPPRESSION OF TALENT INVOLVING THE WHEEL OF THE THE BRAIN OF THE SHIP

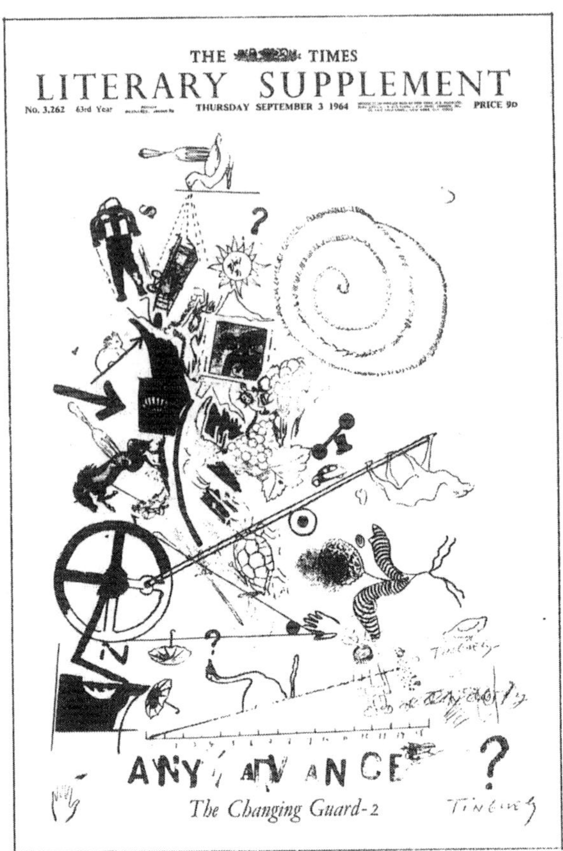
THE TIMES
LITERARY SUPPLEMENT
No. 3,262 63rd Year THURSDAY SEPTEMBER 3 1964 PRICE 9d

ANY Y, AV AN CE ? *The Changing Guard—2*

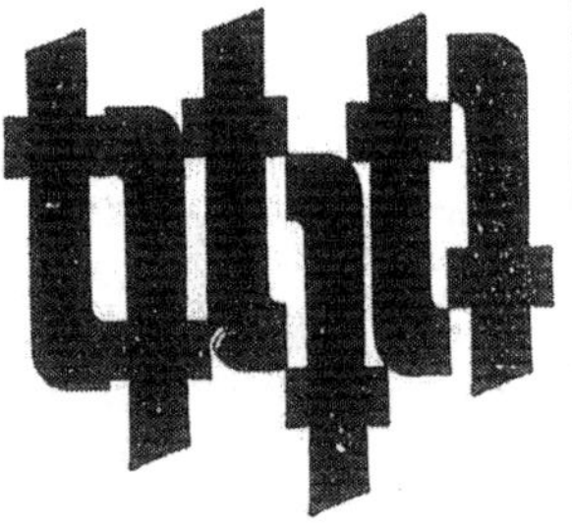

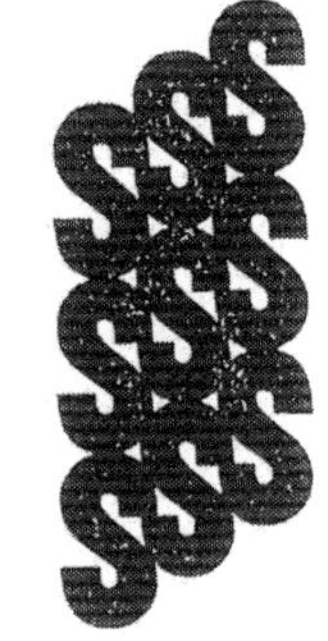

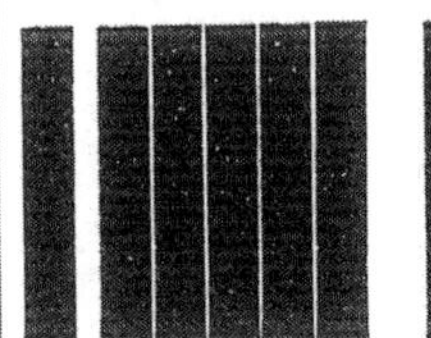

MICHÈLE BERNSTEIN:

The Situationist International

THE Situationist International was founded in 1957 at a conference held in Italy and attended by a number of artists from several European countries. Some of them came from those avant-garde movements that had emerged around 1950 but were still almost completely unknown at that time: *Cobra* in northern Europe and *lettrism* in Paris.

As a start they aimed to go beyond artistic specialization — art as a separate activity—and delve beneath that whole movement for breaking-up of language and dissolution of forms that had constituted modern art at its most authentic. It was decided that the first field of their future creativeness would embrace experiments in behaviour, the construction of complete settings, moments of life freely created.

As any definition of such researches is simply another way of criticizing not only the whole of our present social life but any hierarchical social pattern at all, the situationists at the same time were rejecting the ineffectiveness and mystification of political specialization as a means of transforming the world. They claim that the creative activities initiated by them over the whole range of everyday life are the one and only basis for a new definition of the revolutionary ideal in our time.

This operation to which the situationists had committed themselves was so large in scale that the movement initially concentrated mainly on the formation of a new coherent theory of the modern world, as originally worked out in the Situationist International's reviews "*Internationale Situationniste*" (nine issues to date. P.O. Box 75-06, Paris), *Situationistisk Revolution* and *Der Deutsche Gedanke*. This theory at once sets forth—and attacks—our culture's trend towards organization of passive "spectacles" and all other aspects of the life of consumer society, outlining new counter-forms, from *distortion* of our artistic language—"communication containing its own criticism"—to *unitary town-planning* "which is not a doctrine of town planning but a criticism of town planning". Our International, the I.S., coming after the development both of our philosophy and of our art, at once refuses to proclaim any sort of doctrine and rejects the term "situationism" as used only by enemies of the situationist programme.

The working-out of this theory goes hand in hand with the practical organization of collective activity. The situationists refuse to accept disciples; insist on recruiting only geniuses for the avant-garde task they have set themselves; reject any compromise and even any contact with conformism or with the repetitious mock-modernism of the culture we now have.

The situationists immediately exclude those of their number who fail in practice to maintain any of the strict positions of the group; they have often been reproached for this as a sign that they take their own declarations too seriously. As a result the situationist label has sometimes been usurped by certain intellectuals who have been expelled from the I.S. or even never been members of it: e.g., the followers of Nash in Sweden, the Germans who published the magazine *Spur*, the Dutch Nashists grouped round the *Situationist Times*, or technocratic town planners in the style of the architect Constant. True situationists are much more strongly opposed to all the prevailing mechanisms of culture and information; and so far they have carried out the main part of their work underground.

Important undertakings by the Situationist International are at the moment in course of completion. There are three books on the point of publication: Raoul Vaneigen's *Traité de savoir-vivre à l'usage des jeunes générations*, Guy Debord's *La Société du Spectacle*, Rudi Renson's *L'Architecture et le Détournement*. There is also the reversal of "pop-art" practised by the painter J. V. Martin in his series of *nouvel irréalisme*, and some experimental documentary films. At the same time, the situationists flatter themselves that they influence radical minorities in certain revolutionary waves observable in Spain, the Congo, Scandinavia and Japan.

In a short space it is obviously impossible to develop any argument about situationist principles, or even to explain them with the necessary precision. The need to show their mutual interdependence and its relation to the whole forbids any summary by means of a few isolated points. Among the first intellectual groups who have so far had a chance to get to know these theses, the usual reaction is to ask if the situationists are serious, or if they are utterly mistaken and destined for unparalleled depths of stupidity. The situationists can guarantee that none of these doubts about them will be tenable in a hundred years' time.

Times Literary Supplement, Special Issue, September, 1964

The Changing Guard
The Times Literary Supplement
August and September Issues, 1964

Special issues devoted consecutively to the contemporary avant-garde in Britain and abroad.

Who are the Situationists?

Jorgen Nash

THE first manifestation made by the second Situationist International after it broke away from the IS was a leaflet signed by Jaqueline de Jong, Ansger Side and myself. Shortly after the group Seven Rebels was formed at Bauhaus Situationiste Drakabygget, founded in 1965 in southern Sweden. It is asituationistic centre for experiments in film, painting, décollage, urbanism, poetry, archaeology and music . . .

The Franco-Belgian situationists base themselves on the same principles as Pascal, Descartes, Croce and Gide. Action precedes emotion. You only begin to feel religious after you have muttered your prayers. According to Scandinavian situationist philosophy action is the result of emotion and arises out of emotion. Emotion is a primary, non-reflective intelligence; passionate thought/thinking passion. We are not saying that the French method is wrong or that it cannot be used successfully. We merely say that our two outlooks are incompatible, but they can be made to supplement one another.

The second Situationist International is a freely organised movement. It is a voluntary association of autonomous work groups. At the moment there exist four such groups on the Hallandsåsen in the southern part of Sweden, and two more in Denmark and Finland. It also works together with the German avant-garde group SPUR in Munich, whose books have partly been published at Drakabygget . . . A periodical against popes, politicians and atomic bombs called *Drakabygett* has been edited since 1962, with the journalist and painter Katarina Lindell as editor. The following declaration is a quotation from this magazine:

1) I promise that I shall never, personally, under any circumstances set foot in an atomic shelter. It is better to die standing with all the cultural heritage of humanity, the perpetual modification of which must be our task. The labour movement was once considered to be the salt of the earth. Today it is more like a milch cow, whose udders are being pumped in an effort to get more and more material benefits – at the expense of the mind . . .

2) I refuse to have anything whatsoever to do with the aristocracy of the caves, and never to drink in the company of an owner or a builder of an atomic shelter; for this subterranean aristocracy, even if it manages to survive the disaster, will be of the quality of sewer rats, and could in no case be considered a continuation of the human race.

3) At this point in our present situation it is not so much the thermonuclear war, but rather the threat of this war, which shows the absolute bankruptcy of all the politicians in the world. The capitalist or bureaucratic leaders of both east and west already make use of their bombs every day, in order to secure power for themselves. Only if one realises that they have placed themselves beyond the law can one establish a new legality. I therefore pledge myself not to expect the necessary upheavals of society by any of the existing formations of specialized politics.

This is part of the Mutant-manifesto, signed by all the members of the movement. But as we are no missionaries, and our movement is absolutely anti-authoritarian, we don't run around forcing people to sign our manifesto. The Bauhaus production of books, booklets, lithographs and periodicals is thoroughly non-commercial. Our job is to produce – then our public has to act to get hold of our publications! . . .

In the manifesto of the Second Situationist International we wrote the 'Modern industrial society has so far been organized along classical lines as developed in Greece and in Rome. During the industrial period following the French revolution there have been cycles in which all the different forms of such a method of government have been explored. This has been a valuable experience. It has shown that the enlightened autocracy of Plato and the more or less aristocratic military dictatorship which replaced legal government, as well as the various forms of democracy (including the latest edition, the so-called 'people's' democracy) – that none of these have been capable of creating a form of government to meet and satisfy human needs, still less to allow life to flourish and prosper. The new phenomenon which has dominated industrial society from the beginning, despite some pioneer romanticism, is a growing socialization of all the means of life – which is itself the ineluctable consequence of machine techniques. By socialism we understand the inclusive principle which makes society the centre, meaning and purpose of all human activity. It is all the same whether one takes this evolution to mean progress or whether one interprets it as a growing threat to human freedom. Both attitudes amount to the same thing. Socialisation will spread in one way or another. Man can only dominate his future environment if we face this fact. We must use this knowledge to evolve the means of liberation. In order to win it is essential for us to extricate ourselves from the principle of fatalistic necessity and to regain a new potential of choice and self-determination.

The social structure which fulfils the new conditions for freedom we have termed the situcratic order. The point of departure is the de-christianisation of Kierkegaard's philosophy of situations. This must be combined with British economic doctrine, German dialectic and French social action programmes. It involves a profound revision of Marx's doctrine and a complete revolution whose growth is rooted in the Scandinavian concept of culture. This new ideology and philosophical theory we have called situology. It is places on the principles of social democracy inasmuch as it excludes all forms of artificial privilege. It is the only existing guarantee which ensures that human life can exist in all its cultural variety and without crushing the special abilities of the individual in an anonymous society designed for the unfit. Sartre says that we should always ask what would happen if everyone acted like me. Our answer is that we should all die of boredom.

We want to make it possible for man to be free to gamble his life. This can only happen if everyone is allowed to have individual freedom of action. Greco-Roman thinking is rooted in political and social theory. It is opposed to our own way of thinking because we believe that man as a human being, an individual stands at the centre of all worthwhile activity. Sartre's scolasticism has been called humanistic, but in fact his human being is a socio-centric creature.

There are some people who will fail to grasp the significance of the Situationist struggle. The head-on collision in which we are involved will strike them as inexplicable. But we are convinced that one day this phase will be seen as an event of primary importance for Europe: the moment before a decisive breakthrough. To those who think that a verbal battle is not worth fighting, we would like to say this: A word war is better than a world war.

Times Literary Supplement, Special Issue, September 1964

Fall Out: A British Inheritance

1966-1988

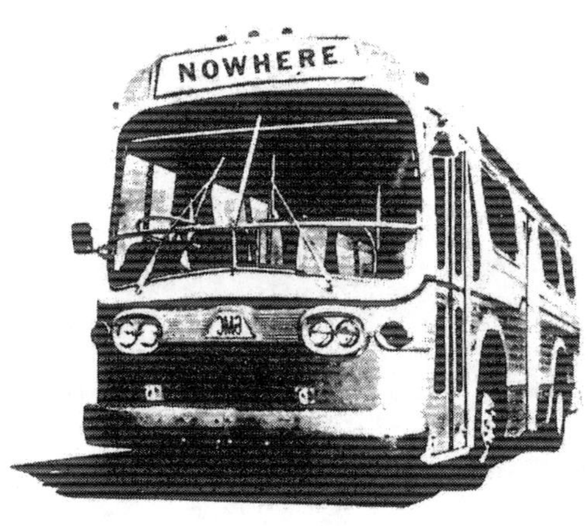

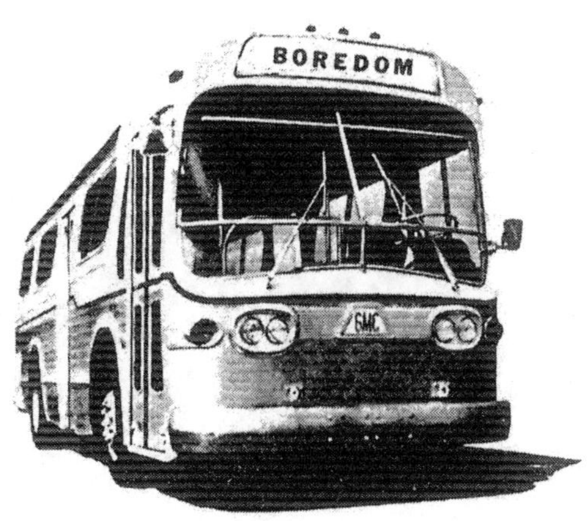

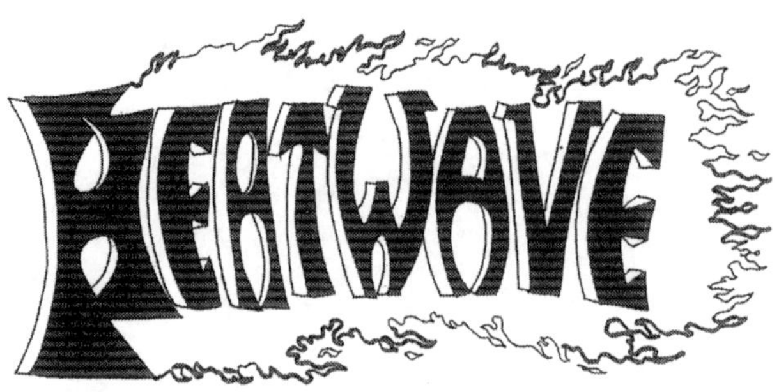

HEATWAVE is a new magazine, but it has a past. On May Day, the first Anglo-American edition of the Chicago wobblies' The Rebel Worker was published here because a group of us felt there was an audience in Britain for an experimental, perhaps slightly crazed libertarian socialist journal.

The Rebel Worker will continue to be published from Chicago; the London group will publish HEATWAVE.

HEATWAVE's policy will obviously reflect the ideas of the people around the magazine but we are not a splinter group. We intend to cooperate, ideologically and practically with our Chicago co-dreamers; we see our task as being the same as theirs -- to run a wild, experimental libertarian-socialist journal which will attempt to relate thought, dream and action whilst pointing the significance of movements, ideas and creations which are ignored by the stagnant, fin-de-siècle revolutionaries.

HEATWAVE is not a rival to existing publications on the libertarian left, but an addition to the libertarian press and an extension of its ideology, both conscious and unconscious, into new fields. HEATWAVE wants to generate heat in every field. We believe the time is ripe for an explosion of revolutionary energy which would alter the face of the earth. HEATWAVE advocates the use of any and all means that may bring to a climax the crisis of capitalism and authoritarianism, and result in the total extinction of all forms of exploitation or authority.

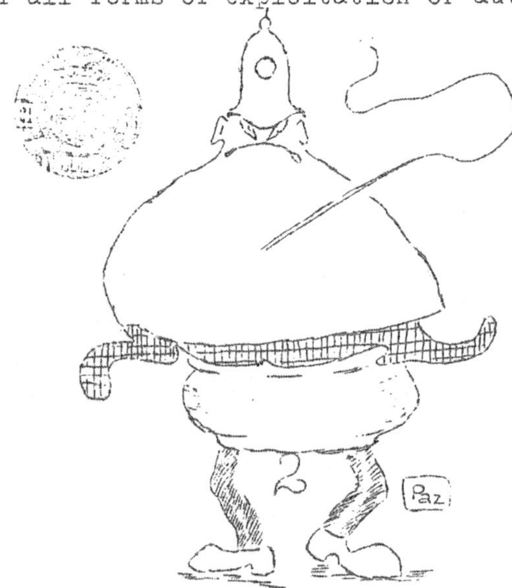

All or not at all

Christopher Gray & Charles Radcliff
September 1966 in *Heatwave* No 2; October 1966
Excerpts

Opposition has degenerated into a series of disparate and fragmentary protests – against nuclear war, against colonialism and racial discrimination, against urban chaos etc. – lacking any grip on the whole of modern society and presenting no serious challenge to the dominant set-up. *What should be criticised is, on the contrary, our normal everyday experience of life.* It is this that is so boring, disgusting and senseless. Why worry about the risk of humanity immolating itself in a nuclear holocaust when everyone, everywhere, sacrifices their real nature, their real desires, their real will to live every minute of every day? All that we can see anywhere is a grotesque travesty of human life, half nightmare and half burlesque; a degraded labour we never chose in order to produce an empty, passive, isolated leisure we never wanted. Life has been reduced to living death. We reject the *whole* system of work and leisure, of production and consumption, to which life has been reduced by bureaucratic capitalism.

But in different terms: it is the concept of *total revolution* which has been lost. It has degenerated into a theory of the rectification of economic and political structures, whereas all the most radical periods of the past revolutionary movement were animated by the desire *to transform the whole nature of human experience,* to create a world in which the desires of each individual could be realised, without restriction. The only real problem is how to live life in the full. Burn, Baby, Burn!

New revolutionary theory must attack production and consumption as a whole, showing that exactly the same alienation exists in both, and showing that their transcendence can only lead to the creation of *a new kind of human activity.* The basic demand is for a society based on the almost-total leisure that mechanisation and automation have not made possible; that is to say, on a new culture corresponding to human desires and not simply dissimulating and sublimating their frustration. It is precisely the early stages of this revolt which can be seen in the revolt of contemporary youth, in their refusal either to work or consume as is ordered, in their permanent strike and in their experiments, however confused they may be, to create *an alternative use of life.* What would a revolutionary society be like? An endless passion, an endless adventure, an endless banquet.

In this issue we have tried to show some of the phenomena of this international revolt and we have tried to relate them to the last radical period of the revolutionary movement (the period 1910 – 1930) whose importance the main revolutionary movement must re-discover and criticise. As the crisis of contemporary society develops, as it becomes more and more acute and less and less easy to dissimulate, revolt can only grow. Things have already reached the point where if anyone wants to live at all *they can only revolt.* The problem now is to make such acts radical and coherent, to relate the fragments seen by more and more individuals to the alienation of social life as a whole, to place them within a perspective which can only serve to expand consciousness and to introduce to each and every rebel the outlines of revolt in which his act can be mirrored along with all other acts of revolt. Finally to create the revolutionary praxis by which this society and this civilisation can be destroyed, once and for all.

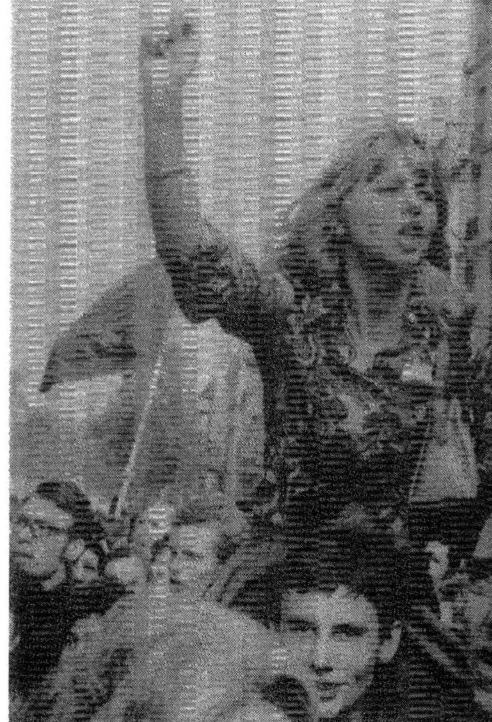

Books behind the barricades

George Steiner
Sunday Times, 1967
Excerpts

A voluminous literature has sprung from the May-June apocalypse in France. French publishers have poured out black books, white books, pamphlets, anthologies of revolutionary verse, collections of polemic and utopian graffiti. The Rue Guy-Lussac has joined the Mur des Fédérés of 1871 in the repertoire of insurrectional songs and ballads. Trotskyists, Maoists, UNEF, Situationists, SNE, Anarchists, JCR, Guevarists, The Mouvement du 22 mars – all have issued manifestos, pasquinades, wall-posters, libels for the dawn. As one combs this material, the intellectual background to the whole student revolt looks far more interesting than the papers made out . . .

Behind the most radical elements in the student movement lie the fantastications, the lyric anarchy, the Dada gestures and search for hallucination which mark symbolist literature and the art and drama of the 1920s and 30s. The world is a collage subject to spontaneous rearrangement, a Kurt Schwitters assemblage to be taken apart and brushed in the corner.

The notion of the 'spectacle' (drama, happening, mask) is crucial to the theories of what is probably the furthest out of the radical factions. Founded in 1957 and claiming branches in Paris, Copenhagen, London and New York, the 'Internationale Situationniste' is centred in Strasbourg. The quickest way to getting the flavour of the movement is to look at the texts reprinted in the current issue of that very intelligent little magazine 'Circuit'. Two of its leaders, Guy Debord and Raoul Vaneigem, have produced books. Debord's 'La Société du Spectacle' (Buchet-Chastel, Paris) redefines the Marxist concepts of alienation and fetishism in terms of dramaturgy. In our consumer-technologies life is merely a bad plan. Like Osborne's 'Entertainer' we strut about in a bankrupt side-show playing parts we loathe to audiences whose values are meaningless or contemptible. Culture itself has become frippery and grease-paint. Our very revolutions are melodrama, performed under stale rules or make-believe; they alter nothing but the cast. Hence the Situationist-Surrealist battle-cries; 'Revolution must derive all its poetry from the future . . . Work must be suppressed and replaced by a new type of free activity . . . Infinite multiplication of real desires and their gratification . . . The only real subversion lies in a new consciousness'. Ask what this new consciousness will contain, what a 'true' as against a 'mountebank' society will be like and the answers are depressingly banal. Debord comes up with a Rousseauist-Marxist pastoral, a state of nature free from economic fetishism and personal alienation. Vaneigem's millennium in his 'Traité de savoir-vivre à l'usage des jeunes générations' (Gallimard) is rawer: 'We must destroy the enemy, not judge him . . . we know there will be no one left to judge us, that judges shall be for ever absent, for we shall have devoured them'. But Vaneigem breaks through his turgid creed to a genuine insight. He sees that no revolutionary movement can be really new so long as its aims are dreamt, programmed, in the vocabulary and grammar of the past. Old words carry an 'old future' in them. There will be no overthrow until language itself is made new, until speech as we know and use it ceases. He is right . . .

Once again, England is left out, so far, of the large-scale disorders, human waste, police brutalities and student destructiveness. But left out also of the intellectual ferment, out of the exhilarating internationalism of the European student movements, out of their artistic-literary rediscoveries and inventions. To the young men and women of Berlin who fought the police with quotations or misquotations from Mayakovsky on their lips, to the students of Nanterre and Paris who chanted bits of Jarry and Eluard while being hauled off by the flics, England is a patch of northern mist that has stumbled out of history. The old men do not want her in their Common Market: the young have no reason to include her in their 'commune'. The consequences could be sad – on both sides of the Channel.

Two Letters on Student Power, *King Mob*, November 1968

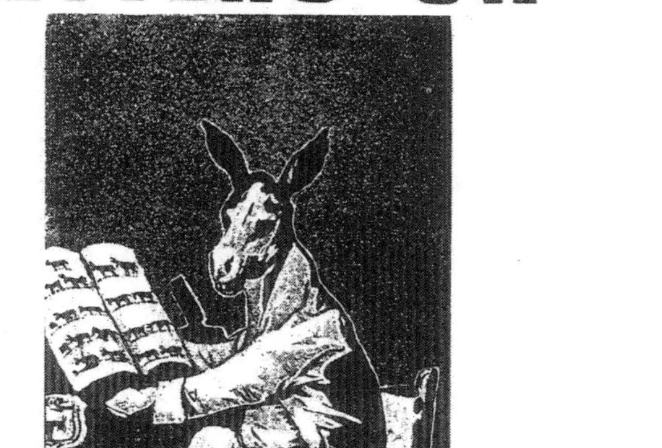

King Mob Echo, April 1968

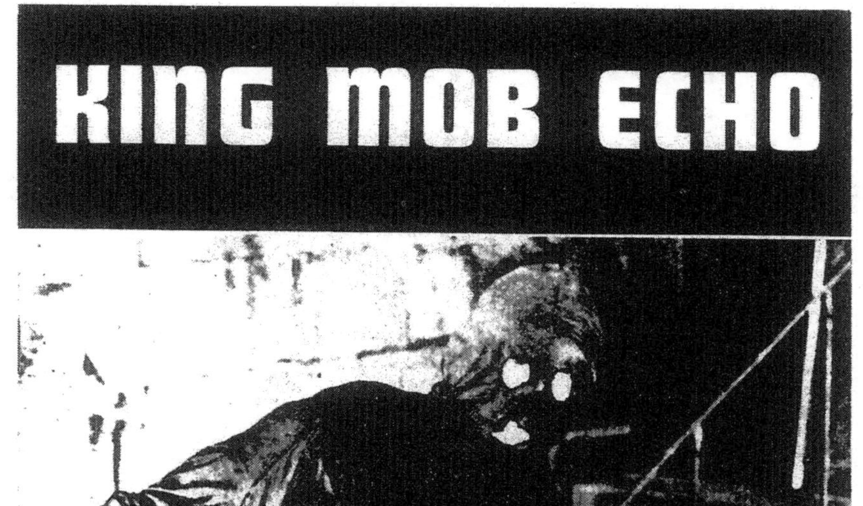

THE RETURN OF THE REPRESSED

So much has changed
perhaps the message is instability
permanent instability in the mind
corresponding to the permanent revolution in things
instability to be accepted as an eternal truth
like Heraclitean flux —

But in this Heraclitean flux, or fire,
there is for me also a Heraclitean Logos
the logos, the word, is One, or oneness
unity
unification
the unification of the human race.

Logos seeks unification; and the fact it faces is
Division —
Alienation, in the old Marxist vocabulary
the rents, the splits, in the newer Freudian vocabulary
the schisms
the schizophrenia.
Now — if I may make a Great Leap Forward —
alienation is schizophrenia
The outcome of the collision between Marx and Freud
is their unification
the perception of the analogy between the two
the analogy between social and psychic
society and soul
body and body politic.

In the mythology of Marxism, the revolution is from
below:
Those lower classes, lower depths, are the depths of
depth psychology
an underworld repressed by the bourgeois ego
a cauldron of energy and violence with the lid on
an anonymous mass, or social id —

If you take the psychoanalytical idea of projection
seriously
the proletariat (if and when we perceive one) is us
projected
a collective projection
a collective dream, or nightmare.

If you take the psychoanalytical idea of projection
seriously
the ego constructs itself by projecting the other
the ego constructs itself by drawing an imaginary line
between inside and outside
an imaginary boundary-line.
And this imaginary boundary-line is the reality-
principle
The reality-principle is the distinction between inner
world and external reality
and it is a false distinction.
"The false reality-principle"
This is to take psychoanalysis more seriously than the
psychoanalysts do
or to pass beyond psychoanalysis
Beyond the reality-principle is poetry
taking metaphors seriously
(metaphors and analogies)
that way madness lies.

The disintegration of the boundary-line
between inner and outer
self and other
is the disintegration of the ego
the disintegration of the ego of the ego-psychologists
in Marxist terms, the disintegration
of the bourgeois ego
of bourgeois individualism
or, alienation overcome —
The split between inside and outside
is the primal split
is the origin of alienation.

Already in Marxism
the intellectual was to go to the masses
bourgeois individualism, the separate self, was to
be drowned in the proletarian ocean
Marxist thought substitutes for the reality of individuals
the reality of classes
but classes, as external realities, mutually external,
are not real either.
It all really takes place in one body.
Marx, who, like Freud, is a genius who surpasses his
own limitations, once said: "The head of this emancipation is philosophy, its heart the proletariat."
He means ego and id. Of course proletariat, if you look
at the word, must also be genital.

At any rate, it all takes place in one body
one body that has been mysteriously dismembered
and needs to be remembered
to knit again these broken limbs into one body.
It must be some kind of embrace
overcoming alienation.
Emerson used to say, There is only one Man —
After Emerson, what happened, on the American
continent, to this intuition?

To perceive that it all really takes place in one body
is to transvalue the old political categories
to pass from politics to metapolitics
or poetry.
The proletariat is dead
but the proletariat is us
long live the proletariat.

—Norman O. Brown, author of *Life Against Death.*

King Mob Echo, April 1968

ART SCHOOLS ARE DEAD
IN IT'S ADVANCE THE FIRE SHALL SEIZE AND JUDGE EVERYTHING

A spectre is haunting art, it is the spectre of annihilation All the powers of the old order have entered into a holy alliance to excorcise this spectre : Police and principals, sculptors and painters, poets and philosphers, designers and architects, art historians and sociologists.

The 'art' offered to us in the galleries, art schools, Lush mags. etc. cannot possibly last much longer.

The sit-ins at various Colleges of Art last year were the first sign of imminent collapse.

However, the proposals put forward by the students failed to grasp the fact that Art Schools are part of an empty, meaningless, culture of death which must be subverted and destroyed on every level.

The atmosphere in the art schools has been getting steadily worse over the last few years. The American dream, media blow out, de-luxe gadgetry, pop art, car styling, acrylic minimalism only served as a front for one-up, put-down gangsterism. Gear and style was (and still is) everything : making out, THE BIG TIME (where you may get a fuck, but you'll always get fucked). Those who manage to keep in the running have to suffer the grind of arse-licking, sherry-drinking, contacts, empty talk. And if you do get a job in an art school then you had better learn to cultivate deceit, ignorance, and keeping your trap shut.

Those who aren't in the running either drop out, end up as bums or become resigned to a dismal job at a grammar school or sec. mod. in the back end of nowhere.

And for what ? It's particularly unbearable knowing that the petty rules of official hierarchies conceal an aching void left by the collapse of the old shit. The fable of the Emperor's clothes could be applied to the whole of the art school set-up. For the fine arts, the game's up - no possibility of a last minute transfusion.

ART'S FINAL MASTERPIECE WILL BE IT'S OWN DESTRUCTION (Soffici)

The Dadaists savage programme of total subversion and the relentless deranged coherence of Surrealism's early revolutionary days.

MUSICIANS - SMASH YOUR INSTRUMENTS

THE NEW ARTIST DOES NOT WRITE OR PAINT BUT CREATES DIRECTLY, THE NEW ARTIST PROTESTS (Tzara)

King Mob, circa 1965

THE DEATH OF ART SPELLS THE MURDER OF ARTISTS. THE REAL ANTI-ARTIST APPEARS

ON JUNE THE 4TH IN NEW YORK, VALERIE SOLONAS SHOT ANDY WARHOL IN THE GENITALS, WHILE KING COOL SCREAMED, "DON'T DO IT...NO.....NO" THE FORTUITOUS PRESENCE OF MARIO AMAYA, EDITOR OF LONDON BASED "ART AND ARTISTS" WAS A CHANCE TOO GOOD TO BE MISSED AND SO SHE PLUGGED HIM TOO. SEVERAL HOURS LATER SHE WENT TO TIMES SQUARE, TAPPED A TRAFFIC COP ON THE SHOULDERS AND SAID, "I BELIEVE YOU ARE LOOKING FOR ME" AND HANDED OVER TWO 38'S.....VALERIE, OF COURSE, IS A WELL KNOWN MILITANT OF S.C.U.M.(SOCIETY FOR CUTTING UP MEN)

A RECENT COMMUNIQUE FROM U.A.W.-M.F.(UP AGAINST THE WALL MOTHER FUCKER) AND S.C.U.M. IN EXILE SAID,

"NON-MAN SHOT BY THE REALITY OF HIS DREAM – THE CULTURAL ASSASSIN EMERGES – A TOUGH CHICK WITH BOP CAP AND A 38 – THE TRUE VENGENCE OF DADA – TOUGH LITTLE CHICK – THE HATER OF MEN AND THE LOVER OF MAN – THE STATUE OF LIBERTY RAPED BY A CHICK WITH BALLS – THE CAMP MASTER SLAIN BY A SLAVE – AND AMERICA'S WHITE PLASTIC CATHEDRAL IS READY TO BURN."

SO DON'T THINK TWICE IT'S ALRIGHT.

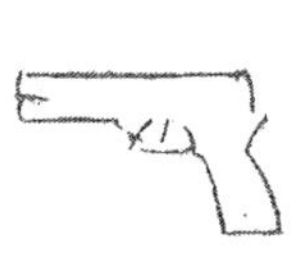

~~ANDY WARHOL~~	~~MARIO AMAYA~~
YOKO ONO	DAVID HOCKNEY
MICK JAGGER	MARY QUANT
BOB DYLAN	TWIGGY SHRIMPTON
MIKE KUSTOW	MILES
RICHARD HAMILTON	MARIANNE FAITHFUL

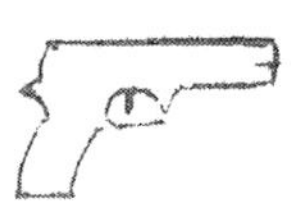

WE APOLOGISE FOR THE INFERIOR QUALITY OF THE ENGLISH COP OUTS, PARASITES AND MERCENARIES NAMED ABOVE.

...........SISTERS FIGHT FOR FREEDOM...................

KING MOB
THE BLACK HAND GANG

King Mob, circa 1968

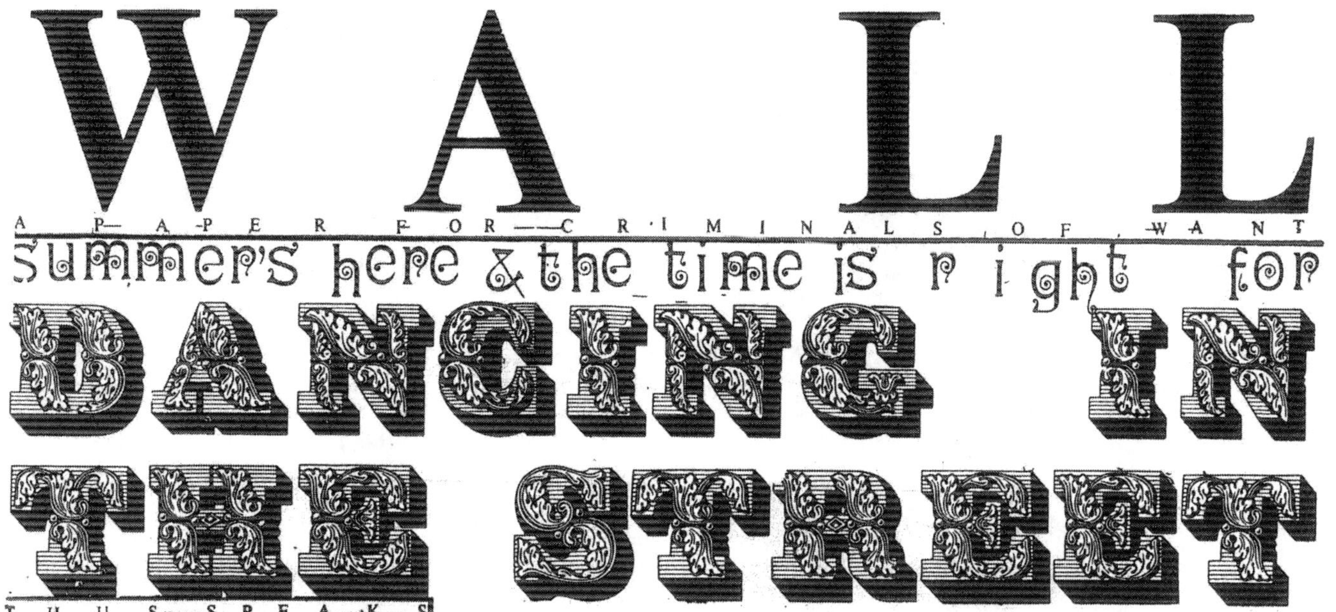

THUS SPEAKS ZARATHUSTRA

The jangling of vocal chords is the negation of history. Jangle Jangle. Music. You know the score, don't you, John Ablett? "We have a rendezvous with Death At some disputed barricade", don't we, Alec Cairncross? Marx's theory of value? You're exams are coming up soon. And all the academic shits--including Trevor-Roper, who must think the Dennis Potter affair is gone forever. But watch this space. Watch this space. "A man who can't fuck can't fight, said George Lincoln Rockwell. In the end, the darkness is the light. And who's waiting for the sun? It's not you, Malcolm Aish. Back into your sepulchre, whitey! The Oxford City fuzz, with Alcadin do they roam, Into some deserted joint. Strike a light, Bill ,if that ain't the nearest thing we seem to a petrol bomb... There are no fields of cannabis this side of the grave, O Pat. Heard the sound of one hand clapping recently? Zip down your flies, let the bullets fly. Who is the Phantom Flasher, Enid Starkie? You have a friend who knows doesn't she, Ruth? He still wants his bread. "How does it feel To be on your own", Charles Radcliffe? The only truth is parody. No parking.

THE WALL IS PUBLISHED BY THE OXFORD MOTHERFUCKERS, A SECRET SOCIETY, WITH THE ASSISTANCE OF KING MOB. MISINFORMATION ABOUT THE EDITORS OF THE WALL WAS CONVEYED TO CHERWELL BY ONE ROBERTA HUNTER-HENDERSON, WHO IS NOT KNOWN TO ANY OF US. THE WALL WILL PRINT NEWS (IF ANY) AND POLEMIC BUT WILL PROBABLY EXIST CHIEFLY TO CHRONICLE ITS OWN FATE. WE HOPE SOON TO HAVE A BCM ADDRESS BUT AT THE MOMENT HAVEN'T. WHEN WE DO WE SHOULD BE ABLE TO SUPPLY ALL ISSUES OF KING MOB, "TEN DAYS THAT SHOOK THE UNIVERSITY" AND A FEW COPIES OF "COMRADES STOP BUGGERING ABOUT". THIS ISSUE IS A MESS BECAUSE IT'S ASSEMBLED BY GONE PEOPLE.

Remember how we got the feel of '67 hot weekdays in Spring down the King's Road? Lapping up the East Village Other, the new new International Times and Inner Space? Floating along our trippy way with Scott McKenzie and the Airplane's "Surrealistic Pillow"? Remember how we got the feel of '68 on March 17th, when suddenly we weren't standing for the fuzz any longer? Non-violence died a very violent death. Then came the Maydays in France, and suddenly Revolution wasn't a sick joke any more. But then came the great missed chance of October 27th, and that was the end of that for a while. So what's the feel of '69? Well, isn't it just beginning to come through? A year of work, a year of play--we're back to '67 again.

Only this time it's going to be different. There's no hope of a resurrection for non-violence, nor for disinvolvement. We tasted blood in Grosvenor Square. This is the year of revolutionary madness. "Soon-to-be-fashionable Situationism", as Oz called it some months ago, is now fashionable, and getting much, much more so. For those of us who dug King Mob before it began edging up on the Black Dwarf in the popularity stakes it's a bit of a drag to have trendiness forced upon us. It's also a bit of a drag that this will certainly be the last year of active Situationism in Great Britain, since Situationism no more than Flower Power can hope to survive its own trendiness. Situationism will sprout and flourish like the Sacred Mushroom. There'll be ghettoes of Motherfuckers, King Mobsters, Werewolves and what have you in every town and university. Even the mods will want in. They dig anything that uses the word 'fuck' as often as King Mob, especially when it's as pill-headed as King Mob also is. Then, when the Press has started beaming, when Situationist musicals have been performed to packed houses, when soft drinks have been advertised with the slogan "Up against the wall, motherfuckers", Situationism will become a mere craze for practical jokes, and will quickly die. This, as I say, is a bit of a drag to the Oxford Motherfuckers, who no doubt display their provincialism in this. King Mob accepts the prognosis with equanimity, if not with glee, proclaiming that the death of an art form is its own greatest work.

Whichever reaction is correct, let

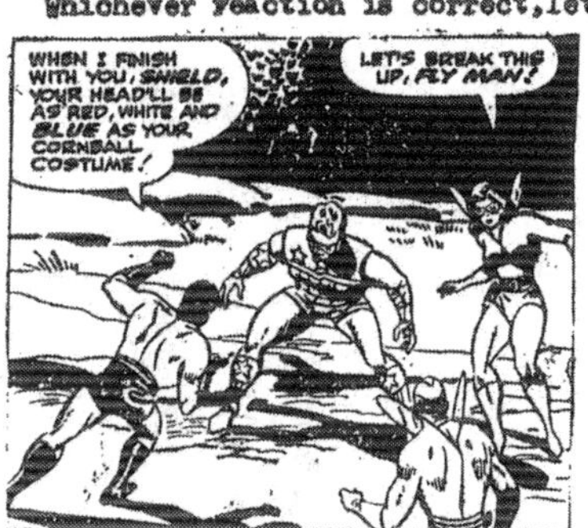

us at any rate seize the day. Situationism--if we must continue to use that severely outdated word--may after all die because it has succeeded. Situationism is becoming popular not only because it is funny, but because it offers an outlet for the disgust of disaffected anarchists. Anarchy is not enough. Anarchy is a soft chocolate. Anarchism is to Communism as the Labour Party is to the Conservative Party (or vice versa). And we all know where the C.P.'s at, don't we Colin Youlden? Colin Youlden, who refused to allow King Mob to be given away free at the Union. Someone told me the other day that Anarchism threw off the shackles of Mutualism through the strength of Bakunin. If that is so, then the process of emancipation, initiated though it may be, has still hardly progressed. Read Bakunin: Bakunin admires Proudhon: there is still in his pages far more talk of Socialism than there is of nameless wildness.

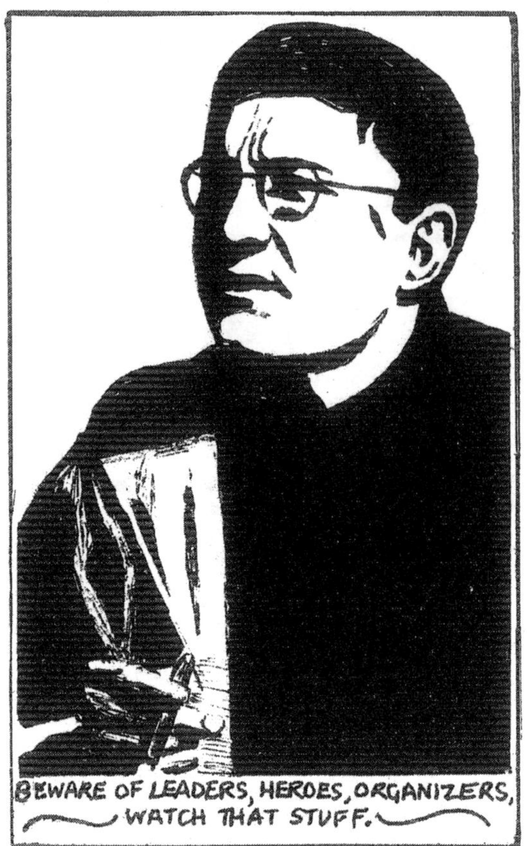

OMPHALOS

OMPHALOS 1 CONTAINS:

THE CONQUEST OF SPACE IN THE TIME OF POWER
[EDUARDO ROTHE]

MASTERS WITHOUT SLAVES
[RAOUL VANEIGEM]

THE END OF THE CHRISTIAN ERA
[ROGER LANGLAIS]

ANTI-COPYRIGHT ©
TEXTS MAY BE USED ACCORDINGLY

"WHEN CONSCIOUSNESS DECAYS, IDEOLOGY OOZES OUT."

2

Any reformism of ideology taking up a position hostile to established society can never be effective because it can never get hold of the forced-feeding mechanisms thanks to which that society still enjoys an efficient use of ideology. Revolutionary thought involves of necessity a merciless critism of all ideologies, including , of course, the ideology known as "the death of ideology" (whose title is already a confession, for ideologies have always been dead thought), which expresses nothing but the ideology of empiricism's celebration over the downfall of an envied rival.

Taking seriously the notion that revolutionaries are neither leaders nor led means translating this into reality by demanding autonomy and coherence, both from oneself and others. "In the global struggle in which we are engaged, to yield an inch on the front of coherence is to allow separation to carry itself over the line we have drawn" (Vaneigem). Autonomy is the precondition for equality, and it depends on the individual's will to define himself as independant and responsible in all that he does, a definition expressed not only verbally but in practice. Revolutionary practice is the appropriation of the means for realising an authentic life, and the theory allows one to consciously dominate the nature of one's own situation and the material means for transforming this situation. The problem of group organisation is the problem of

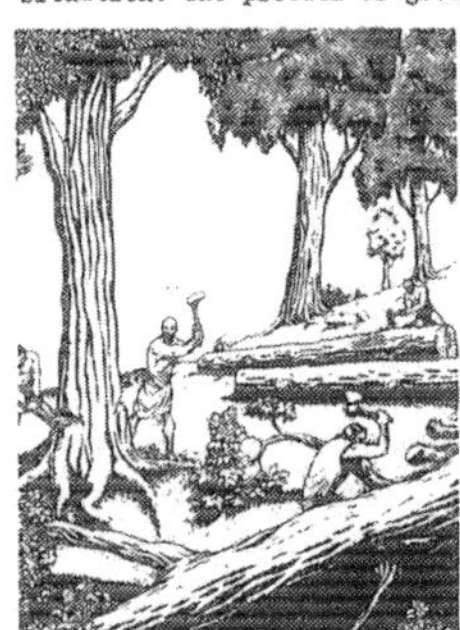
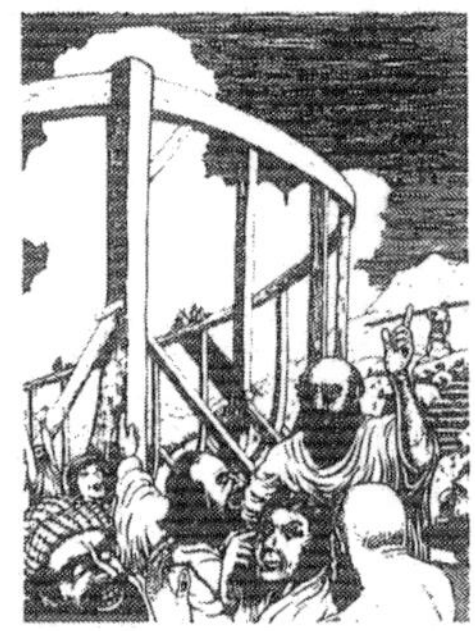

ALIENATED MEN WIN NEW VICTORIES EVERY DAY... FOR WHICH THEY HAVE NO USE.

3

the coherent organisation of collective practice, which is based on the common will and effort to clarify and resolve all contradictions between practical activity and revolutionary theory. It is the application of the radical critique to the real world, the revolutionary's own practical activity included.

Most so called "revolutionary" journals, such as America's "Black and Red", are characterised by an ideological hotchpotch which mixes radical theory with the practice that negates it. The leftist intellectual establishment (New Left Review, etc.) even when it talks of "revolution", is in the last analysis complacent, satisfied if only with its mediocre literary dissatisfaction. It reminds us of a sneak preview audience, sampling in advance the dishes that will sooner or later be served up to all the workers of developed countries - ecological architecture, the welfare state, city planning etc - which will transform the slaves into apparent masters by way of an environmental tranquiliser. (Buckminister Fuller, jaded agrarian romantic, desperately wants to offer man at the end of civilisation fair access to the most vital props of reification. In his global cafeteria, each and every West Afriean village must be provided with non-radioactive colour television, and Do-It-Yourself Plastic Be-Ins equipped with macrobiotic vending machines. The comical degree to which critical ideology has decayed into mere self-affirmation only reflects the decay of the whole of capitalism into a mere spectacle).

The revolution is not "showing" life to people, but enabling them to live.

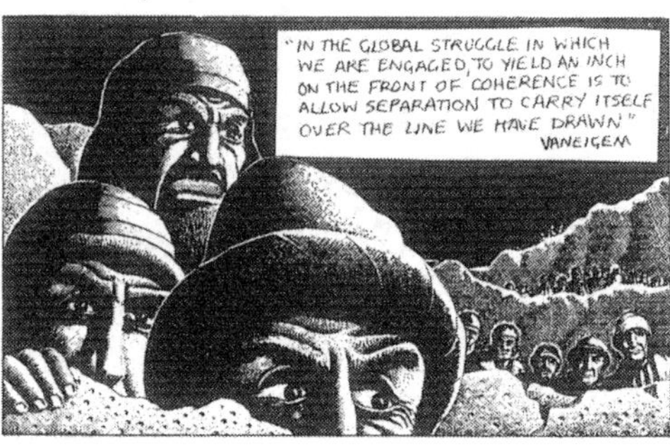

Ramifications of Situationist theory, editorial, Paul Seiveking *Omphalos*, 1970

'Those who make half a Revolution only dig their own graves'

The Situationists since 1969

Christopher Gray
Leaving the Twentieth Century

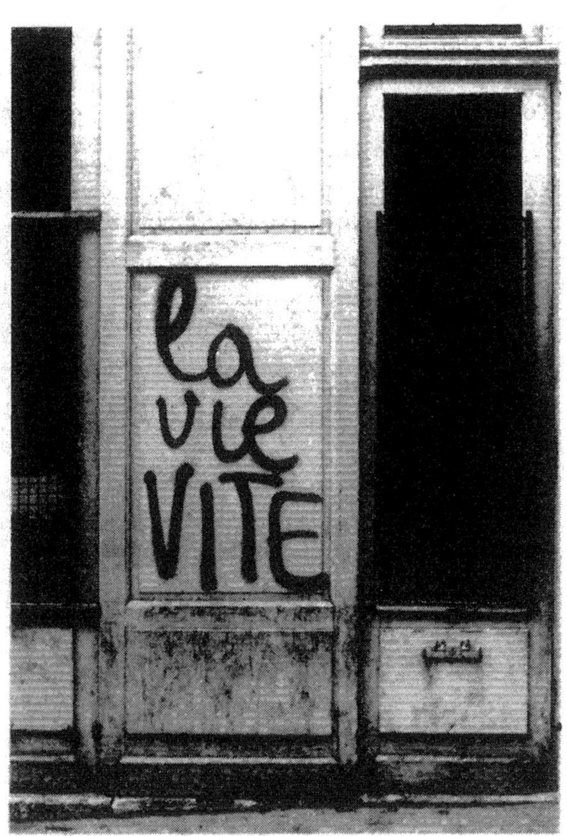

**Nous vivons en enfants perdus
nos aventures incompletes . . .**

Debord, ***Hurlements en faveur de Sade***

May 1968 and France on the verge of anarchy . . . An atmosphere of martial law in Paris and hundreds of factories occupied . . . 140 American cities in flames after the killing of Martin Luther King . . . German and English universities occupied . . . Hippie ghettoes directly clashing with the police state . . . The sudden exhilarating sense of how many people felt the same way . . . The new world coming into focus . . . The riots a great dance in the streets . . .

Today – nothing. The Utopian image has faded from the streets. Just the endless traffic, the blank eyes that pass you by, the nightmarish junk we're all dying for. Everyone seems to have retreated into themselves, into closed occult groups. The revolutionary excitement that fired the sixties is dead. The 'counter-culture' a bad joke. No more aggression, no more laughter, no more dreams. 'To talk of life today is like talking of rope in the house of a hanged man.'

Yet there were thousands and thousands of people there. What has happened to us all?

The Paris May Days were the end for the SI. On the one hand, the police state pressure on the French Left after May made any overt action virtually suicidal. On the other hand, the SI, because it couldn't think its way beyond the debacle, finally received the cultural accolade it had always dreaded: it entered 'the heaven of the spectacle' by the scruff of the neck, and that was that. The atmosphere in France after May was one of utter defiance coupled with complete impotence, and 'situationism' was the perfect ideological expression of this frustration. The SI became famous, and its truth stood out in all its bitterness: a brilliant theoretical critique of society without any grasp of the real problems of what to do about it. What is to be done? Reread Korsch and Duchamp, *mon vieux*.

The movement disintegrated. The last copy of the magazine came out in late 1969. The only significant text to emerge in four years is *La Veritable Scission dans l'Internationale* (1972) by Debord and Sanguinetti – a laboured and increasingly desperate attempt to come to grips with French students' attitude of passive and lifeless worship of revolutionary ideas, but remaining silent on the vital issues of organisation and activity which alone could lead them out of their dilemma. The organisation itself broke up amidst bitter tactical wrangling over 1969-70. Khayati and Vienet resigned. Vaneigem fried, predictably enough. The others went their different ways.

At present there are said to be between two and four members of the SI – including the poor Chtcheglov in his Central European madhouse. Perhaps one should add there are stories that the SI remained intact and really just disappeared owing to police pressure and is now working on a real underground organisation. Sounds a bit like King Arthur and His Knights, but you never can tell. Certainly it seems unlikely that the last has been heard of either Debord or Vaneigem.

The presence of the SI never made itself properly felt in either England or America. The English and what could well have become the American sections of the SI were excluded just before Christmas 1967. Both groups felt that the perfection and publicisation of a theoretical critique was not sufficient: they wanted political subversion and individual 'therapy' to converge in an uninterrupted everyday activity. Some of this they saw, though on a very limited and local scale, the following year: the Americans as *The Motherfuckers* and the English as *King Mob*. Neither group survived that apocalyptic summer of 1968.

Henceforward the dissemination of situationist ideas in both countries was dissociated from the real organisation that alone could have dynamised them. On the one hand this led to obscure post-grad groups sitting over their pile of gestetnered situationist pamphlets, happy as Larry in their totally prefabricated identity. On the other, the more sincere simply went straight up the wall: *The Angry Brigade*, very heavily influenced by situationist ideas (translate *Les Enrages* into English . . .), destroying themselves at the same time as they took the critique of the spectacle to its most bloodcurdling spectacular extreme.

One of the first English members of the SI writes from the States:

> Seen from over here, the SI has a lot to answer for: it has spawned a whole stew of 'revolutionary organisations', usually composed of half a dozen moralists of the transparent relationship; these have inevitably foundered after a few months – though not without bequeathing weighty self-criticisms to a breathless posterity. Idiots. Worse: cures. Yet their traits are undoubtedly linked organically, genetically, to the original SI in its negative aspects: the SI is responsible for its monstrous offspring. Somehow or other, the SI's 'original sin' is tied up with a shift from the sardonic megalomania of iconoclasm to the true megalomania of priesthood. Moving, justifiably, from 'culture' to 'politics' the SI threw the baby out with the bathwater. One day somebody (I forget who) took refuge up a lamp-post, while freaked on acid, from a derive-cum-discussion-of-Lukacs with a merry band of situationists. How is it conceivable that this act could be greeted with blank incomprehension (and – *c'est bien la mot – displeasure*) by Debord, drunkard extraordinary? Yet it was so.

What then remains of the SI? What is still relevant? Above all, I think, its iconoclasm, its *destructivity*. What the SI did was *to redefine the nature of exploitation and poverty*. Ten years ago people were still demonstrating against the state of affairs in Vietnam – *while remaining completely oblivious to the terrible state they were in themselves*. The SI showed exactly how loneliness and anxiety and aimlessness have replaced the nineteenth century struggle for material survival, though they are still generated by the same class society. They focused on immediate experience, *everyday life* as the area people most desperately wanted to transform.

Rediscovering poverty cannot be separated from rediscovering what *wealth* really means. The SI rediscovered the vast importance of visionary politics, of the *Utopian tradition* – and included art, in all its positive aspects, in this tradition. People today will never break out of their stasis for the sake of a minor rearrangement. There have been too many already. Only the hope of a total change will inflame anybody. Who the hell is going to exert themselves to get another frozen chicken, another pokey room? But the possibilities of living in one's own cathedral . . .

What was basically wrong with the SI was that it focused exclusively on an intellectual critique of society. There was no concern whatsoever with either the emotions or the body. The SI thought that you just had to show how the nightmare worked and everyone would wake up. Their quest was for the perfect formula, the magic charm that would disperse the evil spell. This pursuit of the perfect intellectual formula meant inevitably that situationist groups were based on a hierarchy of intellectual ability – and thus on disciples and followers, on fears and exhibitionism, the whole political horror trip. After their initial period, creativity, apart from its intellectual forms, was denied expression – and in this lies the basic instability and sterility of their own organisations.

In the last analysis they made the same mistake as all left-wing intellectuals: *they thought that everyone else was plain thick.* The poor workers don't know what's going on, they need someone to tell them. But people in the streets, in the offices and factories know damn well what's going on, even if they can't write essays about all its theoretical ramifications. *The point is that they can't do anything about it.* What needs understanding is the state of paralysis everyone is in. Certainly all conditioning comes from society but it is anchored in the body and mind of each individual, and that is where it must be dissolved. Ultimately the problem is an *emotional,* not an intellectual one. All the analyses of reflection in the world won't cause a neurosis to budge an inch. Certainly a massive propaganda campaign to publicise the possibility of a revolution, of a total transformation of the world, is vitally important – but it will prove totally ineffective if it isn't simultaneous with *the creation of mass therapy.*

Look, after so many, many pages, let's try and be honest, just for a moment. I feel very fucked up myself, and I know it's my responsibility. Yet whenever I go out on the streets my being somehow reels back appalled: these terrible faces, these machines, they are me too, I know; yet somehow that's not my fault. Everyone's life is a switch between changing oneself and changing the world. Surely they must somehow be the same thing and a dynamic balance is possible. I think the SI had this for a while, and later they lost it. I want to find it again – that quickening in oneself and in others, that sudden happiness and beauty. It could connect, could come together. Psychoanalysis and Trotskyists are both silly old men to the child. Real life is elsewhere.

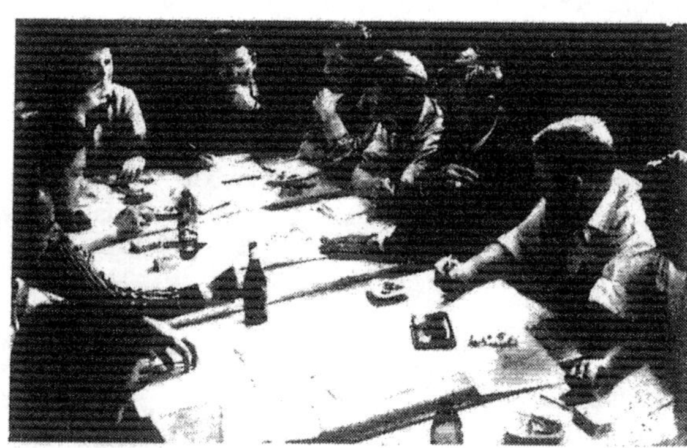

5th conference of the IS, Goteborg, 1961

The society of spectacle An interview with Brigitte Bardot

Ron Hunt and Chris MacConway
Klepht, 1968

Q We've heard the events here last May really changed your life. In what way? Are you still filming?

A Oh yes. Sure. I mean bread can be pretty useful. I channel it all into the Revolutionary organisations. An exposed nipple can become a Revolutionary book (cf Vaneigem's 'Traite de savoir vivre' . . .) or other weapons. I'd even work for all those pseudo-revolutionaries who are so busy trying to recuperate the revolution as it's made – you know from the Fugs to Lindsay Anderson. That way I re-recuperate; that's real cybernetic thinking – feedback picking up a Capitalist profit.

Q Why was it May that specifically changed things?

A Well, it was all suddenly obvious. You know we want to be able to lead our lives as we think we should; for that the C.R.S. are mobilised against us. At school you learn of the end of the Divine Right of Kings; nobody tells you the right was simply transferred to the bourgeoise and status quo. I remember thinking we had all but stopped the system – it was based on our passivity, a change of will and it could be stopped. It was then clear to what a systematic suppression our wills had been subjected. Then there was the graffitti – 'Society is a carnivorous flower' – Hell, I should know that. Here am I a living illustration of the Situationist thesis *The Society of the Spectacle*, I mean it extends indefinitely from the obvious examples – you sitting passively watching me on the screen – wanting a flesh that is celluloid; me playing at being somebody else – somebody dead or imagined. Alienation has surpassed itself. Same of course with the other side of alienation – with the workers separation from his product – this has gone even further than Marx could have imagined.

Q But the system does deliver the goods, can we survive without them?

A We can live without masses of them. Start by distinguishing false needs and real ones. The 'Spectacular Commodity Society' multiplies needs because it can fill none. The 'necessities' that surround us – cars, telys, gear, cameras, paintings, the fantastic acreage of kitsch – are spewed out in a never-ending stream; no one thinks of its purpose other than those making a packet out of it. So we really have become a commodity-dominated society, peoples' relationships are made via objects – ton-up kids; stamp-collectors; cottage-in-the-country-owners; pot-smokers . . .

Q Is this what you mean by the poverty of everyday life?

A Yes, from the factory-worker to the druggy, its generally a matter of survival, not living; an administered survival kit in place of the realisation of desire. Take the poor sod in the factory who says – like so many do – 'I wouldn't know what to do with myself if I didn't work'. God, it is the apotheosis of alienation when life is so boring people think of nothing more exciting than the daily 8-5 grind to make a profit for someone else. Talk about the colonialisation of everyday life; they pull out of India to entrench themselves a little more deeply in your skull. And what's this big underground society. Just another market area, a variation in the range of consumer goods. There is now a 'Gear' and Arts Lab in every swinging town, all indistinguishable, the same processed commodities. The latest goods and poses being exhibited, envied, bought and exhibited again. The city itself is dying; death by commodity asphyxiation; Marx's prediction come true – 'The dead hand of technology strangling humanity'. Everybody knows it and no-one does anything about it – they are too damned scared of a little revolutionary euphoria. And even the goods themselves could be one of the means for the initial transformation to a qualitatively different form of life. Think of all the goods stacked along the Blvd. St. Germain. They could transform the city – lampposts swathed in fur coats, the pissotiers hung with jewellery and paintings, all those lousy books put into great heaps for the real 'battle of the books', the trees and houses wearing all the trendy gear from the boutiques . . . Anything you fancy. I mean no one needs all that junk, so let's free it, and us too from its domination. We saw the first attempts at transforming life in May and as the UN Report concluded – 'This is only the beginning of the youth unrest which will sweep the world clean.' Of course we are working backwards – from youth to children. The Surrealists, Buckminster Fuller etc. all knew it – return to childhood, overthrow the reality principle.

Q You used to have a largish collection of paintings etc. I remember seeing a photo of your house with a Caro and Poons in it. Now you've sold up. Why?

A Why? Need you ask. Art now is so patently reactionary. As an aspect of society (arts purity is a real myth) it has always allied itself to the prevailing social conditions or functioned as their negations. Now it is fully integrated into a consumer society, complete with middlemen and market-researchers. The revolt of the avant-gardists is nothing but the cosy spectacle of what passes for freedom in minds stultified by an acceptance culture working at full capacity. One can only realise art by transcending it. Moreover it is important to oppose the absorbent power of society the fact that one cannot overthrow art without realising it. And the project to realise art is the same as the project to reconstruct everyday life. Those moments of imaginative resistance to the external organisation of life contain at least as much poetry as the best volumes of poetry and prose. Poetry is present in everything that does not conform to that morality which to uphold its order and prestige has nothing better to offer us than banks, barracks, poisons, schools, churches, brothels, and theatres. It is a society sick enough to buy back my Bridget Rileys etc. at an obvious profit to me. Again the money goes into the project for the destruction of hierarchical power. Beyond the power structure and the ideologies it has fed is another reality. Let it flower, a ferocious flower bursting through the shit of the given.

Q What about . . .

A No. no more questions about art, economics, politics etc. The day of the partial critique is over. We are asked our opinions of the details so we ignore the totality that matters. They tell us to look after the pennies, while they look after the pounds. But their days are numbered. The truth is in the whole and the whole is false. Those new tremors running through the atmosphere are in my body. C'mon.

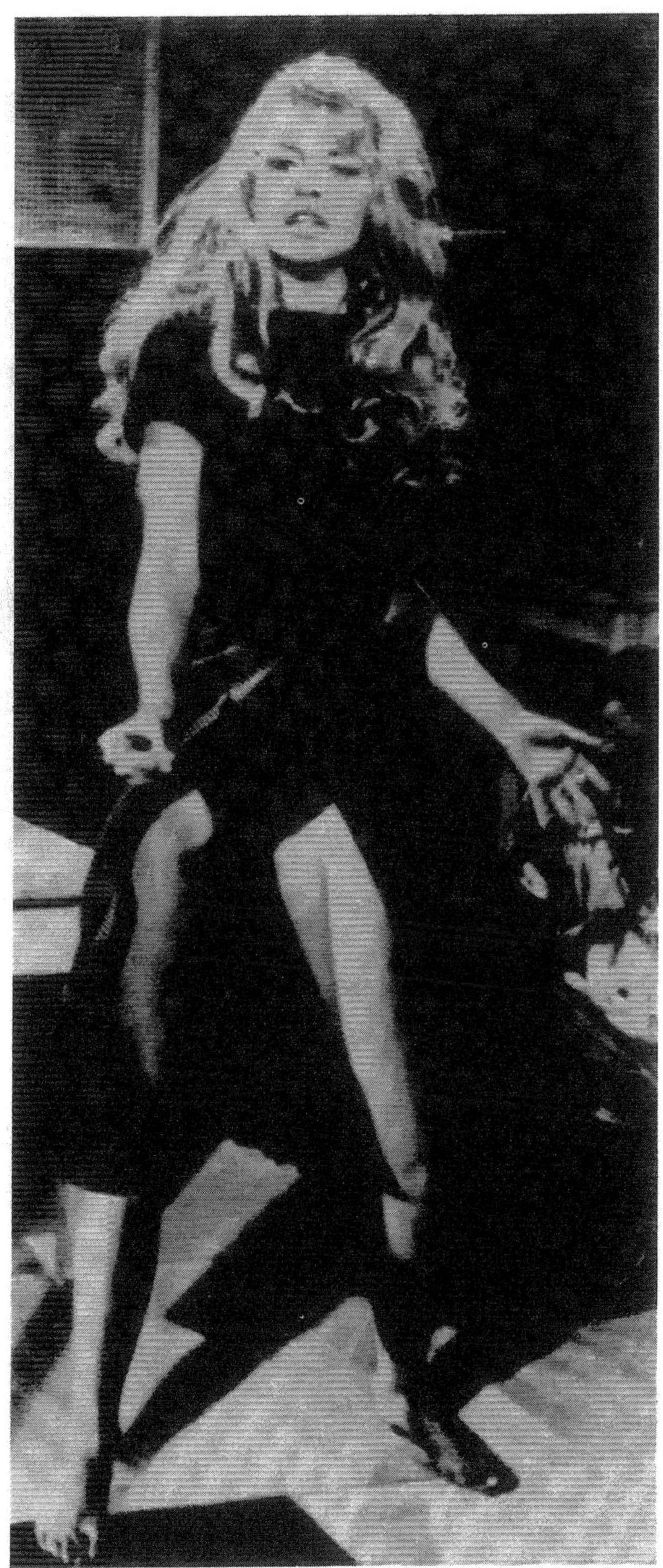

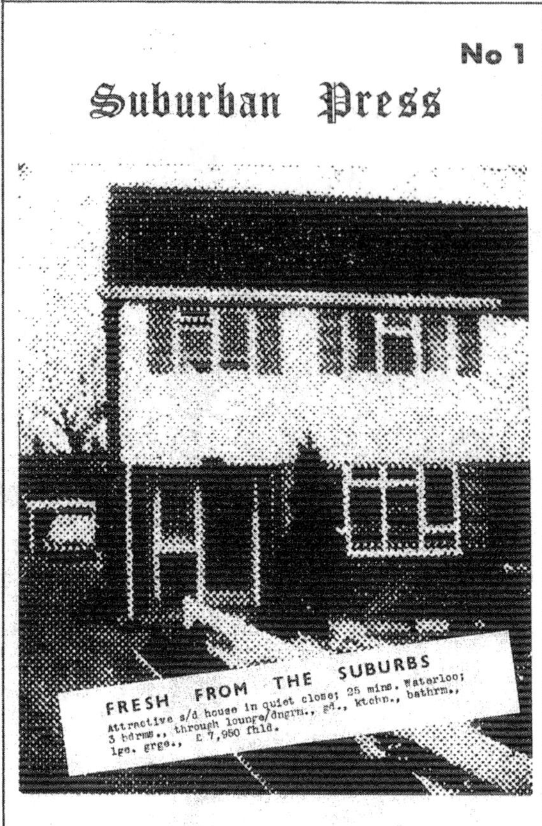

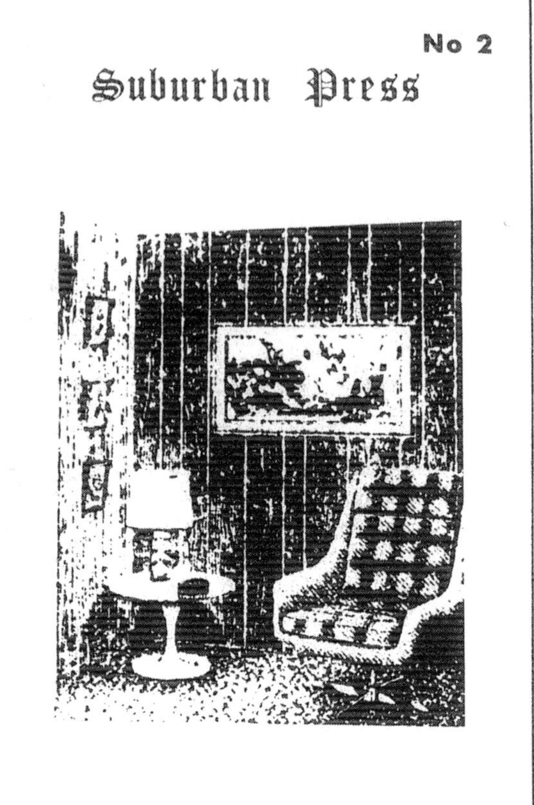

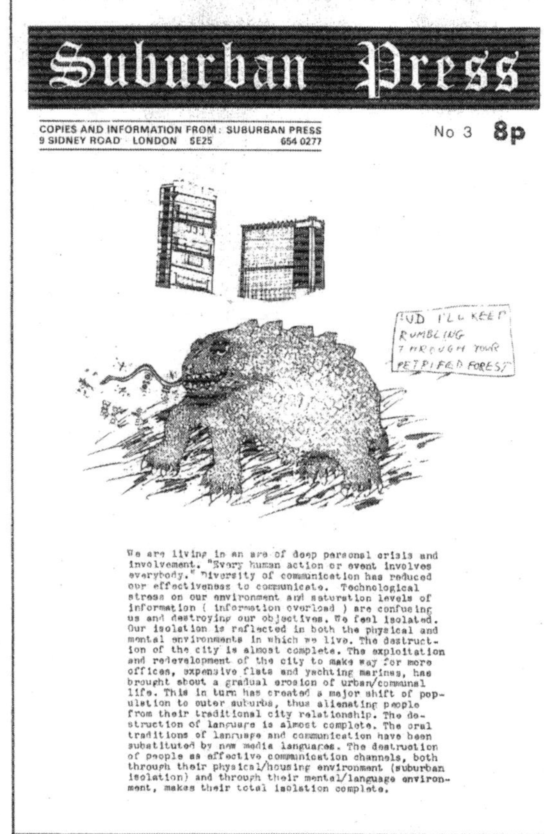

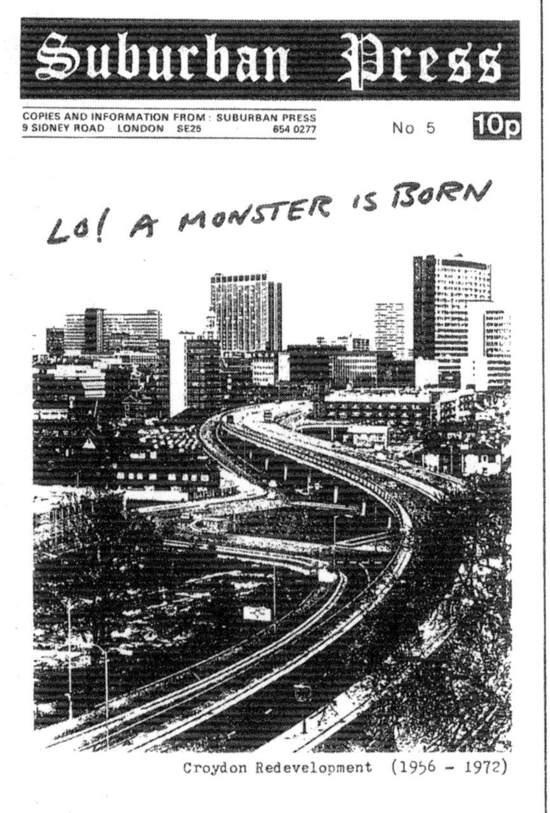

Suburban Press covers, 1970–1975

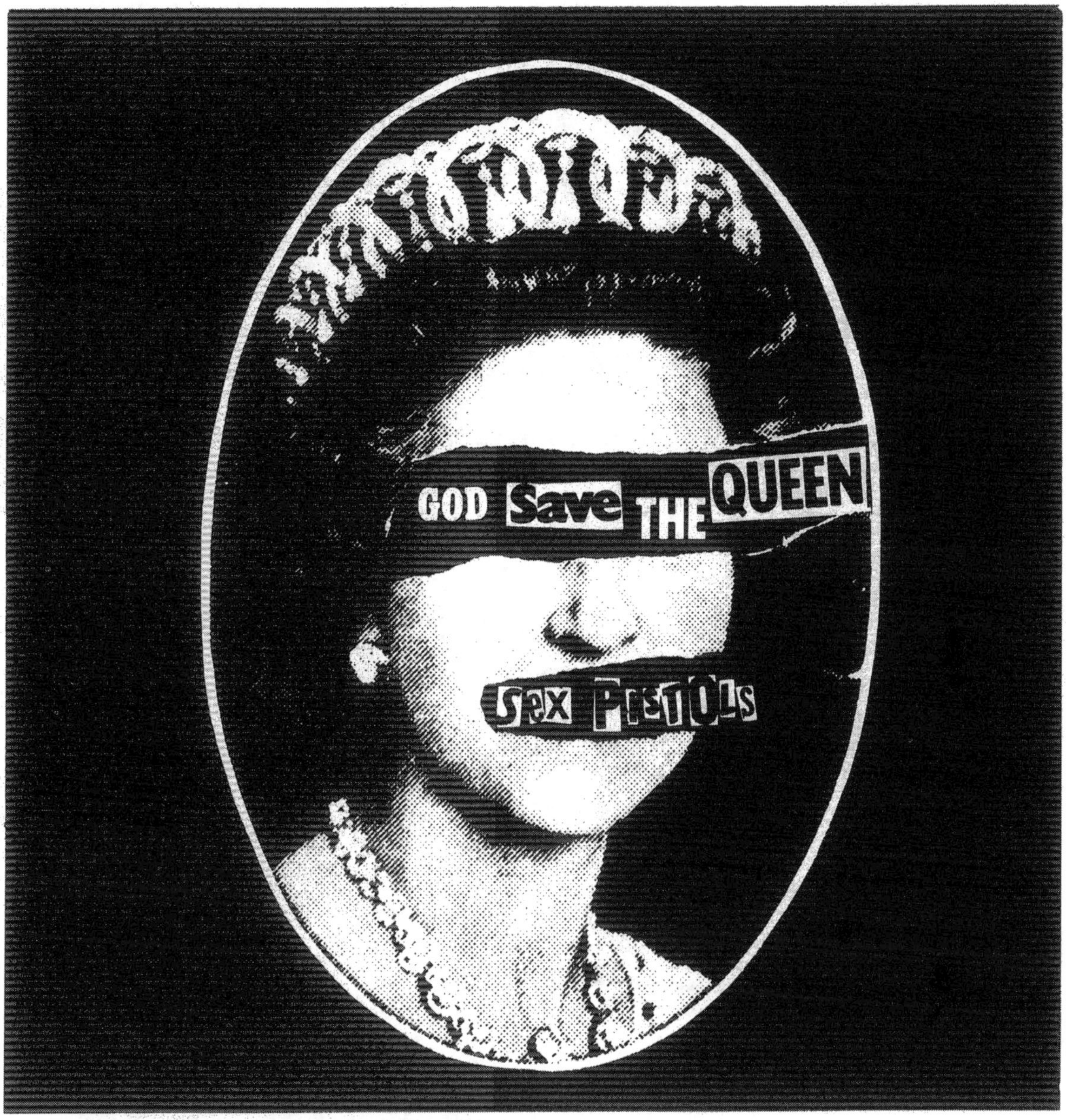

God save the Queen, 1976

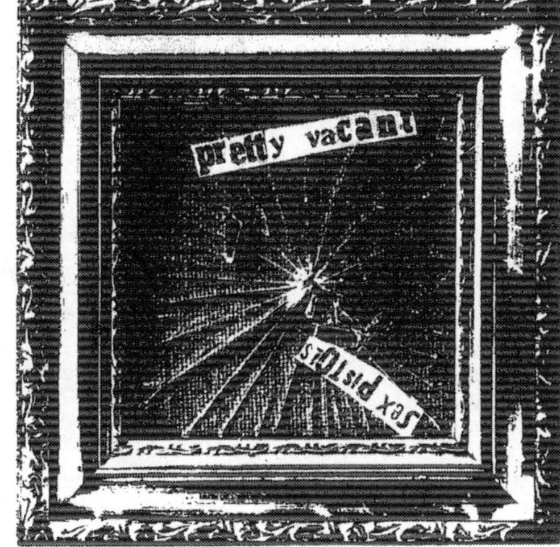

Pretty Vacant, 1977

Jamie Reid

SEX PISTOLS BULLETIN

EMI 2566

ANARCHY IN THE UK

ROCK GROUP START A 4-LETTER TV STORM

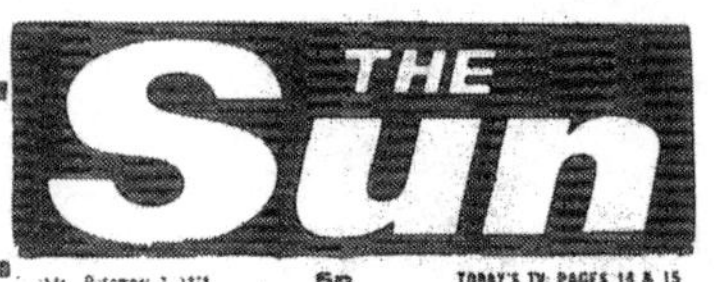

5p TODAY'S TV: PAGES 14 & 15

By BARRIE MATTEI

VIEWERS jammed a television company's switchboard last night after an interview with a rock group ended in a string of swear words.

And TV personality Bill Grundy was accused of encouraging the language that shocked thousands.

He was talking to the "punk rock" group Sex Pistols on Thames Television's Today programme.

Viewers in big protest over shock outburst

Four-letter Punk Rock group in TV storm

Sex Pistols

DAILY MAIL REPORTER

ANGRY viewers demanded the sacking of TV interviewer Bill Grundy last night after

The bizarre face of Punk Rock

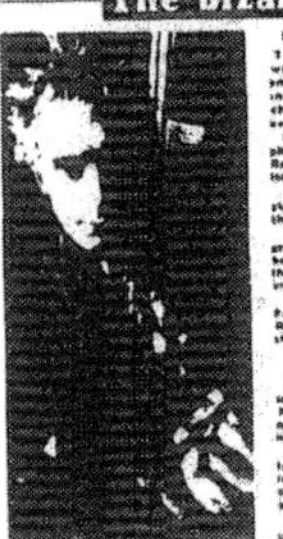

Johnny Rotten, Sex Pistols singer

Siouxie Sioux

Steve Jones

Daily Mail Reporter

THE Rolling Stones were rebels. The Who smashed everything in sight. Alice Cooper chopped up dolls with an axe.

But the latest pop phenomenon called Punk Rock makes all the rest look like nursery rhymes.

Uniform

Daily Mail

THURSDAY, DECEMBER 2, 1976 7p

Evening Standard

WEATHER: Cloudy. Lighting-up time: 4.34 p.m. to 7.16 a.m. Details—Back Page.

London, Thursday December 2 1976 6p

Sex Pistols inquiry over four-letter w...

THE FOUL MOUTHED YOBS — by TV's Bill Grundy

BILL GRUNDY leaves today—"You can't do..."

'Worthless, decidedly inferior, displeasing...'

The Punks—Rotten and proud of it!

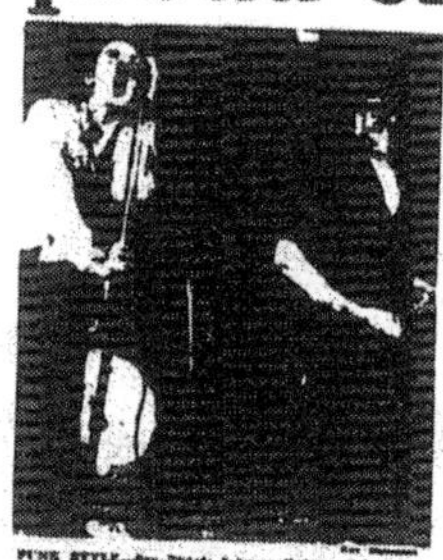

PUNK STYLE—Sex Pistols Johnny Rotten (left) and Steve Jones in action recently at Notre Dame Hall, Leicester Square.

NEWS ON CAMERA

"PUNK — Worthless, decidedly inferior, displeasing, rotten."
—Partridge's Dictionary of Slang and Unconventional English.

PUNK ROCK, which exploded last night in the TV screens in a string of four-letter words, is a bizarre movement which combines rock and revolution, writes Jacques Johnson.

DRIVERS PAGE

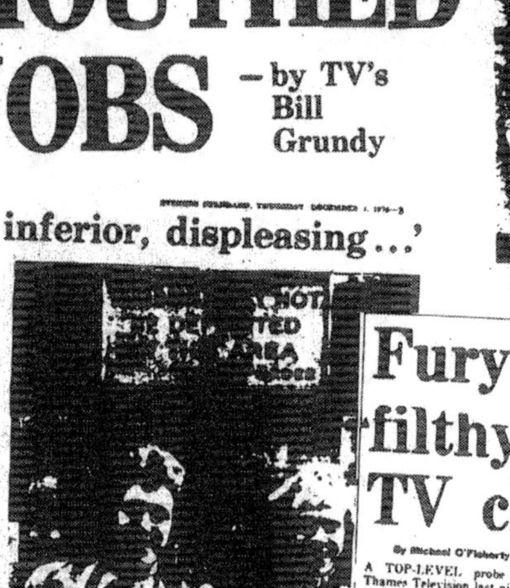

Fury at filthy TV chat

By Michael O'Flaherty and Gill Martin

A TOP-LEVEL probe was ordered by Thames Television last night after a "punk-rock" group delivered a stream of four-letter words on the air.

The group, Sex Pistols, let rip while being interviewed live by Bill Grundy on the early evening programme Today.

Grundy—"disgusted"

The theme

Obnoxious, arrogant, outrageous.. the new pop kings

WHO ARE THESE PUNKS?

THEY wear torn and ragged clothes held together with safety pins.

Daily Mirror

BRITAIN'S BIGGEST DAILY SALE

Thursday, December 2, 1976 No. 22,616

TV's Bill Grundy in rock outrage

?!★!

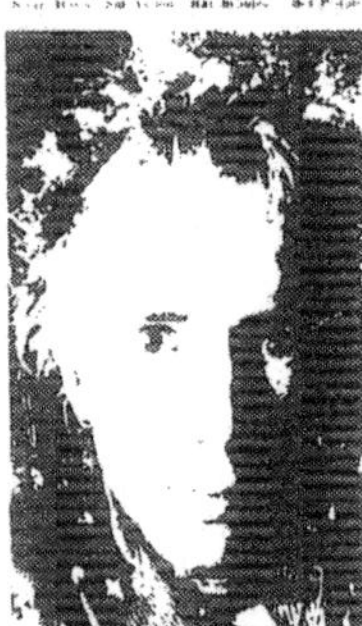

ROTTEN: Johnny the Sex Pistols leader

Anarchy

Banned

THE RAGGED REBEL

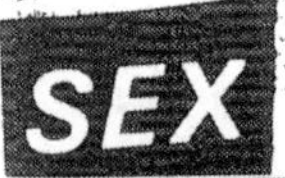

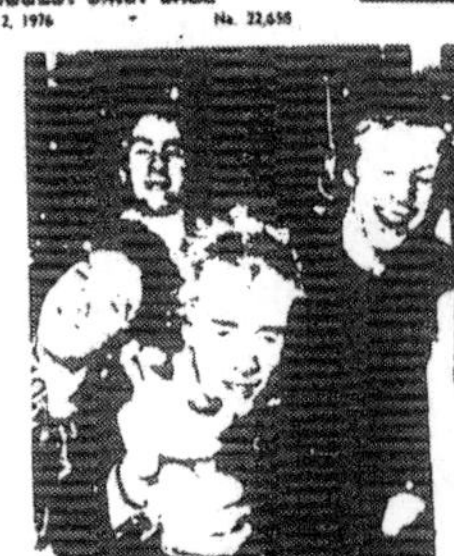

THE GROUP IN THE BIG TV RUMPUS

Johnny Rotten, leader of the Sex Pistols, opens a can of beer. Last night their language made TV viewers froth.

When the air turned blue..

THE FILTH AND THE FURY!

A POP group shocked millions of viewers last night with the filthiest language heard on British television.

Uproar as viewers jam phones

By STUART GREIG, MICHAEL McCARTHY and JOHN PEACOCK

Shocker

London's biggest evening sale

Evening News

LONDON THURSDAY DECEMBER

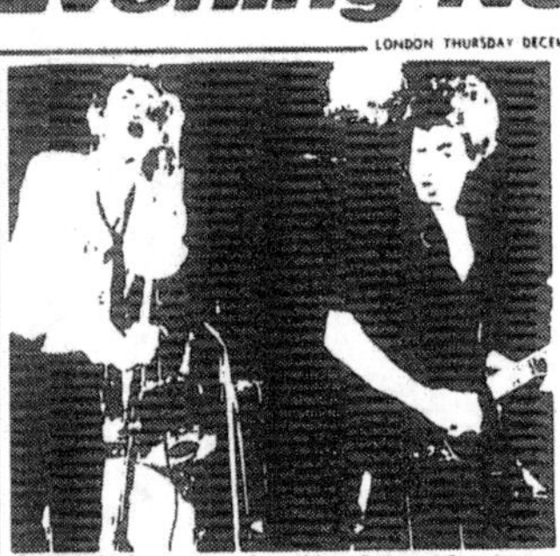

Two of the Sex Pistols group — Singer Johnny Rotten and Steve Jones

GRUNDY GOADED PUNKS SAYS RECORD

By PATRICK STODDART

'On stage the Pistols are the most aggressive, nasty band ever.'

WHO ARE THESE PUNKS? PAGE

Vivienne Westwood

'We were writing on the walls of the Establishment, and if there is one thing that frightens the Establishment, it's sex. Religion you can knock, but sex gives them the horrors.'

Vivienne Westwood
Fashion Guide, London, 1978

'We were not here to sell toys and fetish clothing but to convert, educate and liberate. We are totally committed to what we're doing and our message is simple. We want you to live out your wildest fantasies to the hilt'

Vivienne Westwood
Forum, June 1976

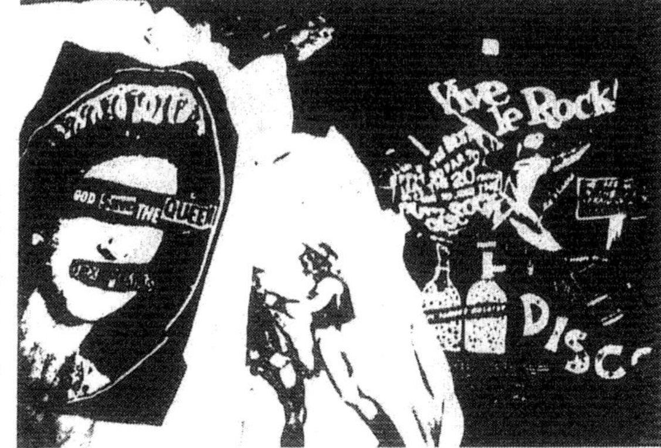

Sex Shop T-shirts, 1975-76

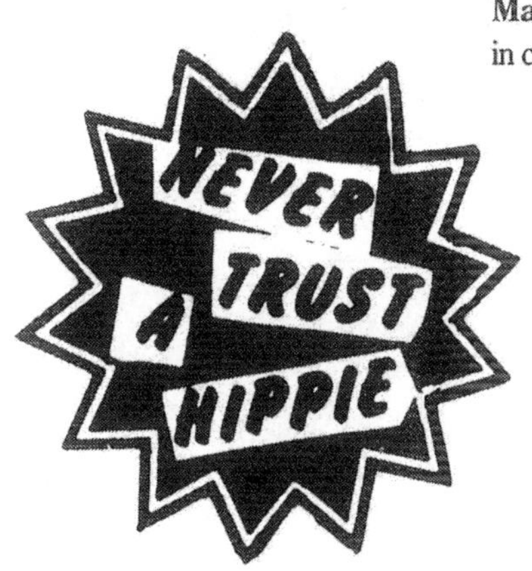

Malcolm McLaren

'They are Dickensian-like urchins who with ragged clothes and pock marked faces roam the streets of foggy gas-lit London pillaging. Setting fire to buildings. Beating up old people with gold chains. Fucking the rich up the arse. Causing havoc wherever they go. Some of these ragamuffin gangs jump on tables amidst the charred debris and with burning debris play rock 'n' roll to the screaming delight of the frenzied pissing pogoing mob. Shouting and spitting 'anarchy' one of these gangs call themselves the **Sex Pistols**. This true and dirty tale has been continuing throughout 200 years of teenage anarchy and so in 1978 there still remains the **Sex Pistols**. Their active extremism is all they care about because that's **what counts to jump right out of the 20th century as fast as you** possibly can in order to create an environment that you can **truthfully run wild in**.'

(signed) Oliver Twist
Malcolm McLaren
Handbill/manifesto for the Sex Pistols, 1978

'Punk rock couldn't be sold . . . It was too much to do with Do-It-Yourself. As soon as you get a Do-It-Yourself force out there, you spawn 5,000 other groups. The record industry never wanted 5,000 groups. They only want one group. One group is more manageable. It's one dictator telling you what the culture is all about rather than 5,000. They don't like the socialist idea that everyone can do it.'

Malcolm McLaren
in conversation with Paul Taylor, 1985

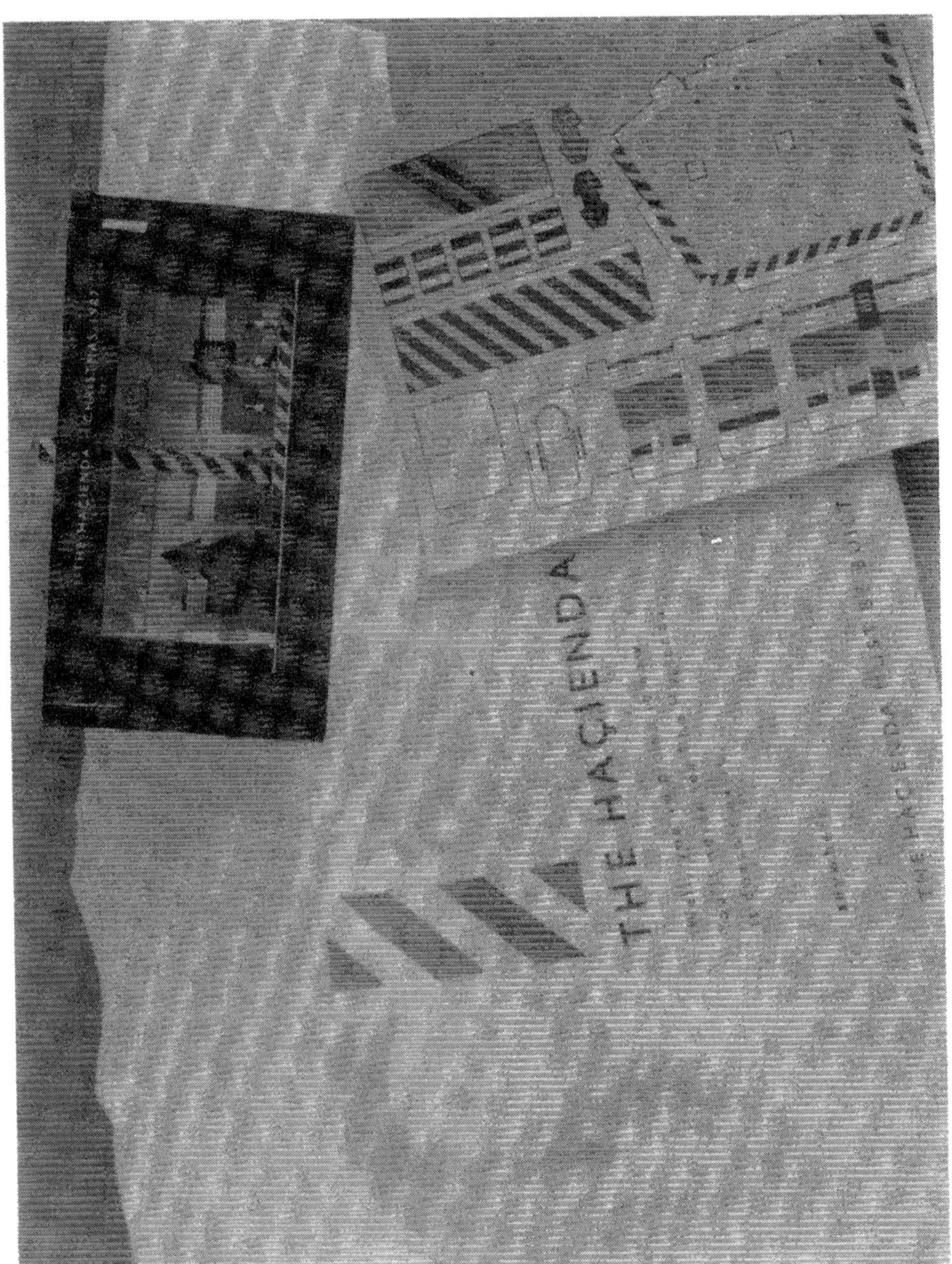

FAC 51 The Hacienda Christmas 1987
Pop up and T-shirt designed by Trevor Johnson

Hacienda opened in May, 1982 – club designed by Ben Kelly and Sandra Douglas.

Factory Records and Hacienda founded by Tony Wilson.

The revolution of everyday alienation

Dave and Stewart Wise
End of Music, 1978
Excerpts

Punk coincides with the long, protracted end of the post second world war capitalist re-construction. The relatively affluent base of previous rock eras is no longer there. Primary poverty is returning with a vengeance after an epoch of capital expansion. It was thought there was no end to a surfeit of commodities – hence the critique of the poverty of abundance in the 60s which was a major factor in the potentially revolutionary explosions of the 60s among alienated youth (though not necessarily of the productive working class, where combating productivity deals played a greater part as a subversive departure, than immediate aesthetic/ecological objections to frozen chickens, mini cars, and T.V. shows).

Punk, like previous rock movements, is based upon youth, but a youth which has in increasing numbers been thrown out of work and has become part of the growing surplus population which is allowed minimally to consume through welfare relief and various scrounges. Punk rock uses the desperation of this social base but only finally to re-inforce this desperation. As long as the spectacle lasts, it will equally be superceded by something different but which sounds very familiar. Probably, more desperate and schizoid – if only to try and hold some attention . . .

A musical situationism was born in the dressed up rebel imagery of Punk and New Wave. While, the Situationists were credited in the one specific instance of the Sex Pistols, the rebellion of modern art forms, first expressed pictorially and in literature, though now recuperated, have increasingly been applied to the production of music . . .

Part of the genesis of punk goes back 16 years to the English section of the Situationists and the subsequent, King Mob – a loose affiliation (hardly a group) of disparate though confused revolutionary individuals in England in 1968.

King Mob lauded and practised active nihilism. 'Revolutionaries, one more effort in order to be nihilists' but most of the active nihilism was directed against the pseudo-revolutionary pretensions of the extreme left of capital, and those who insisted on abiding by a straight job. A tremendous interest was shown in the praxis of deviants – psychotics, the mentally collapsed, (it was somewhat hip to have been through a mental asylum) and petty crooks . . .

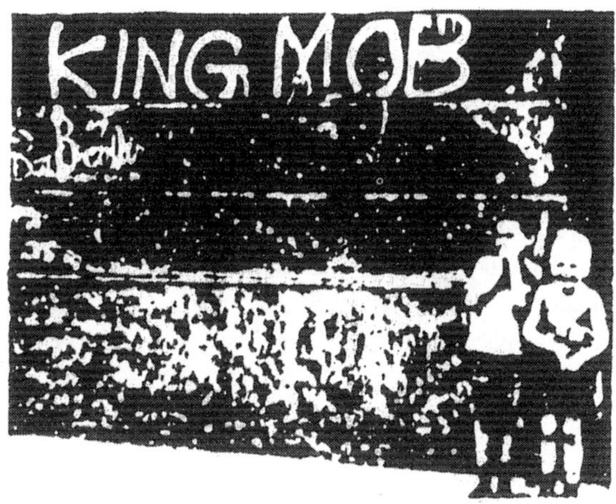

The name King Mob itself came from the Gordon Riots in London in the late 18th century when on the walls of the newly built gutted prison of Newgate the signatories of the insurgents, 'His majesty, King Mob' were placed. On the one hand, 'King Mob' applauded uncritically the Black riots and the activities of the Motherfuckers in the USA, while on the other hand, opportunistically collaborated with a whole consortium of Trotskyists and Maoists, (Maoist spontaneists) under the umbrella of the Vietnam Solidarity Committee. The actions only could have (and did have) reformist conclusions . . .

King Mob's hysterical over emphasis (without adequate explanation) of violence, whether futurist, or contemporary hooligan outbursts, played into the hands of a charismatic romanticism of deeds which, mistakenly equated genuine theoretical development with the dead hand of academia. Without such a distinction the way was open for the grotesque return of English philistinism and the renewed acceptance of the university salon. It was energy itself that was needed, an excess of energy which

NEVER TRUST A SITUATIONIST

The Revolution of Everyday

fostered an apocalyptic fear of the imposed impending passivity; the big sleep; the hunkering down under; the steady job. Fear too, that this fate lay around the corner for each individual who wasn't seen to be radiating personal energy. Do something: it didn't matter that you carried Vaneigem in one pocket, while the other contained a manual on the 'new' participatory social democracy. (Peoples' Associations, Law Centres, Neighbourhood 'Soviets'-sic-in twilight areas, even with a 'militant' market research con for finding out 'the wishes of the people'). In any case one could always threaten bombs and call for the arming of the working classes. The superman/woman militancy and the subsequent vandalism through theoretical and practical confusion caused by having to confront a fresh series of problems. From the breakdown of the King Mob other tendencies have developed. One trying to live out the ideologies of a politically conscious hippy life style, (akin to the Yippees but more honest) became openly terrorist (the tragedy of 'The Angry Brigade') while others became carreerists in the university set up . . .

The overt recuperation of a bowdleralized Situationist critique in the UK was really the capitalizing of deceased active nihilism inherent in the activities of King Mob continuing to exist as a nostalgic, dearly beloved memory, static and un-self critical. In the case of Punk, returning active nihilism to a consumed passive nihilism via rock venues, King Mob eventually gave an extra fillip to the marketing of disintegration, and ironically, became more noticeable in the late 70s than in the late 60s because of the sale of the mass-market of artistic anti-art.

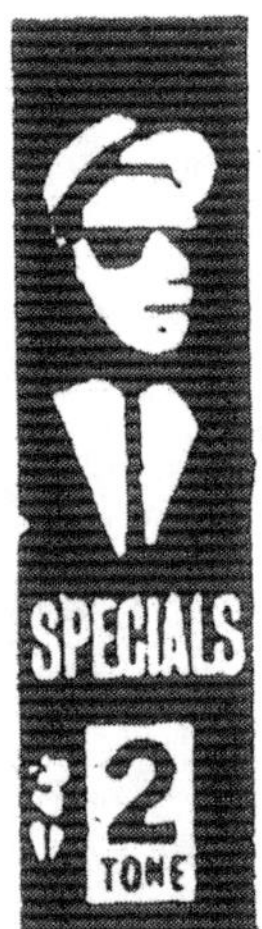

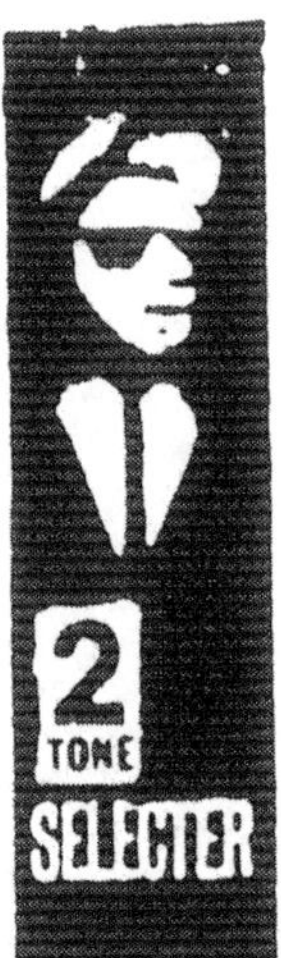

White on black tie: £1.75 + 25p (P & P)
Send postal order/cash/cheque to:

The Sex Pistols

Malcolm McLaren, manager of the Sex Pistols, had been friendly with individuals versed in the Situationist critique in England and had picked up some of the slogans and attitudes of that milieu . . .

The society of situationism is in the process of appearing in the Anglo American world, largely through recent tendencies in pop music, academic situationism in sociology and art history, the new religions, (Sri Bagwhan and the insertion of Vaneigem into Taoism), the sexuality which says anything goes, in production, the mystique of 'self management' and workers control which the experience of the last few years, (Clyde, Lip and the Portuguese co-operatives) has called into question and affects the validity of workers' councils, at least as they have been previously conceived – eg. the Workers' Parliament in Russia and the broadly democratic content of all previous workers' councils. Unlike France or Italy, there are no Vaneigemist town planners or Debordist economists writing for influential journals or esconced in the State apparatus. But no matter, their practice will be broadly the same, that is some kind of modernism whether their forlorn inspiration comes from Schumacher or Debord. The extent of the recuperation is slowly emerging in spite of the economic crisis which one mistakenly assumed would have curtailed such experiment. The gaps in previous revolutionary critique are becoming painfully obvious.

Punk is the admission that music has got nothing left to say but money can be made out of total artistic bankruptcy with all its surrogate substitute for creative expression in our daily lives. Punk music, like all art, is the denial of the revolutionary becoming of the proletariat.

Alienation

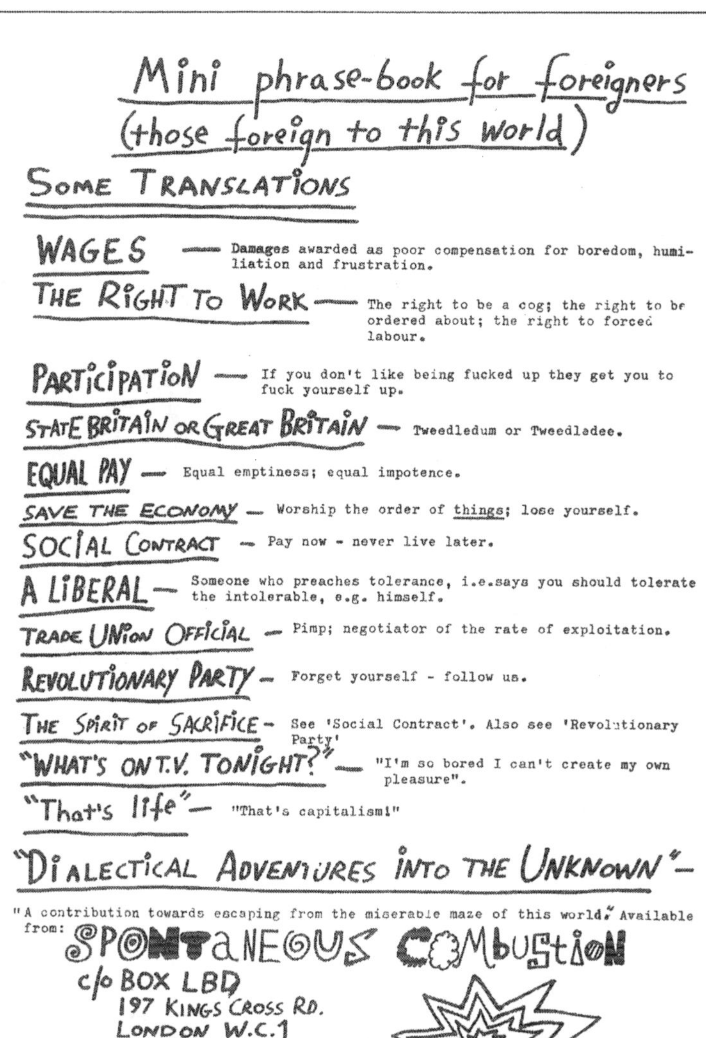

Mini phrase-book for foreigners (those foreign to this world)

SOME TRANSLATIONS

WAGES — Damages awarded as poor compensation for boredom, humiliation and frustration.

THE RIGHT TO WORK — The right to be a cog; the right to be ordered about; the right to forced labour.

PARTICIPATION — If you don't like being fucked up they get you to fuck yourself up.

STATE BRITAIN OR GREAT BRITAIN — Tweedledum or Tweedledee.

EQUAL PAY — Equal emptiness; equal impotence.

SAVE THE ECONOMY — Worship the order of things; lose yourself.

SOCIAL CONTRACT — Pay now - never live later.

A LIBERAL — Someone who preaches tolerance, i.e.says you should tolerate the intolerable, e.g. himself.

TRADE UNION OFFICIAL — Pimp; negotiator of the rate of exploitation.

REVOLUTIONARY PARTY — Forget yourself - follow us.

THE SPIRIT OF SACRIFICE — See 'Social Contract'. Also see 'Revolutionary Party'

"WHAT'S ON T.V. TONIGHT?" — "I'm so bored I can't create my own pleasure".

"That's life" — "That's capitalism!"

"DIALECTICAL ADVENTURES INTO THE UNKNOWN" — "A contribution towards escaping from the miserable maze of this world." Available from: SPONTANEOUS COMBUSTION c/o BOX LBD 197 KINGS CROSS RD. LONDON W.C.1 (PRICE 25p incl. postage)

★ **Dialectical Adventures into the Unknown**
'This new situationist journal is an outrageous attack on all that 'Time Out' stands for: ie concerned left-wing journalism and critical appreciation of all that's best in entertainment. It's condemnation of everything and everyone standing in the way of each individual enjoying their passions and imaginations fully in the world around them, includes, among others, the Left (caricatured as sacrificial altruists out of touch with their experience) and the Arts (belittled as mere soporific compensations for people's lack of creativity). This little slander sheet is available from Box LBD, 197 Kings Cross Road, WC1, price 25p (post paid)'.

Time Out review, 1978

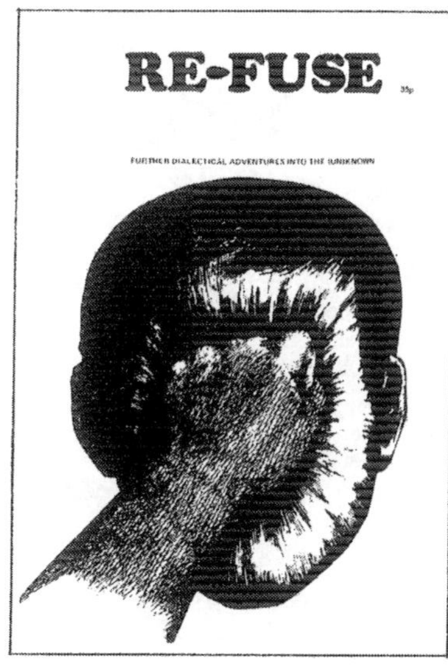

THE FRAUD'S PRAYER

Our Market Who Art On Earth
Hallowed Be Thy Show
Thy State Power Come
Thy Will Be Done
On The Streets As It Is In Work
Sell Us This Day Our Daily Lie
And Justify Us Y/our Property
As We Submit To Those That Assert Property Relations Against Us
And Lead Us Anywhere But Into Autonomous Temptation
But Deliver Us From Anti-Hierarchical Initiative
For Ours' Is The Stagnation, The Cop And The Celebrity
Forever.....Or Never?
Amen.

THE FRAUD'S PRAYER

Our Market Who Art On Earth
Hallowed Be Thy Show
Thy State Power Come
Thy Will Be Done
On The Streets As It Is In Work
Sell Us This Day Our Daily Lie
And Justify Us Y/our Property
As We Submit To Those That Assert Property Relations Against Us
And Lead Us Anywhere But Into Autonomous Temptation
But Deliver Us From Anti-Hierarchical Initiative
For Ours' Is The Stagnation, The Cop And The Celebrity
Forever.....Or Never?
Amen.

Nick Brandt, *Re-Fuse*, BM Combustion, 1978

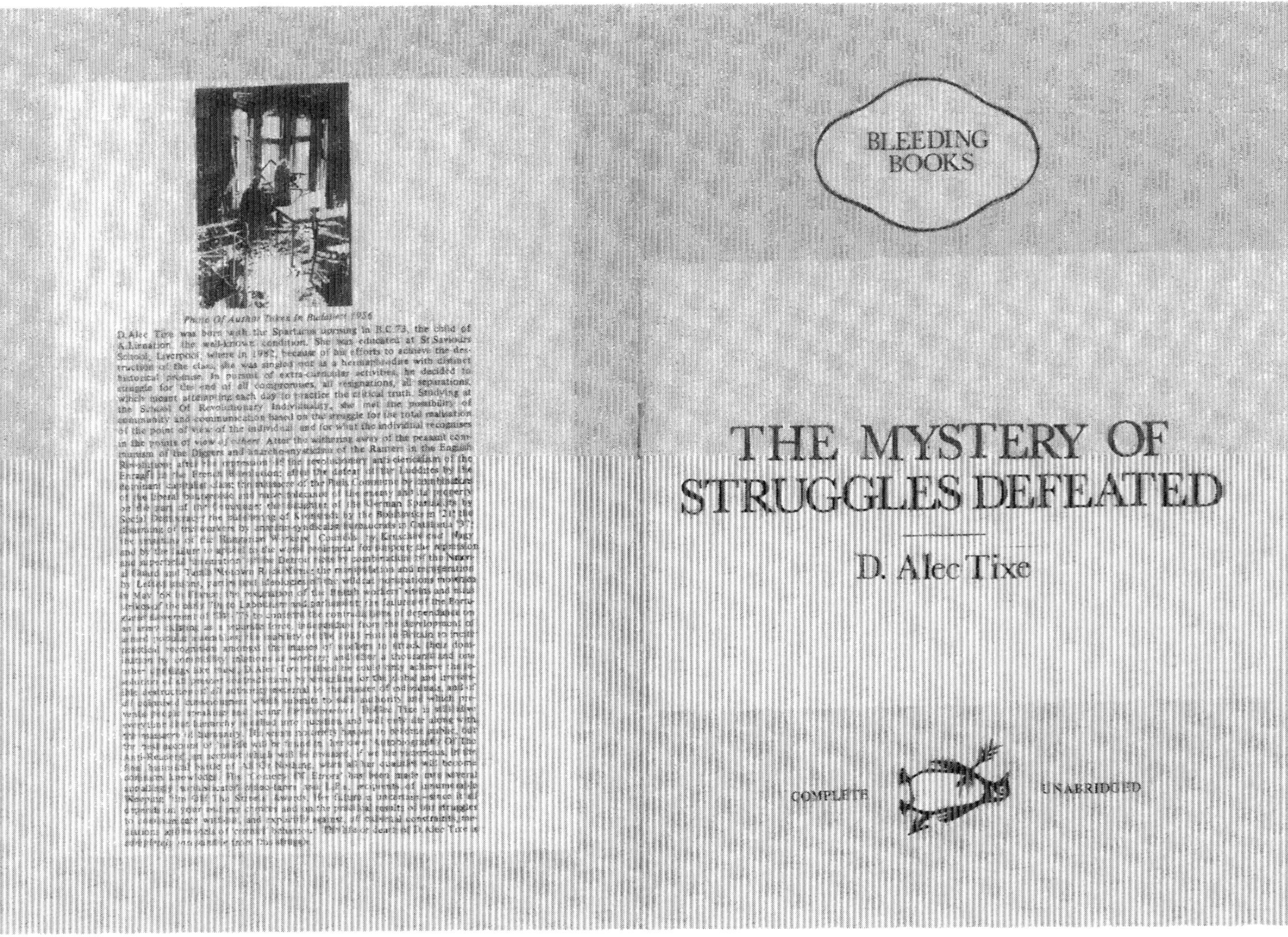

B M Combustion

the road is an arm of the law...
grasping everywhere for
the pollution of money

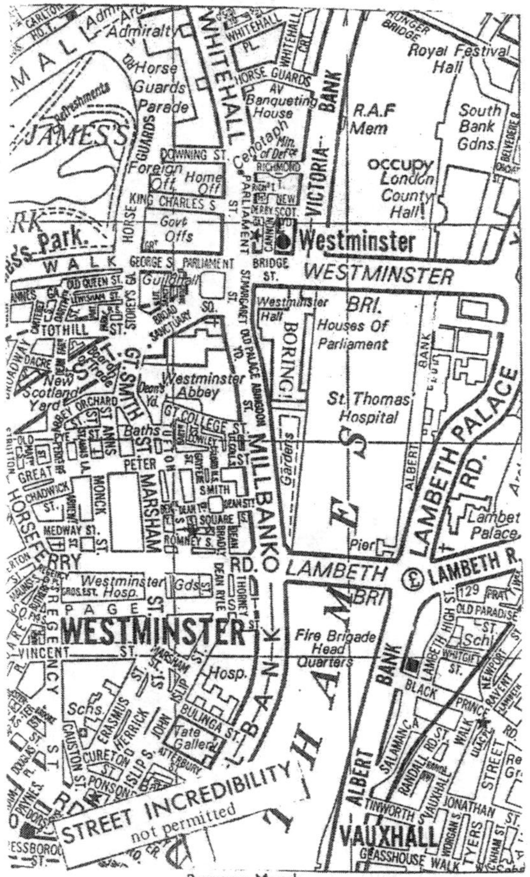

Romney Marsh

FOR A DIGNIFIED AND EFFECTIVE DEMONSTRATION

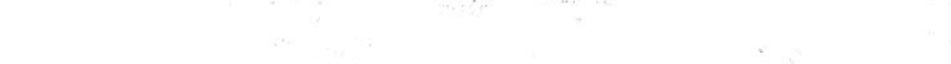

Brought to you by the ALL-LONDON UNITED ALLIANCE OF SOCIALIST CAUCUSES to whom the following are signatories: G.L.C., London Labour Party, T.U.C., S.W.P., W.R.P., I.M.G., C.N.D., Ecology Party, Y.C.L., and B.F.

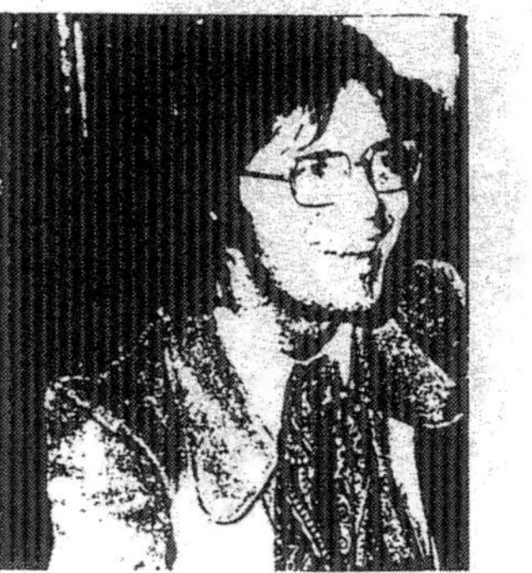

CORRECT

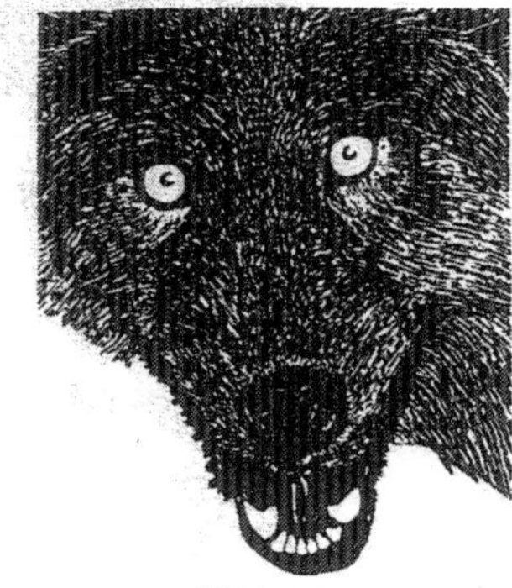
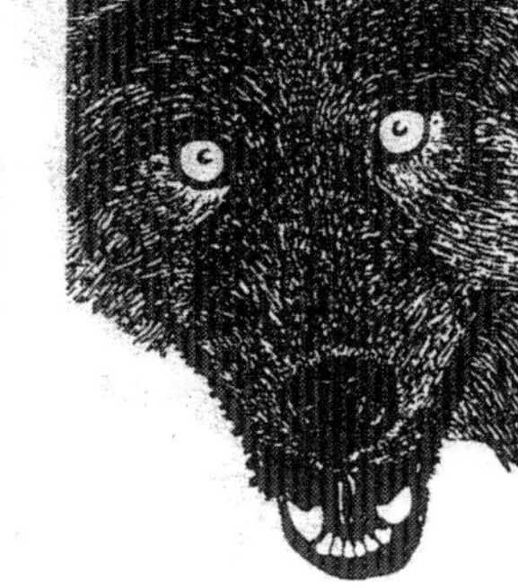

INCORRECT

We welcome everyone to today's demonstration, which we hope will be amongst the biggest London has seen for many years. We are confident that the vast majority of you will keep intact your dignity. A disciplined rally is essential if we are to avoid discrediting ourselves in the eyes of the public and losing the approval of the police. We want to give the media no reason to condemn our campaign by pointing to any over-imaginative acts. To this end, we call on everyone to obey the dictates of the stewards who will be found alongside the police. They will be acting in your interests. They are sensible people – please be sensible with them. Beware of troublemakers – some may be in the crowd with you. If you see any do not hesitate to summon stewards or the police, who, we must remember, are our brothers in work. Comrades! Even in a socialist society we shall still need Specialists-In-Order to combat hooligans and deviants. While it's true that nowadays the police are occasionally over-zealous in their protection of privilege, property, and the violence of the world market, the best way of dealing with this is by demanding public accountability through elected local government or some other representation of submissive community. In the meantime we should recognize that they will only listen to our complaints if we conduct ourselves in the correct manner.

anon circa 1985

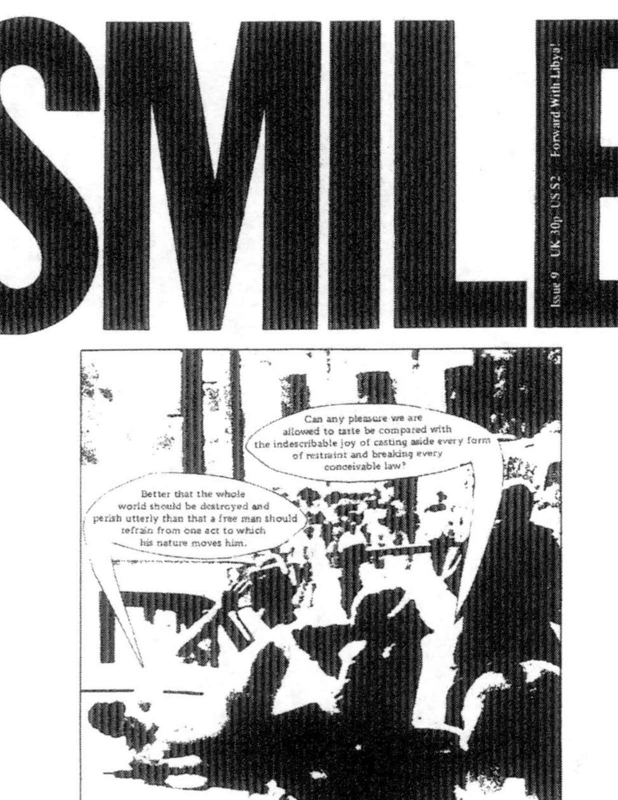
SMILE
Issue 9 UK 30p US $2 Forward With Libya!
Can any pleasure we are allowed to taste be compared with the indescribable joy of casting aside every form of restraint and breaking every conceivable law?
Better that the whole world should be destroyed and perish utterly than that a free man should refrain from one act to which his nature moves him.
TAKE YOUR DESIRES FOR REALITY

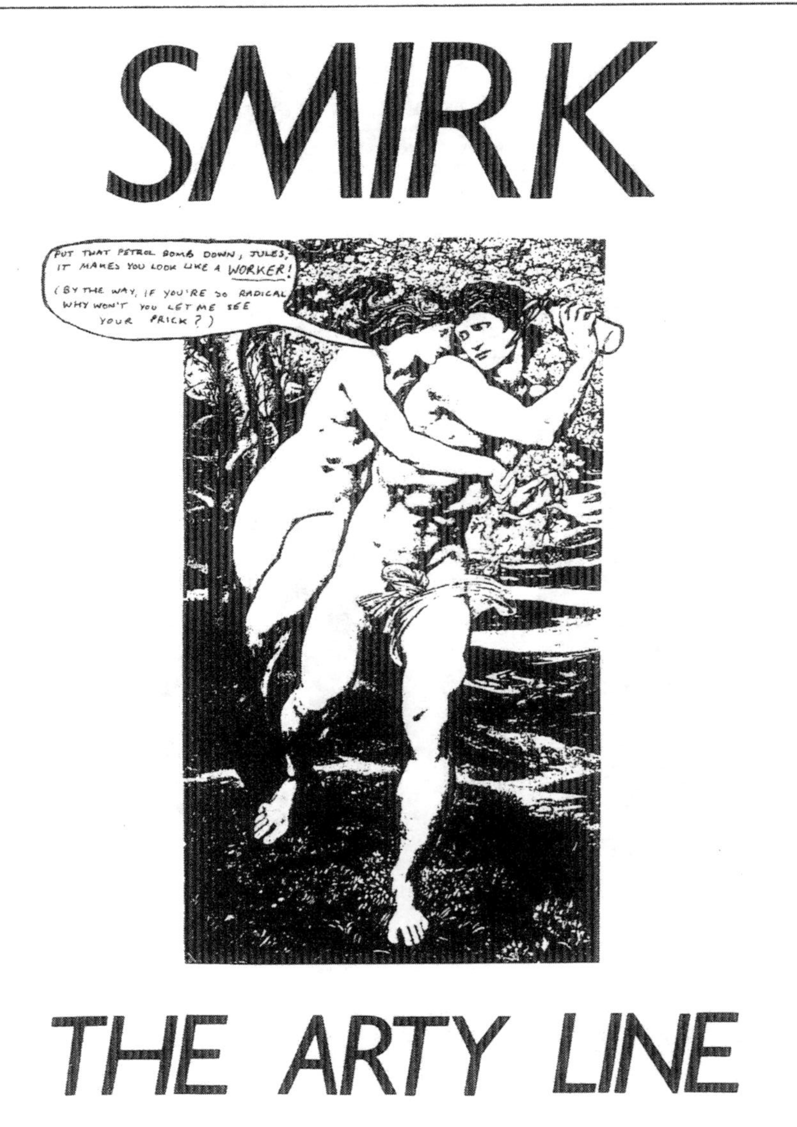
SMIRK
PUT THAT PETROL BOMB DOWN, JULES, IT MAKES YOU LOOK LIKE A WORKER! (BY THE WAY, IF YOU'RE SO RADICAL WHY WON'T YOU LET ME SEE YOUR PRICK?)
THE ARTY LINE

anon, 1987

KAREN ELIOT EDITIONS, 64 GLENTHORN RD, JESMOND, NEWCASTLE UPON TYNE
NE2 3HN tel: 091 281 8314

ORIENTATION FOR THE USE OF A CONTEXT AND THE CONTEXT FOR THE USE OF AN ORIENTATION

The name Karen Eliot can be strategically adopted for a series of actions, interventions, exhibitions, texts, etc. When replying to letters generated by an action/text in which the context has been used then it makes sense to continue using the context, i.e. by replying as Karen Eliot. However in personal relationships, where one has a personal history other than the acts undertaken by a series of people using the name Karen Eliot, it does not make sense to use the context. If one uses the context in personal life there is a danger that the name Karen Eliot will become overidentified with individual beings. We are perhaps heading towards the abolition of the personal, perhaps everything is social and the personal (the individual) is just illusion; this area of activity must be debated, examined. However, previous experiments with multiple names, such as the Monty Cantsin fiasco, indicate that the failure to differentiate between the personal and the social, and in particular over identification by certain individuals with the context, is disastrous. The use of multiple names for pop groups and magazines has proved far less problematic than with human beings.

Karen Eliot is a name that refers to an individual human being who can be anyone. The name is fixed, the people using it aren't. Smile is a name that refers to an international magazine with multiple origins. The name is fixed, the types of magazine using it aren't. The purpose of many different magazines and people using the same name is to create a situation for which no one in particular is responsible and to practically examine western philosophical notions of identity, individuality, originality, value, and truth.

Anyone can become Karen Eliot simply by adopting the name, but they are only Karen Eliot for the period in which they adopt the name. Karen Eliot was materialised, rather than born, as an open context in the summer of 85. When one becomes Karen Eliot one's previous existence consists of the acts other people have undertaken using the name. When one becomes Karen Eliot one has no family, no parents, no birth. Karen Eliot was not born, s/he was materialised from social forces, constructed as a means of entering the shifting terrain that circumscribes the 'individual' and society.

A Karen Eliot curriculum vitae consists of the various activities undertaken by people using the Karen Eliot context. It does NOT contain the personal names of the people who use the context, or dates of birth, or activities undertaken under names other than Karen Eliot. A curriculum vitae of a given 'individual' may contain references to activities they have undertaken as Karen Eliot but this is very different to a curriculum vitae of Karen Eliot. Karen Eliot is a context not a person.

Smile Magazine
Generic magazine title available for plagiarism – the prototype for eighty different versions worldwide – editor Karen Eliot.

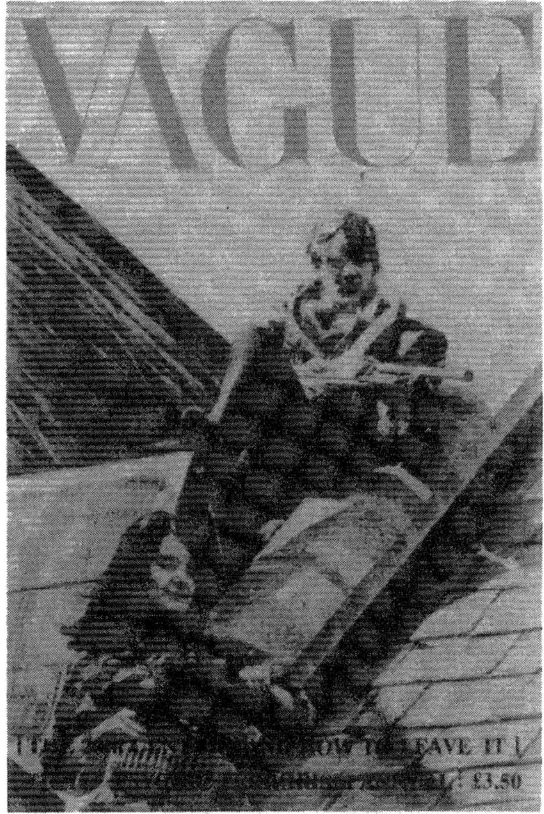

1984

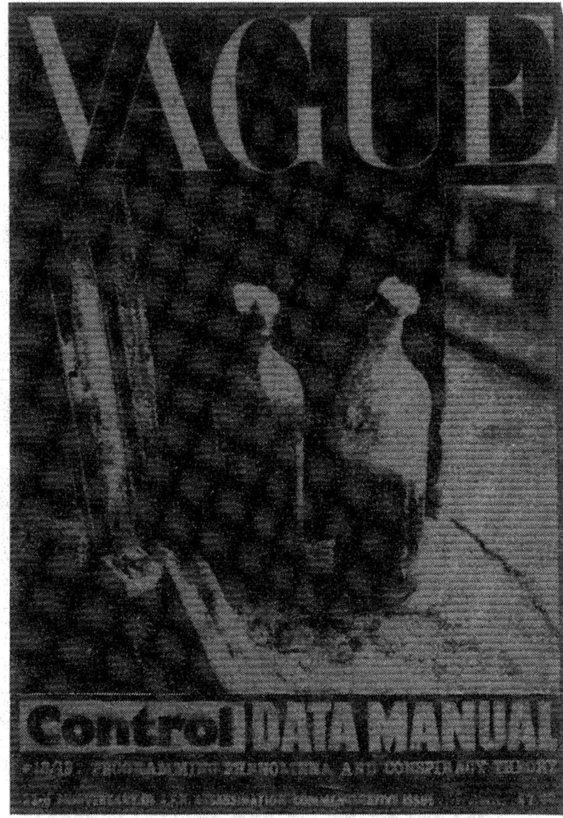

1986

None dare call it plagiarism: nothing is new everything is permissible

Tom Vague

Editorial Vague No 18/19

The great advantage of plagiarism as a literary method is that it removes the need for talent, or even much application. All you really have to do is select what to plagiarise. Enthusiastic beginners might like to start by plagiarising this article on plagiarism. A neo-plagiaristic plagiarist might choose to plagiarise it verbatim; but those of a more creative bent might like to change a word here and donkey, or place the paragraphs in a different sequence.

It is worth bearing in mind that plagiarism is a highly creative exercise because with every plagiarism a new meaning is brought to the plagiarised work. Unfortunately this does not alter the fact that the capitalistic forces controlling Western culture have prescribed as illegal the plagiarising of modern texts, so that the risk of prosecution is ever present. However, do not allow this to deter you from plagiarising modern work. A few sensible precautions will protect you from prosecution. The basic rule in avoiding copyright infringement is to take the idea and spirit of a text without actually plagiarising it word for word. One of the best examples of this is Orwell's '1984', which is a straight re-write of Zamyatin's 'WE' . . .

In short, plagiarism saves time and effort, improves results and shows considerable initiative on the part of the individual plagiarist.

As a revolutionary tool it is ideally suited to the demands of the late 20th Century. Selection of material is the only challenge entailed. To select the very best material one must be a genius.

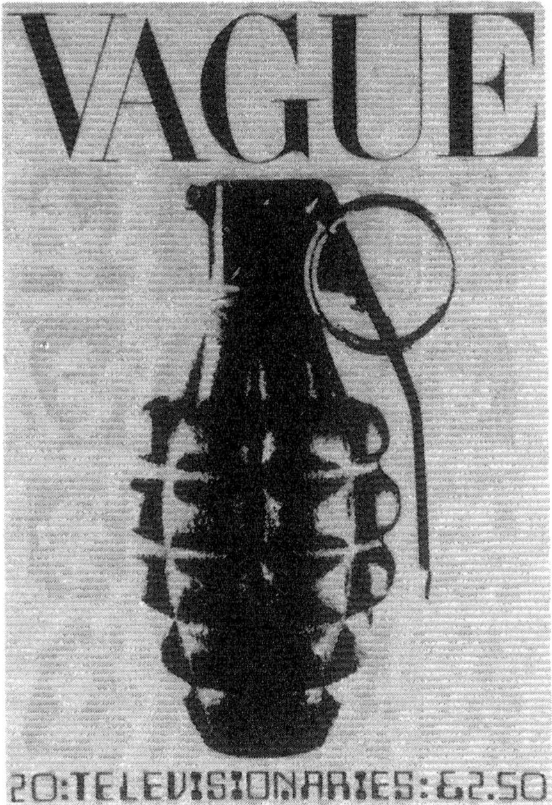

1988

Critical culture and the post-modern condition

Kenneth Frampton

'Place-form and cultural identity' *Design after Modernism,* 1988

Excerpt

The protagonists of Postmodernity, that is to say, those who are convinced that the period of High Modernity has ended, seem to fall, at least initially, into two groups; the neo-Historicists and the neo-Situationists. The first of these, who happen to be the least intellectual and the more prominent in the eyes of the popular press, are those who feel that the entire ideology and stylistic apparatus of the modern avant garde has been discredited and that no choice remains but to abandon this ostensibly inhuman and radical discourse, together with its style, and to return to tradition in every conceivable sense; from figuration and expressionism in painting to tonality and classical form in music, from kitsch historicism in architecture, to outright neo-conservatism in culture-politics and even in politics itself. The neo-Situationists (and I have termed them thus in order to imply that there may be direct or indirect links here to the *Situationist* movement of the fifties) seem to welcome the continuing escalation of modernization as an inevitable and fundamentally radical process; one which, despite its predominantly utilitarian and positive character, embraces a constantly varying and unstable mosaic and hence the latent, liberative conjunctions of the future.

Of the two groups it may be claimed that the second is the more consistent, for where the former is culturally and politically retrogressive it remains committed to the benefits of univeral civilization. It seeks to combine the optimization of techno-science with reactionary culture-politics, exploiting the latter to soften and mask the harsh realities induced by the former. Where the neo-Conservatives are schizophrenic and culturally *anti-modern*, the neo-Situationists are more strictly *post-modern* in that through repudiating the utopian legacy of the Enlightenment (which some of them see as inseparable from political terror) they proclaim the end of 'master narratives', in all fields, including that of science itself. Both groups seem, in fact, to envisage an end of Enlightenment history; the former by embracing historicism and thereby reducing the cultural present to a perpetual and meaningless regurgitation of a petrified past, the latter by renouncing history as the master narrative *par excellence*. Both groups, for different reasons, distance themselves from the redemptive end of bourgeois history prophesied by Marx, and yet in both the master-narrative of techno-science seems to return through the back door; in the first case, by virtue of unabashed reactionary politics, in the second, by assuming an apparently acritical attitude towards the seeming autonomy of techno-science . . .

Despite the spontaneous devolution of power, such as we have recently witnessed in Spain, it would be naïve, to say the least, to underestimate the staying power of the Jacobin state, along with its understandable interest in furthering the 'autonomous' domaine of techno-science, together with its 'value-free' application. In this sense, I would submit, we are finally justified in calling for a culture of resistance, or more specifically, in our case, for a critical practice of architecture, which, without falling into sentimental primitivism, would resist the universal commodification of the modern world and in doing so react against the further centralization of power and control. Here the confrontation between universal civilization and rooted culture takes on a decidedly political potential . . .

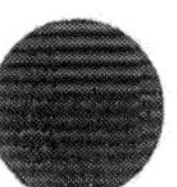

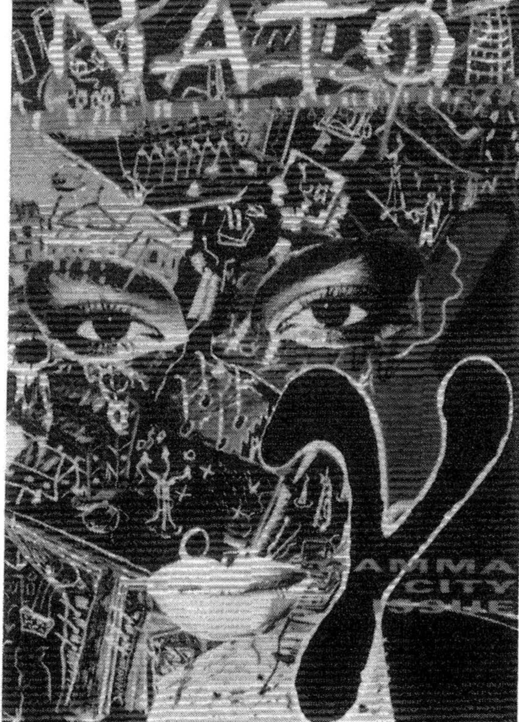

If public views on architecture are lack lustre, those of architects are worse. Both are suffering from modernist-idealist withdrawal symptoms ... When WW2 was in full fling, and cities were crumbling, the architects who'd always wanted to be a bit more 'german' got excited by the possiblilities for planning, neatening and enlarging our cities.

Over forty years later it's easy to say that the solutions were wrong, but even then high rises ideals were out of date. Now, despite all the building, our cities aren't much better, got worse in fact, because the rot is obsolescence ... new silhouettes of twisted steel, a new chaos.

But peoples lives have changed. We work, think, play differently now. Life isn't as clear cut as it was postwar. Perhaps we don't want neat and tidy cities. Cultivated chaos may not be the answer, nonetheless a volatile sense of change has swept into every walk of life ... TV, advertising, music. Lifestyle generally has split into a myriad of tiny parts, each with its own soundtrack and pair of headphones.

Consumption itself has become synonomous with lifestyle, rather than with plain having more. Besides, whether on account of the black economy of your double tape deck, we are all producers. One step further and you switch off the telly because you want to do something for yourself, however makeshift. Exit poverty, enter streetculture, CND, health fetishes, muscle building, car collecting. Poverty from above means possibility, means mobility, means decoding.

Our cities are museums of the old order, based on a system of logical compartments, yet undone and overlayed so often that movement has crept back in by accident. NATO looks for clues under stones ... near railway stations, beneath motorways or on the seventeenth floor of Trellick Tower. Maybe the twisted steel is a signal of the times. We should take a closer look and find the city situations which are smarting for renewal.

Think of city life as a patchwork of events, free from the narrowing effect of blueprint brains. Consider obsolescent structures providing the perfect frameworks for building local dynamos. A subtle combination of energy, archeology, irrationality and even elegance enables 'Gamma situations to tip the balance towards a new urban visibilty. You'll find them everywhere, from faded emblems of the state to deserted street corners and even your own back door steps. And when you've found them ...'

•

Think of an intermediary architecture on that edge between people's lives and the given city, a kind of city furniture poised to refurbish rather than rebuild.

•

The interweaving of diverse function should be seen as positive. Hence look upon tangled road-rail junctions, building sites and converted factories as Gamma-places built by accident.

•

Unpick the situation until bare signs show through, then expand them and spread them out to make space really work as a trigger for experience.

•

Build in fictional gestures and narrative sidesteps, because peripheral ingredients can upgrade reality when thrown in with it.

•

Customise situations with new means and new technologies, not as futurology, but as taking stock. Tape decks, discdrives and VTR's have outgrown their status as commodities. They're spare parts of the architecture of our daily lives.

•

Use materials to exploit their differences. Bend them, stretch them, paint them and erode them, use their contortions to build impulse into dynamic form. We want sensual architecture, architecture which stimulates.

•

NATO's Gamma-City is a get-up-and-go starter pack based on typical sites and probable events. It scrambles uses and meanings ... it bends stereotypes ... it uses double levels ... fictions are used politically. Its city is made active again, putting back the movement that Modern Movement Man forgot about.

Why Gamma? Because gamma-rays emit spontaneously. They radiate strong short radio waves, effecting built mutations.

Nigel Coates

NATO 13

Nigel Coates, *Gamma City Special Issue*, Narrative Architecture Today, 1985

Ralph the Situationist

Art & Language
Artscribe International, Nov/Dec 1897
Excerpt

Situationist texts are very difficult to read, difficult to concentrate on. They often feel like conversations with Ralph. Ralph is twenty three or twenty four. Unemployed. He lives with his adopted father in a rage of despair at the death of his adopted mother. . . Ralph is often to be seen in yellow shorts, with or without shoes, with or without T-shirt on bright days in January and February. He cadges cigarettes and tries to catch your eye. He converses, when you can't turn your eye away from his mild but wild surmise, of peace camps, religion, travels and psychogeography. He writes poetry and letters to the Queen. He is sometimes to be seen on the Post Office doorstep in a detourned (or anyway 'displaced') business suit with an even more displaced executive briefcase. He waits with the mysterious aplomb of an official of the local authority. He sometimes plays football with the kids in the Baptist churchyard. He menaces objectors, not the kids. Ralph is no idiot. But nine times out of ten you quicken your pace only to be checked by the inward threat of moral cowardice or some similar dishonour. You also check your step by the outward threat that you are suddenly a representative of business-as-usual, suddenly a 'straight' generated only (or not, and it is worrying) by the proximity of Ralph. But the conversations are always the same and it's them you fear: intricate unaccultured messes, empty but teleologically replete. Ralph is, as it were, a second-order aphasic. It is as if he gives an aphasic's account of the world in a second-order language which simulates the normal *and* the aphasic in one grammatical sequence. But Ralph's voice has little menace. He voices opinions of others only in his anger at his mother's death.

Reading Guy Debord in particular is like trying to converse with Ralph . . .

In some ways, the often menacing voice is a match for the strangely self-assured optimism of quasi-technical promise. The voice is directed often with excessive force upon what seems to be hastily discriminated targets. But while the heckle is directed somewhat randomly, its targets are specific and the voice is emphatically violent. The futurology of desire, by contrast, is expressed in allusive and evasive terms. The voice is modified to speak of the feeblest generalities and to bluster . . .

Situationist texts are very loose stitched, theoretically porous, exciting rather than informative, and so on. But somehow the texts themselves seem to absorb this kind of observation with a shrug or to threaten it with a Ralph-like (but more menacing) flood of words and abuse. The texts are effectively incorrigible and self-insulating and then some. At the same time they are (at least partly) dressed in the clothes of referential, sequential and therefore corrigible discourse. Quite exotic . . .

The constructive metaphysics of the Situationists – their ethos – was a form of anger. But this anger was not the sort that reverberates in the ironical language of *Class War*: muggings perpetuated on the young things who colonize the razed docklands of London with smart apartments are called *yuppie tax*. This is anger which incorporates irony: the act is dismissed, its 'standard' symbolic value displaced. But the ground of the irony, the cold displacement, *is* anger. The menace is redoubled in being trivialized; a Stendhalian execution. Debord's texts are not ironical in this sense. They are the jeering but not self-displacing signs of anger which utilize irony but which do not displace themselves. To menace is one thing. To detourne or to dérive loudly might carry a certain threat. To speculate or appear to speculate as to its 'laws', to lay down guidelines for the practice, is to reduce it to a little preserved fragment of French culture; the flâneur, remade with a fake psychological vocabulary and a 'revolutionary' pretention . . .

The question is whether these bits of late surrealistic taste, bathetically self-dignified showings-off, whiffley architectural programmes, and so on, constitute a textural aporia on the real surface of the Situationist text (and a reason to read on) or simply a bland incoherence – a self-contradicting absurdity – and a moral ground to give up reading and remembering . . .

To interpret the Situationist texts as going no further than words – as failing, as refusing, to reference the world – is not to render them non-political. It is to point to their symptomaticness as culture politics and as politics in general and also to point to their specific political content . . .

The future, or rather the grammar of futurity, is both a first-order feature of the Situationist writing and a *hypogram* elaborated like a cliché. The first-order 'referential' mode is almost always to the future – to the merely possible and necessarily general. Laws are laws for what will be iterated possibilities. It is as if Debord had already made Riffaterre's misreading of Hegel concerning the disappearance of the *here* and the *now* in being written down, and in the realization that followed abandoned the referentiality of his own text. But only just abandoned. If referentiality had been subsumed we would be left with a dreamwork of the theatre of dreamwork. The 'constructive' or positive coquetries would be consigned to a dream of the future or to a theatre – a non-literal event situated by some sort of temporal index far away from the here and now. If this is where the 'practice' of 'détournement', 'psychogeography', 'experimental behaviour', 'the dérive', etc. are to be found, their bathetic relationship with the voice and grammar of menace is transformed. The voice of menace is the prosopopeic presence of some sort of past in an action detached from the reality of here and now. Organizing and writing are merely forms in (or of?) the dream. This detachment is an inescapable characteristic of the Situationist form. As a consequence of this it becomes a real contradiction of a real cruelty that the Situationist might have played a 'concrete' role in the events (the spectacle) of 1968 so long as these events are construed as concretely historical. But for the Situationist these events are subsumed by the order of the theatre or the text of the not now. If this is not so, then there is no cure for Situationism: it was simply a prototype for contemporary official culture in France. The dreamwork reading provides an interpretation of the technico-socio-anarchic-futural-world-domination-style language . . .

If 1968 was the time that International Situationism woke up, then its dream was *always* of an official French culture, and the dream is now a sort of reality. But *if* it didn't really wake up, if literal epistemological consequences or concrete practical acts are continually deferred, mere adjuncts to the delivery of the dream, then is not official French culture being made to dream the same dream? . . .

If we argue that the dream is over, then we can try to interpret it as a dream. That a failure to interpret it as a dream leads to bureaucratized official mystification is not the same as saying that the dream is not to be interpreted as a madness – a dream of an official and coercive culture. The dream may be a dream of official French culture. That is to interpret it as a dream and not to attempt to continue it awake. To take such a dream as a blueprint for a cultural practice is to attempt a totalitarian act: to turn a dream of culture into culture. Can we get rid of that thought merely by retrodicting the wakers into dreamers?

Martin, Strijbosch, Vaneigem and Viénet wrote that 'art can only be realized in being suppressed' and that it can 'only be suppressed in being realized.' The Situationist project obeys the same unparadoxical rule . . .

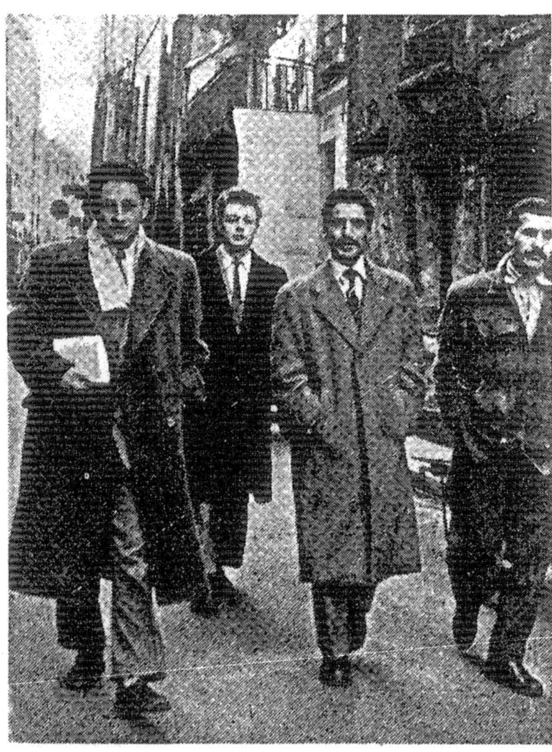

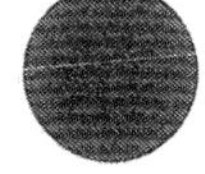

'The first priority in the spectacle's domination is to obliterate all knowledge of history, starting with just about all reasonable information and commentary on the most recent past. The evidence for this is so glaring it hardly needs further explanation. With consummate skill the spectacle organises ignorance of what is about to happen and, immediately afterwards, the forgetting of whatever has nonetheless been understood. The more important something is, the more it is hidden. Nothing, in the last twenty years, has been so thoroughly coated in obedient lies than the history of May 1968. Some useful lessons have indeed been learned from certain demystifying studies of those days; these, however, remain state secrets.

'It's now some ten years since a president of the republic, long since forgotten but at the time still basking on the spectacle's surface, naively expressed his delight "knowing that henceforth we will live in a world without memory, where images flow and merge, like reflections on the water." Convenient indeed for those in business; and who know how to stay there. The end of history gives power a welcome break. Success is guaranteed in all its undertakings, or at least the noise of success.

' . . . The precious advantage which the spectacle has acquired through the *outlawing* of history, from having driven the recent past into hiding, from having made everyone forget the spirit of history within society, is above all the ability to cover its own tracks – to conceal the very progress of its conquest of the world, its power already seems familiar, as if it had always been there. All usurpers have shared this aim: to make us forget that *they have only just arrived.*'

Guy Debord
Commentaires sur la société du spectacle, Editions Gérard Lebovici, 1988

Compiled and edited by Iwona Blazwick in consultation with Mark Francis, Peter Wollen and Malcolm Imrie. With special thanks to George Robertson, Steve Radmall, Jamie Reid, Stewart Home, Paul Seiveking, Jon Savage, Tom Vague, Martin Poole, Ingrid Swenson and James Lingwood for their invaluable advice and/or loan of materials.

This publication accompanies the exhibition **On The Passage of a Few People Through a Brief Period of Time.**

Presented at the Musee National d'art Moderne Centre Georges Pompidou/ICA, London/ICA, Boston: 1989–1990. Conceived and realised by Mark Francis and Peter Wollen, with Paul Hervè Parsy. In consultation with Tom Levine, Greil Marcus, Elisabeth Sussman.

The exhibition has been supported by the Association Française d'Action Artistique; the Ministry of Culture in Copenhagen; the Netherlands Ministry of Welfare, Health and Culture; the Instituto Banco San Paulo of Turin in co-operation with the Italian Institute; Becks Bier; Visiting Arts; Assorted Images; and the Friends of the Situationist International.

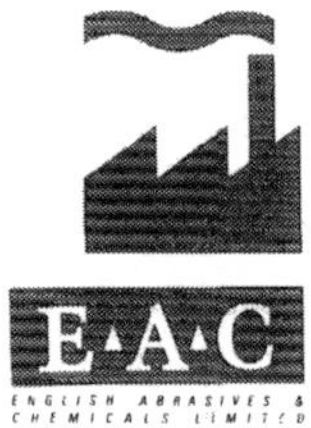

This publication has been sponsored by Factory Records; sandpaper cover donated by English Abrasives and Chemical Limited.

Edited reprints compiled and published by Verso/ICA Publications, London 1989.

Verso
UK: 6 Meard Street, London W1V 3HR
USA: 29 West 35th Street, New York, NY 10001-2291
Verso is the imprint of New Left Books

ICA
The Mall, London SW1Y 5AH

Verso ISBN 0 86091 983 8

British Library Cataloguing in Publication Data available.

Designed by John Mitchell and Jane Harper
Typeset by C Leggett and Son Ltd
Printed and bound by CPI Group (UK) Ltd, Croydon, CR0 4YY

Printed and bound by CPI Group (UK) Ltd, Croydon, CR0 4YY

06/07/2026

02160639-0001